STOCKS OR OPTIONS?

STOCKS OR OPTIONS?
PROGRAMS FOR PROFITS

ROBERT FISCHER

With an Appendix on United States Tax Considerations
of Options Transactions by Joseph Ross, Merrill Lynch, New York

Translated by Claudia Ott

A Wiley-Interscience Publication
JOHN WILEY & SONS, New York • Chichester • Brisbane • Toronto

Library of Congress Cataloging in Publication Data:

Fischer, Robert, 1941–
  Stocks or options?

  "A Wiley-Interscience publication."
  Includes index.
  1. Put and call transactions. 2. Stocks.
3. Investments. I. Title.
HG6041.F5713   332.64'52   80-11669
ISBN 0-471-05599-9

Printed in the United States of America

10 9 8 7 6 5 4 3 2 1

To
Rosemarie
Jens and Claudia

PREFACE

What this book is all about is, simply, Money. The behavior of that mysterious commodity has fascinated people of all ages, of all classes. This book intends to help the investor apply two investment methods successfully: capital investment in stocks and negotiable options on stocks. After an extensive analysis of the stock market, emphasis will be placed on the trading of options since this is a relatively new and little understood method of investment.

Generations of investors have tried to find the optimal method of capital investment tailored to their individual needs and financial resources. The traditional methods, until 1973, were investments in treasuries, bonds, or stocks. In 1973, however, the Chicago Board Options Exchange was founded, marking the beginning of the trade in easily negotiable options. Since then, it has become famous or, to some, infamous, and resulted in new criteria for investment decisions which could in part be called revolutionary. This book intends to help the investor in making investment decisions and in becoming ultimately successful in the money game.

The stormy development of options trading since 1973 has shown that many investors are very much attracted to this new medium. Subsequently, more options exchanges have been initiated in the United States and in Canada. The enormous success of options trading will in all probability be repeated in Europe as well. On April 4, 1978, an options exchange for Dutch, British, and American stocks, modeled after the American predecessors, was established in Amsterdam. Options trading on German stocks was started on Feb. 14, 1980. Thus possible investment strategies with options will become of interest to the investor who holds predominantly German stocks in his portfolio. The investor to whom the **vii** names Jim Walter, Kennecott or Skyline have relatively little significance will probably be much more interested when he encounters the names Basf, Siemens or Daimler.

This book deals with the possibilities of American options exchanges and establishes the connection between the American and the European options markets. In-depth knowledge about the factors that determine the success or failure of investments is required in order to take a successful position in options. This is more exaggerated with options than with any other form of investment. Options trading offers a wide range of investment possibilities with great opportunities to the well-informed investor, but it can mean quick ruin to the uninformed trader speculating in this extremely dynamic market.

This book aims to give comprehensive information about the specific opportunities and risks of options trading and thus provide the basis for well-considered decisions in this market. Certain ideas which, because of their wide publication, tend to confuse the public about the real conditions of options will be shown for what they are, as prejudices. The notion that the options trading offers fast and enormous profits without much risk is dangerous and must be corrected in just the same way as the idea that any trade in options is the exclusive domain of the highly speculative trader.

Obviously, attention will focus on the American stock- and options markets since it is only here that empirical data are available. But inasmuch as the American market will serve as a blueprint for the European options market, these data are representative. Both calls which have existed since the beginning of the CBOE and the more recently introduced puts will be extensively analyzed. In addition, numerous possible trading strategies will be introduced.

The reader may wonder why the book starts with an extensive analysis of the stock market. He should keep in mind, however, that all option strategies will fail if the underlying direction of a particular stock and the general market in general are not taken into consideration. The investor unfamiliar with the stock market will, in the long run, only encounter failures in the options market. A systematic analysis of the stock market is essential, so that the advantages and disadvantages of options trading strategies can be correctly evaluated.

A basic question to be answered is one of stock pricing. Who are the participants confronting each other in the market? How is the constant balance of supply and demand maintained at all times? What are the factors—logical, psychological, technical—that influence the market? A thorough knowledge of the rules that affect the process of pricing in the market may result in above-average returns and continuing success. Investment success in stocks or options based on information can only last if the stock market permits information advantages. This then relates to the question of whether the stock market can be considered an efficient market and becomes the starting point for an on-going controversy between theorists and practitioners. The theorists' hypothesis that "everything is a random walk" is contradicted by the practitioners who endeavor to achieve a sufficiently dependable price forecast through the use of a suitable selection of analytic devices. It will be shown that price forecasts can be made more dependable by dividing the entire market into economic, monetary, technical, and psychological sections and by evaluating industrial groups and stocks. However, price forecasting within probable limits by means of these analytic tools alone is not enough. Evaluating and measuring the risks and rewards of stocks is just as important. It is inadvisable to enter into the options market unless a risk evaluation is possible, since it is the basis for determining if, under what conditions and to what extent capital investment in options would be preferable to simply entering a position in stocks. The crux of the matter is: does the investor really possess the character traits required to deal intelligently and successfully with options, that is, does he have the "knowledge" and—above all—the "discipline":

ROBERT FISCHER

Schwelm
West Germany
January 1980

ACKNOWLEDGMENTS

Originally, this book was intended as a thesis to complete doctoral requirements for the University of Trier. However, extensive and in-depth
discussions with Professor Kromschroeder of the University of Trier
proved conclusively that a scientific doctoral thesis was not the way to
pass on the experiences derived from my years of intensive work as a
broker.

The extraordinary readiness of several stock market experts to stand by
with advice gave me the chance to write the book in its present form. I
must make special mention of Dipl. Volkw. Michael Ott of Bad Honnef,
Germany, and Dr. Gerhard Landert of Zürich, Switzerland, who helped
me with the original German edition. Long discussions and the important
material which they provided, along with their concerned criticism,
helped the book become a success in Germany.

My wish to see the book published in the U.S. would never have been
realized if it had not been for my former teacher, Joseph Ross of Merrill
Lynch, New York, who provided valuable support. I am delighted that
Joseph Ross also agreed to write the Appendix on tax problems. Any book,
however interesting the subject matter, is wasted if the reader has to plow
through material that is studded with mistakes. My special thanks go to
Claudia Ott, who managed to translate so many dry topics into such read-
able style. Every translation, however, has its limitations when the trans-
lator does not have daily contact with the subject matter and language.
This is particularly true for the unique language of the stock market. Steve
Bradley of Salomon Brothers, New York, was of special help in reviewing
the terminology and translation with admirable precision. Ira Wilkow,

Interactive Data Service, New York, has done a great deal of sound work on the computer charts in the options strategy section.

The best intentions of the author would have been in vain if questions and problems were not resolved on the spot, as they arose. I am especially proud and grateful that Perry Kaufman of New York, the author of several excellent books on commodities, provided that help and found the time to review the book. Because of his critical comments and suggestions the American edition was improved upon considerably.

R. F.

CONTENTS

1 *STOCK PRICING AND INVESTMENT OPPORTUNITIES IN THE STOCK MARKET*

No other market is subject to the many events, arguments and upheavals that occur on the many levels of economics and finance as the stock market. Not only does it reflect the economic situation but also the successes and failures of a government. The stock market is considered the arena of capital supply and demand, but although some people see it simply as a playground for the speculator, its real significance becomes apparent only when one appreciates that the stock market is a major reflection of a nation's economy.

The effectiveness and influence of the big stock exchanges cannot be doubted. This holds true particularly for the New York Stock Exchange. The daily volume traded on the exchange shows a wide diversity. The biggest daily turnover was achieved in 1979 with approximately 86 million shares, and even volume of that magnitude presents no severe technical problems. It is, however, debatable whether sufficient marketability could at all times be guaranteed for all listed stocks. Even on the New York Stock Exchange, it would be a difficult undertaking for large shareholders to sell or buy several hundred thousand shares a day of one company without temporarily influencing the price trend of that stock. Various kinds of influences that affect prices of stocks are discussed in this chapter.

1

WHO INFLUENCES PRICE MOVEMENTS?

Pricing on the stock market depends on supply and demand. If the demand for a certain stock is higher than the supply, prices go up, and vice versa. This explanation may seem so obvious as to be superfluous, but many investors pay no attention to this fundamental rule. The state of supply and demand is reflected in the tactical behavior of the investors. This behavior includes the whole gamut of emotions and intuition, the use of rumors, and the systemic publishing of information, be it correct or manipulated. Buyer and seller are engaged in a continuous confrontation. Only this diversity of interests makes it possible to maintain a liquid and functioning market and thus determine the pricing of stocks.

Price movements come about because of the large number of market participants whose motives for buying and selling may vary greatly. Those market participants are for example:

◇ **Firms** that for reasons of company policy acquire *minority interests*. Completion of the vertical integration, distribution of risks by diversification, strengthening of the company in economic competition, or ousting an irksome competitor from the market are the compelling reasons for this procedure. Quite often the acquisition of such interests is less risky and less expensive than building up a new production branch from scratch.

◇ **Long-term capital investors** who buy stocks as stable investments in order to achieve a rate of return on invested capital, a combination of price appreciation and dividend returns, which is expected to be above the average of that which was be achieved from bonds or treasuries. Investment funds and insurance companies also belong to this group. They invest income from premiums or financial reserves in obligations, stocks, and the like, according to legal regulations and statutes and often hold them for a long time. Company reserves that are used as a security bolster and guarantee for the company's credit rating have to be counted in as well.

◇ **Speculators, traders, and small investors** who, according to their psychological makeup and readiness to take a risk, try to make fast gains in stocks and play the market, keeping their eyes solely on their own interests.

◇ **Brokers and members of the stock exchange** (floor traders, specialists, market makers) who have been bound by the exchange to guarantee the continuity and liquidity of trading. Because of the rules of the United States Stock Exchanges, specialists, for example, must continually bid and offer prices on a particular stock and be willing to take issues that have found neither a buyer nor a seller within their own orders.

The common denominator of all these investors is their desire for profit through trading the stock market. They differ, however, as to the extent of knowledge, character, time horizons, and financial resources, as well as to the role they play in the market.

A rather extreme example will serve to demonstrate how pricing is actually carried out. At the beginning of April 1977 Credit Swiss Zürich (bearer's shares) were quoted at SF 2,700. The average daily turnover in this stock on the Zürich exchange amounted to approximately 150 to 300 units. When the "Chiasso scandal" broke, excitement began to spread. Rampant rumors mentioned losses in a range of between 200 million and 2 billion Swiss francs. Speculative trading and an extensive press campaign made the daily turnover jump to 3000 to 6000 units—not counting the orders that banks handle internally and that do not have to be publicized. Increasing volume caused the stories and gossip about the scandal's effects on both the bank and Zürich itself as an international finance center to multiply. Some played down the problem, believing the losses to have been anticipated in daily prices. Other people wondered whether the losses admitted by the bank were just the tip of the iceberg and what sort of other problems would surface. Another group predicted that this would give the entire Swiss banking world a bad reputation. The panic sales of the pessimists occurring at one time caused the price of the stock to plummet from 2750 to 1980 Swiss francs. The optimists, however, came to the rescue, stemmed the tide of the stock's decline, and filled their own portfolios at bargain prices. Those investors who panicked did not trust the bank's bulletins and saw a confirmation of their pessimistic attitude in the fact that the Swiss National Bank was prepared to put up a helping credit of 3 billion Swiss francs—which, incidentally, was never used. The buyers, on the other hand, estimated the bank's substance and earning power and trusted in its ability to absorb even large losses fairly quickly. Beyond that, these investors counted on the cooperation and support of other Swiss banks who would certainly fight, with the entire system at their disposal, to maintain the public's confidence in Swiss banking. This was a case of rational consideration winning over emotional actions. Heads rolled, an extensive stockholders' meeting helped smooth the troubled waters, and the price finally stabilized. By October, the price was up to 2400 Swiss francs and 50% of the original price loss had been regained.

The example of the Credit Swiss proves that really very few shares compared to the total number of units change hands even in extreme situations. During the entire crisis, which lasted from April to October, only 5% of the stock had changed hands. Long-term investors with strong capital backing do retain their stocks in their portfolio for years, unconcerned with price movements. Every attempt at short-sale profit comes up against a resistance, since these long-term investors tend to increase their holdings when the stock is at a low rather than liquidate their position.

Most speculators count on the shortcomings of the market and want to profit by them (speculation in the sense of short-term trading is attempted). Differences in level of information, evaluation of the market situation, and risk preferences cause price movements. Aside from that, there is absolutely no consensus as to what constitutes a "profit" in the market and at what point one should be

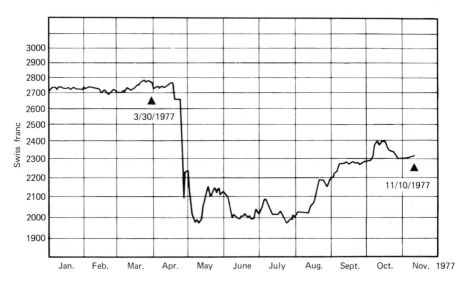

Figure 1   Price of bearer's share "Credit Swiss," January–November 1977.

satisfied. The intense desire to "hit the jackpot" often induces investors to take risks they would not even dream about and which would send shivers down their backs if contemplated in daylight.

Many short-term investors do not even intend to stay with the positions entered or sold short for any length of time, since this would constitute too big a risk, considering the size of their financial resources. They rarely bother about specific conditions of the companies whose stocks they hold, and they are not particularly interested in the long-term, fundamental developments of the company, just as long as the price trend goes in the right direction. For them, only the present economic situation is of importance. Thus sudden developments can easily surprise them because, due to their short-term commitment, they would have to react to sudden large purchses or sales of rival investors.

Having a speculating public, however, is an absolute requirement for the market, not only because it creates volume and liquidity, but also because it brings the necessary diversity of opinion into the market. Since small investors assume that, compared with the alleged "insiders," they get the information too late anyway, they tend to buy very early, just to be "in on the deal." Rising prices, on the other hand, certainly do stir up the buyers. That means that the public buys most when prices are highest. With falling prices, investors frequently sell out in near-panic. Even more often, though, they watch their stocks lose 50% or more of their value because they delayed selling in the hope of recovering their losses in a renewed rise in prices later on. In contrast, investors engaged in short sales frequently lose their nerve and cover their position when prices have risen by only 10% (or even less). The psychology of the many investors who always bank on rising prices simply cannot imagine anything else is an essential factor in determining the pricing of stocks.

Many investors rely on the advice of brokers, bankers, newspapers, or "hot tips" from acquaintances when making a commitment. They rarely take into consideration that this information nearly always has to be outdated, and they are surprised when the expected price movements are not realized. Those investors who have discovered that following the news media alone is insufficient to judge accurately the market in general as well as specific stocks tend to ask not only one but several advisors before taking a position. Here the decision really becomes difficult, since it is extremely unlikely that all the advisors will hold the same opinion. The investor usually is filled with optimism. The well-considered advice not to buy the stocks he has in mind or even to hold off investments for the time being is hardly ever palatable, and the investor usually prefers the advisor who shares his optimism. Now, brokerage houses naturally are more interested in their commissions than in their customers' profits. However, since they all want the business, the investor will, for psychological reasons, in most cases get the answer he wants to hear. Of course, any sensible advisor knows that each and any opinion on the investment can be right on the market. The investor will again and again forgive his advisor, even if prices do not develop as expected—just as long as the advisor has fallen in with the customer's opinion. If, however, prices rise as the customer had foreseen and yet he had followed the diverging opinion of his advisor, he will never forget that grievance. The conceptions and difficulties of investors searching for advice can probably best be summed up this way: "Give me good advice, but don't dissuade me."

Many investors cannot spare the time to follow the market intensively and therefore entrust their capital to investment companies who do this more or less professionally. Both in Germany and the United States the administration of the big funds is in most cases conservative and growth oriented. The results are nearly always the same: diversification and the buying of blue chips create a gain that matches the increase in the rate of national growth. These funds are long-term oriented and possess an equalizing influence on stock pricing. As long as these funds are not subject to heavy selling or do not replenish their portfolios when prices are at a low (which would be easy because of the constant money flow) fluctuations in prices will keep within reasonable bounds.

The market scene in the United States changed drastically in the 1960s when Gerry Tsai filled his aggressive growth fund—colloquially known as go-go-fund—with stocks that promised quick capital gains rather than dividends and long-term growth. Preference was given to a concentration in few investments and a fast turnover over a wide distribution of stocks of various industrial groups. Since investors flocked to these promising "go-go funds" and supplied them with incredible amounts of money, stocks like Xerox, Polaroid, and Fairchild Camera—which the aggressive funds had declared their pets—began to move. Prices rose dramatically to several hundred dollars per share. Fairchild, for example, jumped from $28 to $220. When the fund management began to feel that these stocks really were overvalued, they tried to get out faster than they had gotten in. Consequently, the prices dropped, occasionally by as much as $100 per share, within a few weeks. There are numerous examples of this sort in the second half of the 1960s. The pricing of these stocks no longer had anything in common with the actual growth of the companies, which offered the stocks. Only a fraction of the outstanding stock was passed from one poor blockhead to the next. Whoever got caught holding the bag could in the end just sit and watch the prices drop to rockbottom, only to discover finally that, on top of all, the exchanges could no longer guarantee regulated dealing because of lack of liquidity. In the final analysis, these aggressive investment funds failed everyone with the exception of the funds' managers whose management fees made them wealthy men. Only those funds that diversified with growth-oriented issues and that to a great extent had been established long before the "go-go funds" are still triumphantly alive today.

Development in Germany was a bit different. High-efficiency funds were hardly feasible in the tight stock market situation. As a result, large amounts of free capital moved into the "gray investment market"—first into the IOS funds, later into depreciation funds and commodity options trade. The case of the "Zollerngesellschaft" who, in 1976 lost their total investment of 30 million deutsche marks within five months, was by no means the last of the big failures. More and more investors found out to their chagrin that their money had "gone down the drain" or simply disappeared. This in turn called the public prosecutor and the CID into the battlefield.

According to the motto "invest as little time as possible and reap the biggest gains in return," investors often entrust their capital to companies that are fraudulent by intention. In Germany, one only has to go to the commercial registry, apply for a listing as a firm, and then can shortly afterward advertise: "And again we've doubled our capital within one week!" People responding to those advertisements very often are talked into purchases by high-pressure salesmen who, with an incredible amount of smooth and cold-blooded persuasiveness, give them fabricated details and downright lies.

Unknown to the general public, the monies entrusted to these companies quite often are not even invested but immediately transferred into a special account outside the country. Such companies have mushroomed in Germany during the past few years, since there are hardly any laws restricting their activities. And too many of them work on the same psychological principle: "Spin the customer the right yarn, promise him a return of at least 50%, maybe even 100% or more, and you can hardly cope with the flow of checks coming in through the mail." Since the duped investor has no legal recourse (in Germany losses in commodity trading and earnings fall under the gambling law and cannot be recouped by suit) he usually prefers to keep quiet about it. After all, nobody likes to admit that he has been had—especially in this type of "investment."

At the most, the details of the above examples are new. In 1935, Lord Keynes had already described the situation in one of the most pertinent passages ever written on the subject:

> It might have been supposed that competition between expert professionals, possessing judgment and knowledge beyond that over the average private investor, would correct the vagaries of the ignorant individual left to himself. It happens, however, that the energies and skill of the professional investor and speculator are mainly occupied otherwise. For most of these persons are, in fact, largely concerned, not with making superior long-term forecasts of the probable yield of an investment over its whole life, but with foreseeing changes in the conventional basis of valuation a short time ahead of the general public. They are concerned, not with what an investment is really worth to a man who buys it "for keeps," but with what the market will value it at, under the influence of mass psychology, three months or a year hence. Moreover, this behavior is not the outcome of a wrong-headed prepensity. For it is not sensible to pay 25 for an investment of which you believe the prospective yield to justify a value of 30, if you also believe that the market will value it at 20 three months hence.

> Thus the professional investor is forced to concern himself with the anticipation of impending changes, in the news or in the atmosphere, of the kind by which experience shows that the mass psychology of the market is most influenced . . . [thus] there is no such thing as liquidity of investment for the community as a whole. The social object of skilled investment should be to defeat the dark forces of time and ignorance which envelop our future. The actual, private object of the most skilled investment today is "to beat the gun," as the Americans so well express it, to outwit the crowd, and to pass the bad, or depreciating, half-crown to the other fellow.

This battle of wits to anticipate the basis of conventional valuation a few months hence, rather than the prospective yield of an investment over a long term of years, does not even require gulls amongst the public to feed the maws of the professional; it can be played by the professionals amongst themselves. Nor is it necessary that anyone should keep his simple faith in the conventional basis of valuation having any genuine long-term validity. For it is, so to speak, a game of Snap, of Old Maid, of Musical Chairs—a pastime in which he is victor who says Snap neither too soon nor too late, who passes the Old Maid to his neighbor before the game is over, who secures a chair for himself when the music stops. These games can be played with zest and enjoyment, though all the players know that it is the Old Maid which is circulating, or that when the music stops some of the players will find themselves unseated. [Quoted in Adam Smith, *The Money Game*, p. 240. New York, Random House.]

Adam Smith, author of *The Money Game*, underlines Keynes' explanation:

Nothing, for the foreseeable future, is going to hinder the impulse to volatility. If all the fund managers have been piling into airlines, and if (as they did recently) the funds own more than 40% of Northwest Airlines, and if a number of funds want to get out of Northwest Airlines at the same time, it may be hard to find buyers, and Northwest Airlines is going to have some wide swings.

There are some corrective forces at work. For one thing, at the rate they are now being consumed, there may not be enough Gelusil and tranquilizers to serve all the fund managers with their triggers filed hair-thin. More reasonably, some fund managers are going to bring in the factor of the other fund managers, and expand their intended holding periods back again to a more manageable distance. The legal beagles may even make some rules, though if history is any guide, they will be rules that treat the situation as it was when people began thinking of rules, and not with the situation as it will develop to be. [Adam Smith, *The Money Game*, pp. 217–218, New York, Random House, 1967.]

THE MARKET—*A GAME OF CHANCE*

Many people think of the market as of a game of chance, comparable to roulette. This comparison is completely wrong, though. Roulette is a game of sheer chance. It is characteristic of this game that one player is pitted against the bank and that the results cannot be predicted. Furthermore, to guarantee an equal chance for each player, croupier and ivory ball are changed at regular intervals. The introduction of the figure zero ensures the long-term gain of the bank. Every attempt to "beat the system" has failed to date and will continue do so in the future. The only people who have made a fortune on roulette systems have been the authors of books propagating their systems. What is essential: the outcome of the game cannot be influenced; no matter how great an effort one makes, it remains a matter of luck, with the "chances" always the same.

In terms of comparing the market to a game, an analogy to horse racing would be much more apt than roulette. When "playing the market" not everything is left to chance, just as with horse racing. With the right information and a certain amount of cleverness, much more can be achieved. One could call it a "strategic game" whose rules permit both rational and irrational behavior. What might lead to problems here are incomplete information and the quick-wittedness, intelligence, and adaptability of one's opponent. This is a real contest of human intelligence in which everyone tries to gain an advantage over his opponent and to maintain and, if possible, increase that advantage. The result of this "game" can be influenced. It is information for the sake of which the battle is fought, and both getting and distributing the information is of importance. The investor has to be able to distinguish between valid and misleading information, and in addition he has to try to determine whether the information he has received is complete. Although this tends to lead to a situation in which all prices are in a state of equilibrium, fresh information discrepancies always come into play because of changes in company policy, new technology advances, or political developments.

The market game is a genuine parallel to economic processes. In addition to the competitiveness of the market, acquisition and utilization of information play a decisive role in this field. In the final analysis, it is of little importance whether a company evaluates possible openings in a specific market, customers' reactions, and earning prospects through location analysis or economic prognosis, or whether an investor can determine the chances of a company by means of good judgment of the market. Both the company and the investor try to find out whether the chances of both horse and jockey are good, so to speak. What makes the decision-making process risky, however, is the fact that it is not sufficient to carry out market analysis, have a dynamic company policy, or do a stock analysis. It is just as important to know what the competition is doing and how it reacts to one's own plans. The company that builds a supermarket in a certain area and, having received a favorable sales projection, counts on solid profits for years to come will curse that forecast when just a year later an even bigger company with better financial resources builds an even bigger supermarket in the same neighborhood. A turf expert who knows all about the horse's condition and has all other salient facts at his fingertips will still fail in his prognosis if he does not know that the jockey has been bribed to lose a particular race (as happened in Germany in 1977). Equally, investors who correctly judge the conditions of companies and the economy will still have bad luck with their investments if some big investor suddenly rejects that particular stock for psychological or emotional reasons and sells out.

Certain elements of a "game" are always discernible in the market. The buyer is the seller's opposing player; the winner is not yet determined. And just as in a game, not everybody can win in the market. You can only win what others lose.

Up until 1970 a viable market game was the "buy and hold" strategy if there was a wide diversification in stocks. Between 1950 and 1970, stocks and dividends yielded approximately 10% on the average in the United States, corresponding to the growth of the economy. As shown in Figure 2, this era of growth slowed down with the 1960s in the United States, and with that in other Western industrial countries as well. More and more economies and companies reached the limits of their growth. Although in 1968 real growth in the United States still amounted to 12 to 15% per annum, it had decreased to 3 to 5% in 1977. Until 1968 the rate of inflation did not rise beyond 3% per year, but in 1977 one had to reckon with 7% per year. Company earnings until 1968 grew in the neighborhood of 12 to 15% a year, but in the years between 1968 and 1977 they fell below 10%. In 1967 the rate of increase in the American gross national product began to level off noticeably. Despite constant expansion of money volume and steadily increasing public debt, no permanent stimulus for the economic growth was achieved.

Various factors such as the energy crisis, unemployment, rate of inflation, and rate of exchange problems for foreign countries force the investor to find new investment strategies. It is obvious that

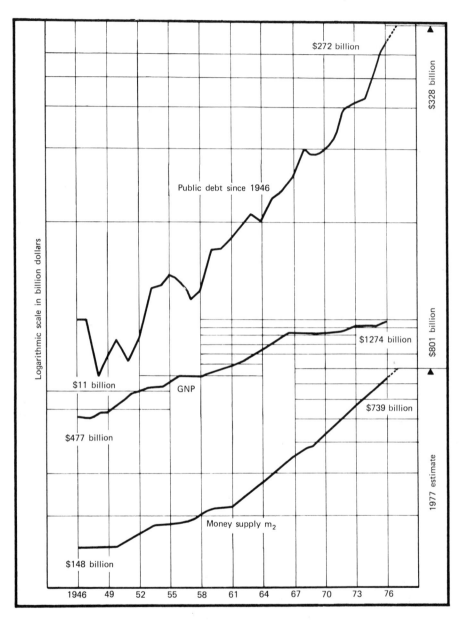

Figure 2 Government debt, GNP, and money supply, 1946–1976 (Richard Russel, Dow Theory Letters, Inc., 1977).

today more than ever before, tools for analyzing and recognizing short-, medium- and long-term trends have become absolutely necessary. In Chapter 2 the question whether such analytic tools can be created is investigated. If the possibility exists, they could be considered *gain strategies*. A rational player would apply such a strategy. But then there would have to be players on the other side who either do not have those rational strategies or refuse to apply them. These could be described as "adventurers" who obey their impulses, stick to their habits, follow the crowd, and take their business to the place where the shouting is loudest. As a rule, this type of investor is the one who gets stuck and can no longer sell his shares profitably since all the more knowledgeable players have already sold. Keynes illustrated these practices extremely vividly by comparing them to the game of musical chairs—the speculator is the one left without a seat when the music stops.

ARE MARKET DEVELOPMENTS PREDICTABLE?

The preceding section discussed the question whether one could really call the market a game. The answer is neither an unequivocal "yes" nor a decisive "no." Contrary to a game of chance such as roulette, the success of capital investment on the market is not predetermined by an illusive and random mechanism. Rather, the investor has the chance to rationally justify certain investment decisions by skillful analysis and interpretation of information and by making a distinction between promising and less promising strategies. On the other hand, the success of each capital investment is determined by a multitude of factors that can be neither completely controlled nor predicted with any amount of certainty by the individual investor. Provided one defines this unpredictability—which cannot be overcome even with the best analytic tools—as being characteristic of a "game," then the market could in that sense be called just that. However, it becomes a game of chance only for those participants who refuse to apply well-established analytic tools and rely exclusively on their intuition.

The majority of those practitioners who deal professionally with capital investment in the market would in all probability agree with this characterization of the market. Theorists in their research of capital and stock market theory, however, have come to exactly the opposite conclusion. Most of them consider the market an "efficient market" that moves as if governed by laws of probability, although it is not exactly guided by random mechanism, as is the case with roulette.

The assertion that it is possible to achieve above-average gains in the market by applying the proper tools of analysis has to be defended against the theorists' arguments. After all, a market that distributes opportunities and risks among the market participants according to a random mechanism offers no chance to distinguish between "good" and "bad" investment decisions.

The theory of the efficient market, which is the subject of the following chapter, has three variations according to literature: it is possible to distinguish between the weakly, the semistrongly, and the strongly efficient market. All three versions are based on the assumption that a market is efficient whenever the following conditions are fulfilled:

◇ Rational behavior of market participants.
◇ Objective homogeneity of all stocks traded.
◇ Complete visibility of the market for all participants.
◇ Information freely available for all market participants.

It is obvious, as most theorists agree, that these premises are unrealistic; they are, however, mainly considered adequate, not essential, conditions for the realization of an efficient market. If, however, the efficient market can also establish itself under different and less-rigid conditions, it is impossible when trying to repudiate the theory to be satisfied with merely pointing out that the premises stated were unrealistic.

Are Stock Prices Random Products?

The weak form of the so-called "efficient market theory" or "random walk theory" is based on the assumption that

> all information that could be collected on the basis of the stocks' past behavior is reflected in present prices. Therefore, the investor cannot profit by knowledge and analysis of past price movements. Pricing follows a pattern that is governed by a random walk. [Burton G. Mal-

kiel, *A Random Walk Down Wall Street,* New York, Norton, 1975, p. 140.]

To support their theory, the academicians choose the example of coin flipping. The probability of a coin's landing heads up is always 0.5; the past pattern does not change this probability. If it landed heads up ten times in a row, the probability of the next toss being heads continues to remain 0.5. Thus the probability cannot be improved by keeping track of the sequence in which heads turn up in a trial run of 100 or 1000 throws. Theorists have compared the Dow Jones average with a simulated random numbers sequence established by tossing a coin. Heads stood for the assumption that the price of a stock would go up by 0.50 point compared to the previous day, tails that the price would close 0.50 point down.

The comparison of such a number sequence to a chart reveals surprising similarities. With a sufficient number of tosses, all patterns that chartists consider certain indicators for the future price movements of stocks could be reproduced.

Tests of this kind have also been made in an attempt to show that all stocks follow a random walk, that is, that the price movement of a stock is completely unpredictable and has no relation to past price movements whatsoever. This thesis is mainly supported by some statisticians who up to the present have found no clear evidence for a correlation between price movements in the past and those in the present. They have arrived at the conclusion that prices have "no memory" and that yesterday's prices have nothing to do with prices of tomorrow. In the theorists' opinion, investors who follow the charts exclusively would in the long run achieve nothing but large commissions for their broker.

Still, even the statisticians have admitted that, when a numbers sequence determined by coin flipping was compared with a chart, differences were discernible provided a stock showed a long-term trend. And this is exactly what the chartists are trying to find out. They do not want to know *why* economic facts such as supply and demand come into play and cause price movements: they want to know *when* and *in what direction* the stock will move. The case of Sea Container Inc., for example, which in 1976 traded from a low of approximately $7 per share to an absolute top of $60 in 1977, illustrates the discrepancies between the opinion of the statisticians (who frequently have no practical experience with the market) and that of the practitioners.

◇ Many theorists maintain that future pricing of stocks cannot be predicted. Prices are random products. Each and every stock analysis is useless. No rules can be established.

◇ Most practitioners do not believe in the random walk theory. In their opinion, rules can be established that—if adhered to—promise above-average profits.

What these rules could be like and what could be achieved by applying them is discussed in Chapter 2.

Do Stock Prices Have a Memory?

The hypothesis of the semistrong form of the efficient market theory is based on the assumption that

all past information is useless for market analysis (contention of the weak form) since the current price of the stock reflects all that is known about a company. [Oldrich Yasicek and John A. McQuown, "The Efficient Market Model," *Financial Analysts Journal*, Vol. 28 (September–October 1972), p. 358]

According to this theory, each stock has an "intrinsic value" reflecting present and future market value of a company that at a given time has been attributed to it by investors on the basis of all public information then available about the stock. The intrinsic value can only change with new information, as all other information is already reflected in the current price. But not all news represents "new" information. A lot of it is simply repeated or has been partially published before. Ordinary events can cause rumors and speculations that, once in circulation, are quickly taken for gospel truth. Truly significant new information is random, never deducible for all, and it changes the intrinsic value of a stock only at random intervals. The price actually paid for the stock is therefore the intrinsic value of a stock plus or minus random deviations.

Numerous studies have tried to prove that all information available is reflected in current stock prices. Two of these studies deal with the effects of stock splits and those of annual earnings announcements and may serve as an example here:

With a stock split of 2 : 1, the price of a share of $100 is halfed. The investor, who before the split owned 100 shares at $100 each, now owns 200 shares at $50. A study of the effect stock splits have had on the rates of return of 622 companies from 1926 to 1960 has been made. It showed that speculating on an increase in rates of return or higher dividends had been unsuccessful despite the decrease in prices. [Eugene Fama, Fisher, Jensen, Roll: The Adjustment of Stock-Prices to New Information, *International Economic Review*, Vol. 10, No. 1, pp. 1–21 (February 1969).]

The deviations from normal rates of return for 261 firms were examined to detect the effect of annual earnings announcements. It was found that the average rate of return for stocks with increased earnings rose throughout the year preceding the announcement. For stocks with decreased earnings the opposite was true. In other words, most of the information in earnings announcements had been anticipated by the market. [Ray Bail and Philip Brown, An Empirical Evaluation of Accounting Income Numbers, *Journal of Accounting Research*, Vol. 6, pp. 159–78 (Autumn 1968).]

Followers of the semistrong form of the efficient market theory maintain that a company's balance sheet, earnings, sales, and the like have no influence on the price movement of the company's stock, since current prices reflect all that is known about the company. If one were to accept this theory, practically all fundamental analyses would be useless for forecast purposes.

It seems more than doubtful that the stock price really represents the intrinsic value of a stock. Can the value of a company really be determined? What kind of criteria would have to be applied? Neither the balance sheet, balance sheet ratios, nor statements by company management can convey a comprehensive picture of the company's value. It is equally impossible that an *accounting firm* can really carry out a valid and reliable company valuation. Even insider knowledge offers no protection against misjudgments. A perfect example for this kind of failure is the takeover of the American company Micron by the German Hussel Holding AG. Hussel had hired an accounting firm of worldwide renown to go over the company's books. They were checked five times with a finetoothed comb and each time given a clean bill of health—but later on a loss of several million dollars was suddenly discovered.

Academic theories totally neglect the strongly diverging opinions of investors and the fact that many investors completely ignore information on purpose. But even with equal information, the investors' behavior depends on individual risk preferences, time horizons, financial substance, and the like. Furthermore, a distinction between the behavior of the private investor and that of investor groups has to be made.

The trend in Mannesmann shares in 1976–1977 created enormous excitement on the German stock market. Along with many other companies in the same industry, Mannesmann's earnings grew at a breathtaking pace from 1974 to 1976: within three years, earnings per share went up by nearly 150%. The price of the stock reflected this trend to nearly the same extent. The company management announced—and quite realistically, as it turned out later—that this trend could not possibly continue. Investors, however, refused to believe it and continued to speculate on rising prices, totally disregarding the actual growth of the company. Disillusionment set in four to six months later: prices were corrected downward by approximately 25%.

Stocks frequently are either "overvalued" or "undervalued". On this point the followers of the semistrong form of the efficient market theory are harshly criticized by the practitioners. In the case of Mannesmann, no inside knowledge was necessary to realize that the stock was extremely overvalued and would eventually correct downward. Some knowledge of the market and a somewhat analytic mind were all that was necessary to figure that one out. The efforts of good analysts center on the attempt to spot possible under- or overvaluations. However, the case of the closed-end trusts that trade below set asset value shows that even the knowledge of a discrepancy between market price and book value cannot always be used successfully. The closed-end United States–Japan trust is a typical example. In 1977 the trust stock was traded at $8½ per share while the book value was $11¾.

The semistrong form of the efficient market theory maintains that current prices fully reflect all information available. It consists of the intrinsic value of a company plus or minus random deviations.

Many practitioners doubt that this assertion is correct because over- and undervaluations of stocks can be so extreme that they can lead to a complete misinterpretation of the intrinsic value. Emotions, intuition, knowledge, and so on, all have an impact on price movements. Such factors no longer have anything to do with judging the intrinsic value objectively. Investors pursue what is fashionable (computers, space science, semiconductors, solar energy) and stocks with a future. They rarely bother to investigate a company's prospects and status before investing; rather, they follow current popular buying patterns. Price movements then develop laws of their own, which can no longer be explained by a company's development.

Is the Insider Better Off?

The strong form of the efficient market theory says

> that stock prices not only reflect public information (contention of the semistrong form) but also what is known of the future. [Burton G. Malkiel, *A Random Walk Down Wall Street*, New York, Norton, 1975, p. 140.]

A number of tests have been made to check this assertion. Studies have been conducted on the performance of big United States investment funds (mutual funds), which reportedly achieve better results because of "better and faster" information. Quite a lot can be said for the suspicion that the big funds can put the squeeze on the small investor: they not only get all the information they want first hand, but also—and even more significantly—they can even "invent" information, that is, manipulate it. With the help of "homemade news" they can cause prices to move and thus make sure of their share in the profits. "Funds are uncanny, anonymous, huge, and they know everything," Adam Smith said in his book *The Money Game,* and he concluded that the private investor has no chance against these investment giants. Many theorists take exactly the opposite stance and maintain that

> no funds manager or top analyst can—over an extended time period—achieve a better selection in stocks than an amateur.

or, more drastically expressed:

> A blindfolded monkey throwing darts at the financial page of the *Wall Street Journal* would come up with results on which no trained analyst could possibly improve.

The mutual funds are supposedly the most professionally oriented investment companies in the United States. They are required by law to publish all information that is needed to check on their performance. Since nearly all mutual funds can be measured by the same criteria, comparative studies have been made to check whether the strong form of the efficient market theory holds. These studies investigated the performance of

◇ 189 mutual funds between 1952 and 1958 [Irwin Friend, A Study of Mutual Funds, prepared for the Securities Research Unit, Wharton School of Finance and Commerce, University of Pennsylvania (1962).]

◇ 34 mutual funds between 1954 and 1963 [William F. Sharpe, Mutual Funds Performance, *Journal of Business, Security Prices*, A Supplement, Vol. 39, No. 1, Part 2, pp. 119–138 (January 1966).]

◇ 115 mutual funds between 1945 and 1974 [Michael C. Jensen, The Performance of Mutual Funds in the Period 1945–1974, *Journal of Finance*, Vol. 23, No. 2, pp. 389–415 (May 1974).]

According to these studies, the performance of these mutual funds was on the average no better than that of funds which were essentially structured the same way but whose management reputedly was not quite so professionally oriented. The results of the funds were equally distributed, half better and half worse than the Dow Jones average. The result of the second study was even more unfavorable: compared to a hypothetical portfolio which included all the Dow Jones stocks, 11 mutual funds showed a better performance, 23 worse. If an investor had bought the 30 Dow Jones stocks and—following the "buy-and-hold strategy"—had left them in his portfolio, he would have achieved a better performance than the mutual funds administered by professionals.

Between 1967 and 1976 the big German funds showed similar performances. Full-page advertisements boasted that capital had doubled—provided dividends were reinvested—over the previous ten years. However, a little mathematical double-checking reveals that the doubling of capital in 10 years corresponds to a return of approximately 7%. During the same time (1967–1976) the FAZ*-Average rose by approximately 4.5%. If one adds the average dividend on German stocks, every investor who had acquired a broadly diversified stock portfolio back in 1966 and held on to these stocks

* FAZ = *Frankfurter Allgemeine Zeitung*, Major German daily newspaper.

until 1976 would have achieved that same 100% increase in value as the funds. The funds, however, use that unremarkable result in their advertising campaigns to catch new customers.

Naturally, the publication of the studies' findings did not exactly send the fund managers into transports of delight. However, when judging the funds, one should remember that

◇ The big funds are required by law to hold broadly diversified portfolios.

◇ They not only compete with their peers but also with banks and insurance companies.

◇ Nearly all investment decisions are thrashed out in engless meetings. This think-tank operation kills all individual feelings of responsibility. Decisions are made on the basis of a conglomerate of conflicting and subjective interpretations of price trends.

◇ Conflicts in interest can come about, since the big funds quite often are affiliated with big banks. (If, e.g., a big German bank wants to place Mannesmann convertible bonds, a fund affiliated with that bank cannot sell Mannesmann stocks on the market at the same time. On the contrary, the fund may be required to buy more of these stocks from the bank if they cannot be placed.) The clash of interests becomes even more pronounced when a big bank has formed an underwriting syndicate and committed itself to distribute new stocks. Quite often, stocks that have not found a buyer are pushed off onto the funds.

◇ The size of individual positions in the fund can hinder free movement. If a fund holds several hundred thousand shares of one stock, it cannot sell a large number at the same time, since this would depress prices—no matter how accurately and exactly they have estimated the market situation.

◇ Further serious limitations for the big funds are: their statutes often are too limited and often do not permit short-sales; the possibilities of buying stocks of various countries with special funds are restricted; when the market is down, the funds can only shift a fraction of their stock investments in cash holdings.

As a rule, the big funds hold such broadly diversified portfolios that their return usually corresponds to the current average return—unless they pursue extraordinary risks. But why should a portfolio manager play it unsafe? As long as he holds even with competing funds, that is, his performance is comparable to that of his rivals, he does not have to worry about getting fired. Even if he were to receive more and faster information than his collegues, he could not be certain that this would lead to instant success. And since the performance of the various stocks held by the fund are compared and evaluated by the fund's management at least once a month, it would not pay to swim against the tide. It might indeed be fatal for a portfolio manager if a new investment strategy were to bring poor results in a trial run. Therefore, it is hardly conceivable that even a single portfolio manager would voluntarily submit to the psychological pressure of defying the whole phalanx of his peers—despite the fact that it is the "Lone Ranger mentality" which promises better returns. He is, however, much better off running with the crowd, since it is highly unlikely that he would reap the fruits of his labor anyway and get a substantial increase in salary—even if performance had been improved thanks to his initiative.

It seems more than questionable whether these studies on the performance of mutual funds really support the efficient market theory. Rather, one cannot help thinking that the hypothesis "everything is a random walk and stock analysis therefore useless" quite often serves as an excuse for bad performance. There are approximately 11,000 securities analysts in the United States. Most of them are only human, too.

CONCLUSION

If there really were persons or groups of "wise men" who could lay their hands on information that would help outperform the market every time, they would keep their secret under their hats and never tell. Certainly, any person of that caliber and ability would not go looking for a job with a fund that *has* to publish its information—and neither would they turn up as little numbers in statistical reports to support or defy academic theories. The theorists "proof" would seem rather inconclusive and fairly wide open to attack.

The constant and determined search of the theorists for someone who would always come out ahead in the market game finally had them doing some research on the "smart money" of the specialists who handle the separate transactions and on the behavior of "company insiders" (members of top management).

◇ Checking the transactions of specialists on the Exchanges provided proof that information obtained from order books can be used effectively in making a profit. [Victor Osborne M. F. M. Niederhoffer, Market Making and Reversal on the Stock Exchange, *Journal of the American Statistical Association*, Vol. 61, pp. 897–916 (December 1966).]

◇ Transactions of "company insiders" showed that stocks would go up within the next six months if that group showed a tendency to replenish their portfolios with shares of their own company. [James H. Lorie and Victor Niederhoffer, Predictive and Statistical Properties of Insider Trading, *Journal of Law and Economics*, Vol. 11, pp. 35–53.]

◇ Transactions of insiders have to be made public. Analysts have become interested in these buying and selling transactions. Although figures on these transactions are only published six weeks after they take place, they still can provide indications whether one should get on the bandwagon. [Consensus of Insiders, Stock Splits . . . Boon or Bane?, P.O. Box 10247, Fort Lauderdale, Florida 33305, October 7, 1977.]

Incidentally, the publisher of the Dow Theory Letters, R. Russell, is living proof for the SEC's strict supervision of the trade in general (the Dow Theory Letter has been one of the most popular market letters in the United States for decades). It is generally known that the weekly market letter had quite an influence on the stocks which it recommended for purchase or sale. Mr. Russell surreptitiously bought or sold the stocks he discussed in his letter shortly before the letter went to press, knowing full well that his recommendation would influence the pricing. He was found out in due course by the SEC and disciplined in 1977. Obviously, the perfect capitalistic market does not come about for nothing—if it exists at all. Supervision by state institutions, created for that purpose alone, obviously is necessary.

The feud between theorists and practitioners is still raging. The results achieved by both are contradictory, as anybody could have foretold. The assertion that stock analysis is useless does not have to be accepted without question—and that assertion is not accepted by the author of this book. A lot of mathematical processes have turned out to be quite valuable for analyzing the market. Experience, character, and extent of knowledge are not measurable and never will be. If that ever were to become possible, the stock market would be at an end, since then everybody would be "right," and the game would be over—forever. In the past decades, however, certain characteristics have crystallized. These features have provided insights, according to which rules could be established. With the help of these rules each investment decision can be made more successful. It can provide the individual investor with better and more concise information. The next chapter discusses in detail the rules for analyzing the entire market, industrial groups, and individual stocks.

2 *METHODS OF FORECASTING STOCK PRICES*

THE LABYRINTH OF PRICE FORECASTS

Speculators really do have the most fantastic, farfetched, and extraordinary mental images of the processes of price forecasting. It is said that if a slump is lurking around the corner, the pews of Trinity Church will begin filling up with members of the Wall Street community. If, however, you have to fight for a table in one of the exclusive neighborhood restaurants, it is considered a certain sign of a bullish market, since everybody is eating up his profits in style. Some people use an analogy, based on an example of Fibonacci (fourteenth century) that the reproduction pattern of rabbits shows a statistical regularity similar to price forecasting. Another group supports the findings of Jevons, who thought he could prove a relationship between the variation of sun spots and harvest cycles. From that, it was only a small step to the discovery that there seems to be a remarkable interrelation between rainfalls in Berne and the movement of the Standard & Poor Average (Figure 3). Slogans like summer rally, yearend rally, or even the proverb "after labor day down, you had better leave town" still retain a comparative forecast value. People believe in being able to make a long-term weather prognosis by observing what the weather is like on June 21, and what the *Farmers' Almanac* is to the meteorologists the *Stock Trader Almanac* (published every year) is to the stock market com-

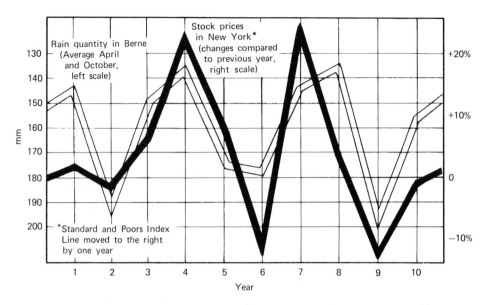

Figure 3 Rainfall in Berne (Switzerland) compared to stock prices in New York (typical 10-year cycles 1890–1940). (Rudolf Frick, Basel, 1972.)

munity. The *Almanac* investigates the usefulness of all "wise sayings" for the past 30 years (the meaning of months, days, hours, farmers' sayings, seasonal fluctuations, and so on).

All this shows how highly conducive the market is for flights of fancy and how difficult it is to get people to come "down to earth" and make them accept scientific forecasts. The stock market simply *is* an extremely complex structure that can be judged properly only if one goes to the trouble of untangling all the details and facets that finally do influence the movement of prices. Every year, industry sinks billions of dollars into market research in an effort to survive competition, to get a lead over any rivals, and to maintain that advantage. They try to analyze the most complicated processes and turn them to their own advantage. Quite often this proves absolutely futile, despite the enormous investment in time and money. Whoever wants to take his money to the stock market should abandon all illusions and keep in mind that the processes of pricing are just as complicated and difficult to analyze as the development of a company.

PRICE PROGNOSIS AND THE INVESTORS' MENTALITY

There is a host of strategies that promise profitable speculation in the market. This is clearly incompatible with the contention of the disciples of the random walk theory who insist that everything is a random walk. The choice of the strategy depends to a great extent on the investor's mentality. A business tycoon like J. P. Morgan made use of his influential connections and continued to increase his fortune in that way. Investors dedicated to investment strategies travel all over the country, talk to presidents and vice-presidents, and are not above checking out factories in person. Quite often it gives them much better insight into the state of inventories and order books than a three-martini lunch. For the investor who will assume risk, it might definitely be a worthwhile strategy to buy only stocks of companies that seem to be on the brink of bankruptcy and whose stocks sell at discount prices. Quite often, large profits are in the offing for the investor who not only can wait but has the luck and the nose for it—provided the company can turn the situation around. The American company Memorex, whose stock dropped from $160 per share in 1970 to $2 in 1974, is a typical example. In 1977 it was back to $30. Similarly, the VW (Volkswagen) which traded below DM 50 not too long ago reached DM 250 by the end of 1978. More often than not, these purchases are the result of sober calculation rather than emotions. Such decisions frequently result in a direct hit, if the investor has both complete knowledge of the company's situation and a feel for economic and political developments. But with all these investment decisions, the investor has to be ready for a long-term commitment and be able and willing to ride out the wave. The drawback with most investors is that they simply do not wait long enough. They think short-term and tend to reverse even carefully planned decisions if the price trend does not show immediate signs of moving into the desired direction.

Most investors are "professional" optimists. Only that can explain the peculiar fact that they simply sit back, watch prices go down by half, and still remain absolutely convinced that they will go up again—some time. On the other side, there are the speculators who panic the minute prices under short-sale conditions run counter to their expectations by no more than 10%. Another stumbling block is the "idée fixe" of many investors that one has to be fully engaged at all times for fear of missing out on an upward price movement. It is nearly impossible to convince an investor that it would really be preferable to invest only 50% or even nothing at all in stocks when the market is down and to put the remainder of the capital into bonds and treasuries until the market has recovered. The greatest virtue and accomplishment of the successful professional in the market are the ability to wait and to control his emotions. Whoever fails in this respect will inevitably and very quickly suffer the fate of the "typical investor" as shown so lucidly in Figure 4.

A mixture of emotions, greed, intuition, and objective knowledge is responsible for the decisions of most investors. Usually it is luck, not knowledge or strategic behavior, to which success must be ascribed. However, nearly all these short-term decisions are based on the type of data that only have long-term effects on price developments, such as changes in earnings, dividend payments, or company sales.

This is the point where the investor especially interested in options has to watch his step, because here the going becomes perilous. The investor who has been lucky enough once to make a fast buck thanks to a "hot tip" or a quick look at a chart quite often thinks himself the "born speculator" in the stock and options trade. In most cases, however, it takes no more than a year to gamble away his capital, especially in the options market.

The investor who is too busy to do stock analysis thoroughly and regularly ought to follow the method of *dollar cost averaging*. That method requires that a fixed number of dollars be invested in a company's shares at regular intervals. In this way, price risks can be considerably reduced—although not totally eliminated—and a relatively favorable average price can be realized. Good-quality stocks cannot always be bought at the lowest price. Usually the "gamblers" succumb to temptation that amounts to addiction and try to recoup their losses by risking ever-higher stakes in their quest for the really big score. And any random hit—which of course cannot be avoided in such a hit-and-miss operation—naturally adds fuel to the fire. If, in addition, the investor suffers from the "idée fixe" mentioned before—that he always has to be fully invested—losses and commissions will gang up on him in the end, and he will come out of the deal like a plucked chicken.

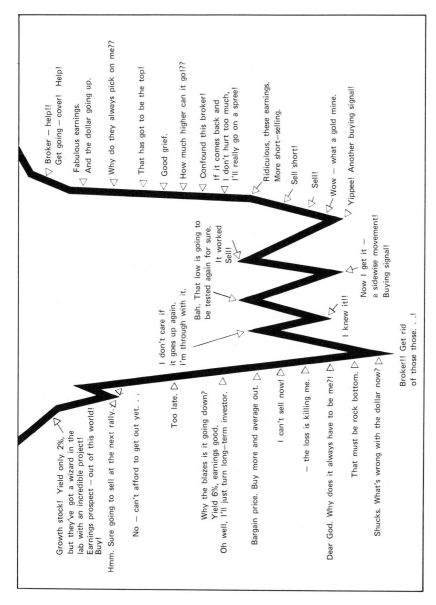

Figure 4   Typical investor's behavior. (Weltwoche, September 1977.)

29

The following example serves to illustrate the method of "dollar cost averaging":

Period	Invested Capital (in $)	Price (in $)	Number of Shares
1	150	75	2
2	150	25	6
3	150	50	3
Total cost	450		
Average price	$40.91		
Number of shares			11

In this sample, 11 shares were bought. The current market value is $50 per share. Total value amounts to $550. Since only $450 was invested, the average cost per share comes to only $450/11 = $40.91, because more stocks were added at a lower price than at a higher price. The most important premises for the success of this investment strategy are:

◇ Long-term planning of the investment.
◇ Investment in the same stocks.
◇ Liquid assets on hand.
◇ No long-term down trend.

This last condition is particularly important, because that is where the snag is: if the investor follows the strategy of dollar cost averaging, he buys fewer "good" stocks when there is a long-term and lasting increase in price. With a continuing decrease in prices, on the other hand, he is buying more and more "bad" shares. Sufficient diversification would be the panacea for this problem.

Not all investors follow the above strategy or similar purely technical methods that purposely exclude any attempts on forecasting. They may think them too conservative, or they may have personal strategies or forecast tools which they consider more promising.

The starting point for each rational decision for buying or selling a stock should be a solid plan—based on either mechanical methods or forecasts. Not only must the method be "good," but also the investor must be absolutely consistent. Here some tempting little devils have to be conquered: who would not begin to doubt his own abilities when the buying limit is reached just at that moment the newspapers, market letters, and brokerage houses begin to report that sales and earnings of that particular company are going down?

The limits of such mechanical methods for price forecasting are examined in the following chapter.

There is absolutely no method of analysis that can guarantee profits to the investor. It is, however, indisputable that a systematic analysis of the entire market, of industrial groups, and their stocks improves the results of investment decisions. It does not pay just to "guestimate" in this business. The investor whose decisions are based on emotions, intuition, hot tips, or the news alone is not going to survive in this market. That kind of haphazard behavior is even more dangerous when dealing with options, which hold an unusual number of pitfalls for the unwary. Any company trying to launch a new product will try to determine its chances by means of market research and customer behavior research before it starts an advertising campaign. Stock analysis follows essentially the same principle. The person who does not understand the past, who has not learned his lesson from past events, will not be able to learn from future developments either. Again, it is simply not enough to watch interest rates, dividends, rate of inflation, sales, earnings, and the like. An analysis combining the various indicators of the general economy, industrial groups, and individual stocks would be much more promising. The indicators involved here can be divided into four subdivisions. For each of these groups, some selected indicators are given:

1. **Indicators for determining the general economic development**

   Leading indicators
   Productivity of the economy
   Gross national product
   Wholesale price index
   Inventories
   Production at full capacity
   Investments
   Balance of trade
   State budget
   Consumer behavior
   Inflation

2. Indicators for determining the monetary development

Trend in interest rates
Growth rate of money supply
Free credit balances in brokerage accounts
Debit balances on stocks and bonds with brokers
Bond market activities
Relation of rate of interest to stock and bond yields

3. Indicators for determining the technical state of the stock market

Market indexes, such as:
—New York Stock Exchange Index
—Standard & Poors 500 Index
—Dow Jones Industrial Average
Moving averages
Chart analysis
Analysis of market breadth by advance/decline ratio
Block activities of large investors
Most active stocks
High/low index
Overbought/oversold
Analysis of divergences

4. Indicators for determining investors' behavior/investors' psychology (optimism/pessimism)

Cash holdings of funds
Margin debt
Free credit balance in brokerage accounts
Behavior of odd-lot investors
Short sales of
—Odd lotters
—Members of the exchange
—Specialists
Insider trading
Trading by members of the exchange
Recommendations of market letters

These four categories by no means represent a comprehensive compilation of aids for stock market analysis. Not only could they be considerably enlarged on, but it can be seen that the different items within these categories frequently overlap. An analysis, however, that makes use of these indicators can at all times provide valid insights into the state of the market. Many indicators can be examined from a short-, medium-, or long-term perspective. For example, the statement that the expansion of money supply per se is unfavorable cannot be accepted without qualifying it. An increase in money supply on a short-term basis can be absolutely favorable because additional liquidity is pumped into the market. From a medium-term point of view, however, rates of interest will tend to decline. Under long-term conditions, that kind of policy will cause a rise in the rate of inflation, to which the market always reacts unfavorably. Such deliberations—which always differ according to the time the conditions were examined—are the reason that analysts disagree in their evaluations. Experience has shown that two of these four subdivisions are of special importance for price forecasting:

◇ Indicators for determining the monetary development.
◇ Indicators for determining investors' behavior.

This is a logical conclusion, since the monetary development—interest rates, liquidity, the credit situation—controls the economy and therefore the stock market as well. It can be deduced from these indicators, for example, whether industry is willing to make investments or whether the investor would benefit from buying stocks on margin. These factors influence investors' behavior, which in turn affects the market. For that reason, the analysis of investors' behavior tries to determine the actions of all those millions of investors with their different preferences, know-how, and financial resources. Do they buy, sell, or prefer to put their money into a savings account? Are they bullish or bearish? At what times do insiders, members of the exchange, or specialists invest, sell, or short-sell—and which stocks? The examination of the four subdivisions with respect to the range of their forecasting abilities shows they can be divided as follows:

◇ Short-term (4–8 weeks) indicators of technical analysis and investors' behavior.
◇ Medium-term (3–6 months) indicators of the technical and monetary analysis.
◇ Long-term (6–12 months) indicators of monetary and economic analysis.

This order of progression can be illustrated with the help of the 1977–1978 decline in the American Stock Market: first, technical and psychological indicators point toward a decline. The market is heavily overbought. Blue chips move rather sluggishly, and the general economy is sustained more and more by secondary stocks. The funds are out of cash reserves; insiders begin to sell; specialists and members of the exchange engage more and more in short-sales. Nothing points toward a decline yet on the monetary or economic sector—on the contrary, everything seems quiet and in good shape. The situation at the end of 1976 was typical: the monetary development gave no cause for alarm. The Federal Funds Rate was approximately 4%. The money supply moved well within its permissible range. The economy seemed to be in marvelous health, which was reflected in the forecasts that were generally favorable. Anybody who, at the end of 1976 when the Dow Jones had risen to more than 1000 had dared to say "I feel in my bones that the market is going down!" would have earned nothing but derision and catcalls. During the second phase in May 1977 the Dow Jones held around 950 points, and interest rates began to climb. The Federal Funds Rate rose from 4 to 6% during the following months. The money supply was greatly expanded, and public debt grew steadily. But although the monetary situation grew continuously worse, the basic economic situation still looked very good. Published earnings constantly increased. The price-earnings ratio of the Dow Jones Industrial Average had hardly ever been so modest. Without exception, the market letters advised averaging down and adding to positions.

It was only during the third phase, in the third quarter of 1977, that the basic economic picture deteriorated too. Earnings forecasts were corrected; the news media began to write about inflation, the closing down of factories, and recession. This was the signal for all those investors who base their decisions simply on the general atmosphere to sell their stocks. In January 1978, the Dow Jones had dropped to 760 points, that is, 25% below the previous year's level. Tempers were short, the mood predominantly pessimistic. Interest rates were high; the money supply had increased enormously; the main topic of conversation in the market was the investors' fears of inflation which, incidentally, also served as an excuse for all other price decreases. More and more companies began to revise earning forecasts downward.

The technical analytic tools were the first to give favorable signs and a promise of better times to come. Slowly, insiders began to buy again.

No matter how good analytic tools are, it is still extremely difficult to really stand by a decision once it had been made. When everybody else plays the confirmed pessimist, an investor will certainly be shaken by doubts whether he should go against the experts' opinion, even though he has received a clear buying signal. For example, the emotional pressure on the investor is tremendous if, at the precise moment he has decided to invest in steel the newspapers begin to report bad prospects for the industry. Indecision caused by uncertainty usually leads to putting off making an investment decision. That way, however, the effectiveness of analytic tools is, a priori, negated.

Analysis of all aspects of the economy, of the monetary, technical, and psychological market situation, is the tool that enables the analyst to differentiate between long-, medium-, and short-term trends of the market and to assess the situation of specific stocks. In the following section we examine the question of how and to what extent methodical forecasts can be made using these tools.

ANALYSIS OF ECONOMIC AND MONETARY INFLUENCES

Indicators for Determining Overall Economic Change

Gross National Product

What is the connection between the price movements of individual stocks and the overall economic environment? American experts estimate that four-fifths of all changes in corporate success are caused by external factors that cannot be influenced by the individual company. These are, among others, the overall economic statistics, economic and structural policy, and changes in monetary and capital markets. King has published a study which showed that 31% of all stock prices move in concert with the general market trend, 37% are dependent on overall economic factors, such as interest rates, 12% are subject to conditions in individual industrial lines, and only 20% are influenced by changes within individual companies. [Benjamin King, Market and Industry Factors on Stock Prices Behavior, *Journal of Business* (January 1966).]

Anybody who tries to tie in the development of the stock market with the overall economic development in order to draw conclusions about future stock price movements has to know the laws of economic processes.

Among the individual interrelations that have to be analyzed are: production, investments, inventories (warehousing), level of prices and wages, supply and demand, full operating industrial capacity, interest rates, liquidity, and credit demand.

The gross national product (GNP) is the most comprehensive denominator by which the overall economy is measured. The GNP represents the market value of all goods and services within an economy. It is the aggregate of all reserves in the economy, such as wages, income, earnings, rate of interest, and rent income, or the aggregate of all expenditures of consumers, industry, and government (including exports). The GNP can be divided into separate components. The condition of these components can give more information about the stock market than the aggregate GNP alone. If, for example, there is a notable wage increase, this will influence company earnings and therefore affect stock prices. This effect on the market could clearly be seen when, in November 1977, the British miners demanded a 90% wage increase. The moment that demand became public knowledge, the market suffered a general slump.

However, future movement of the stock market and of individual stocks is more dependent on the future GNP than on the current one. The actual GNP used for price forecasting is in itself variable and therefore subject to forecasting. Several indicators precede, coincide, or lag behind the overall cycle of the economy. A breakdown could be made as follows:

Economic Indicators

1. Leading Indicators

The index of the 12 leading economic indicators published by the Department of Commerce belongs to that category of data about the United States economy whose publication is always eagerly awaited, especially by the Wall Street community. Each one of these separate indices has its own value. The leading indicator published by the National Bureau of Economic Research is composed of 12 index series:

◇ Average work week, production workers, manufacturing hours.
◇ Average weekly initial claims, for unemployment insurance.
◇ New business formation.
◇ New orders, durable goods industries.
◇ Contracts and orders, plant, and equipment.
◇ New building permits, private housing units.
◇ Change in book value, manufacturing, and trade inventories.
◇ Industrial material prices.
◇ Stock prices, S + P 500 common stocks.
◇ Corporate profits after taxes.
◇ Price to unit labor cost manufacturing.
◇ Change in consumer installment debt.

It is interesting to note that the stock market, too, is considered a leading indicator.

2. Co-Incident Indicators

Aside from the leading indicators, there are a number of indicators that move parallel to economic processes. Among them are the rate of unemployment and retail trade sales.

3. Lagging Indicators

A number of indicators react belatedly to an economic cycle. They reach their peak when the overall economic situation has slowed down and are at their lowest when economic growth has already increased. Among these are the index of commercial and industrial loans and the index of plant and equipment expenditures.

At the moment of their publication, these three indicators give a concise and sharply defined picture of the economy and the trend the economy has taken during the past months. Any changes in the individual indicators should be fully investigated to improve analysis. For instance, if there is a favorable change in 6 out of 12 leading indicators, this would represent 50%. If, during the next month, 8 indicators (not necessarily the same ones) change favorably, there is a change of 67%. In this way, changes in the overall economic situation and that of the stock market can be identified more clearly than by just considering the leading indicators as a single entity.

Indicators for Determining Monetary Change

Overall economic movements do not follow independent natural laws. They are to a great extent codetermined by political decisions. Since the effect of these decisions only becomes apparent after some delay, it is—in order to make a forecast of the overall economy— important to observe the political-economic decision processes of those institutions that have the necessary power invested in them. To that extent, political-economic decisions can take on the character of leading indicators. Among the most important decision processes on the economic-politic level are fiscal and Federal Reserve policies. A Fiscal Policy that is to serve as an economic regulator tries to influence the overall economic demand by means of variations in the budget. The best-known method is "deficit spending," which goes back to Keynes' macroeconomic theory. The government attempts to create an additional demand with the help of a budget deficit that is meant to revive the economy. Fiscal Policy intends to control demand and is handled by the Congress. The Monetary Policy of the Federal Reserve, on the other hand, aims to regulate money supply. The variation in money supply is simply reflected in a variation of the price level. According to the monetarists, however, the money supply represents the main reason for changes in merchandizing and therefore in the cyclical movements as well. They claim that for that reason monetary policy clearly takes precedence over fiscal policy. This bone of contention still lies between the defenders of the various modern economic theories.

Even though the monetarists—from Irving Fisher to Milton Friedman—have had quite an impact on the decision finding of the Federal Reserve, it seems unrealistic to suppose that the movement of stock prices is exclusively dependent on the movement of money supply or the trend in interest rates.

Analysis of Changes in the Money Supply

Lately, the market has been reacting to the money supply figures published every Thursday after the market closes with such an incredible degree of sensitivity that one is tempted to speak of a veritable "money supply fixation." That fact in itself, however, is no proof that variations in the money supply are immediately converted into variations of the national product or stock prices respectively. Rather, it indicates that the majority of investors in the market are convinced that such an interrelation exists. Although the structure of interest rates can be altered by changes in money supply, it is also quite obvious that each week the volume of money fluctuates within a certain spread in a dynamic economy. However, this does not cause a simultaneous change in the overall economic situation. This becomes evident when at certain times the money supply M_1 increases, but M_2 and M_3 go down or the reverse occurs. Only a general trend of the money supply to either expand or decrease will have a decisive effect on the interest rates or on the economy. Incidentally, many investors are extremely hazy about the meaning of the figures M_1, M_2, and M_3. This is yet another indication of the public's irrational behavior in connection with the stock market.

M_1 = demand deposits plus currency held by the nonbank public.
M_2 = money supply M_1 plus commercial bank time deposits.
M_3 = money supply M_2 plus savings deposits.

If the Federal Reserve switches from a restrictive to an expansive money supply policy and there are also other favorable factors, that policy certainly can lead the market out of a slump. This connection is extremely complex and has so far been explored very little in theory, and not properly understood, either.

The problem remains, how to definitely recognize a change in the Federal Reserve's policy. If that were easily done and the consequences from this procedure were plainly recognizable, neither cyclical nor price forecasting would be necessary. The investor would only have to wait for a signal from the Federal Reserve and then go "full steam ahead"—he could be sure of his profits.

Figure 5 illustrates the difficulty of analyzing changes in money supply. An interrelation between trends for changes in money supply and those of the Dow Jones Industrial Average can certainly be deduced. There is, however, a considerable time lag between changes in money supply and the movement of the stocks, which in the end leaves considerable leeway for interpretation.

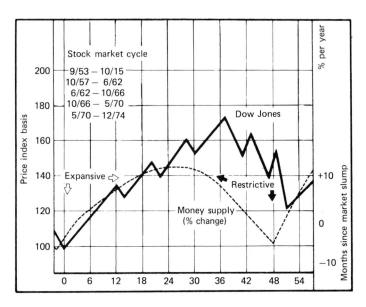

Figure 5   Stock prices and money supply change (per cycle).
(Michael Hays, The Dow Jones Irwin Guide, *Homewood, Ill.,*
1977.)

Technically, the money supply presents the same problems as the GNP: the denominator used for price forecasts can in itself be predicted only with great difficulties. The problem with applying all the overall economic indicators is simply that it is the purpose of the stock market always to anticipate future economic developments.

Analysis of Changes in Interest Rates

The investor observing the actions of the Federal Reserve should not only watch for changes in the money supply but also include other aspects of Monetary Policy as well. This would apply predominantly to:

◇ The open market policy which involves the purchase and sale of government securities in the open market.

◇ The change in discount rates, that is, the interest rate on money borrowed by banks from the Federal Reserve.

◇ The minimum reserve requirement policy, which determines how much money the banks have to deposit with the Federal Reserve (without interest).

The interaction of these three tools of the Federal Reserve, plus a few others, constitutes monetary and Credit Policy. The person who only looks at the changes in the prime rate will never gain proper understanding and insight into the changes of the structure of the interest rates. (The prime rate is the interest rate which United States banks charge their most prestigious clients.) In the spring of 1977 it became obvious how nonsensical it would be to make short-term investment decisions dependent on changes in the prime rate. One week the First National City Bank increased its prime rate, but a week later the Morgan Guarantee Trust lowered its rate. The two banks had used different formulas for calculating the prime rate and therefore achieved different results.

It is much more important to watch the Discount Rate and the Federal Funds Rate. Only when these change will the prime rate begin to move as well.

The level of short-term interest rates is determined directly by the Federal Funds Rate. The Federal Funds Rate in turn is directly determined by the Federal Reserve Board and should therefore be watched very closely. Figure 6 illustrates the relationship of the Dow Jones Average and the Federal Funds Rate. Up to 1965 the rate of interest was never above 5%. After that it was usually higher. Experience has shown that the interest rate has an unfavorable influence on stock prices only if it is above 6% and shows signs of rising even further.

If the Monetary Policy is switched from restrictive to expansive, the result is usually an increase in stock prices. One has to keep in mind that there is often a time lag of several months between a change in monetary policy and a rise in prices. The reason for a change from restrictive to expansive Monetary Policy is quite often an increase in the rate of inflation, and it frequently occurs months before prices react to that move.

The Federal Reserve not only controls the money supply but also determines the margin requirements for those purchases or short sales investors can arrange through margin with their broker. This percentage can vary considerably. In 1977 it was at 50%; that is, the investor interested in a $10,000 purchase could get a $5000 loan

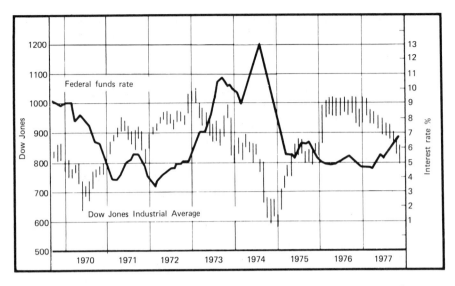

*Figure 6   Federal funds rate compared to the Dow Jones Industrial Average from 1970 to 1977. (**Dean Witter Reynolds Inc.,** **New York, Düsseldorf, September 1977.**)*

from his broker. The Federal Reserve changes these requirements infrequently. It might increase the percentage if there is reason to believe that there is either too much speculation going on or that stocks are overpriced. On the other hand, the percentage can also be reduced if additional buying power is needed in the market.

Investments on margin have both advantages and disadvantages. Whoever uses margin for speculating should remember that aside from the interest he has to pay, he might have to face the danger that additional funds will be needed if there are strong adverse price movements. On the other hand, with a proper forecast, earnings prospects can be extremely favorable. Every investor, however, should weigh carefully both advantages and disadvantages before a margin purchase. The investors' debit balances are published regularly and give a fairly good indication of how future market developments are seen by those investors.

In 1978 the Swiss magazine *Schweizer Wirtschaftsrevue Bilanz* published an article explaining the interrelation between stock market and interest rates.

"The investor is convinced that interest rates determine investments in bonds and that prices of debenture bonds fluctuate according to the level of interest rates. Therefore, the timing is watched by the investor with the necessary diligence. But what about stocks? Prices in the stock market are determined by supply and demand as well. For judgment, both the Monetary Policy and the trend in interest rates are important factors. In order to understand the interrelation between interest rates and stock prices one has to keep in mind that the supply, that is, the number of stocks, remains relatively constant. It is merely the demand that is subject to change. An increase in demand denotes an increase in prices; if the demand goes down, stock prices go down as well.

How can the investor measure the demand? Today, 75% of all stock turnovers are managed by institutions—insurance companies, mutual funds, pension funds, and the like. These investment groups cannot wait and ask themselves whether they should invest at all, but only where and to what extent. Because of the daily stream of money entrusted to them for investing, these institutions are up against constant pressure to invest. Every day they have to invest millions and a pause of only a few days would inevitably lead to a critical state and multiply that pressure. One of the golden rules for the investor is that he should look for an investment that promises a certain yield at minimum risk. For example, you will be quite safe if you invest your money in treasury bills or if you put it into a savings account. If, however, the return is too small for your ambitions, then you would have to risk buying stocks. In 1969, interest rates for bonds, deposit accounts, and short-term Eurodollars rose up to 9%; in 1974 they even reached 13%. In comparison, stocks with their relatively meager dividend returns offered small inducement to the investor and, at that time, most investors thought and acted along those lines.

In such a situation it becomes self-evident that the demand for stocks goes down if the yield of less risky investments increases. The higher the interest rates, the lower is the inducement to buy stocks. The moment interest rates have reached a peak and begin to go down again, money flows back into the stock market, even if the state of the economy is still far from satisfactory. This transition is very smooth, not abrupt, and most investors only recognize it through hindsight. To sum up, there are three essential reasons why decreasing interest rates can have a positive impact on the stock market:

◇ Stocks and bonds are competing investment forms, and they are both purchased because of their total yield. The current stock price, moreover, reflects the discounted total value of future dividends.

◇ Changes in interest rates influence company earnings power directly via financing and also by their effect in the economy. Low interest rates influence consumer demand and propensity to invest in addition to the inventories of companies.

◇ Fluctuations in interest rates have a direct influence on stock prices because of the readiness of the investor and speculator and opportunities given to him to trade on margin.

As Figure 7 shows, long-term interest rates are usually higher than the short-term interest rates, since long-term loans as a rule carry a higher risk. If this ratio of interest rates is reversed, sooner or later the market will deteriorate. Then *why* do most bank experts and investors persist in remaining "bearish" long after they should have turned bullish? Just consider the situation at the end of 1974. There was a worldwide recession. Inflation in the United States and in Switzerland was at a record high. Gold was around $200 an ounce. The stock market barely showed signs of life and just crawled along. Investors were faced with bleak prospects and despair. The economic laws seemed to be completely out of kilter and no longer valid.

In the fall of 1974, more and more countries switched from a restrictive monetary policy, which was instituted to fight inflation, to an expansive monetary policy in order to relieve unemployment. The trend in interest rates topped out even though rates still remained at a high. Investors held on with tooth and nail to their high returns and wanted nothing to do with so fickle a thing as the market. However, the market "looked ahead," started an upward trend, and became generally bullish. The investor who had not heeded the writing on the wall was stranded. Whether interest rates are high or low is not alone important for the stock market. The trend in interest rates and the ratio between short-, medium-, and long-term interest rates are just as influential.

Admittedly, it is not easy to maintain sunny optimism after the stock market has been in a slump for a long period. And pessimism is even harder to sustain if stock market prices are high and wealth seems to be imminent. But here one has to watch out and make certain that wishful thinking does not take precedence over reality.

The level of interest rates is influenced by the following facts:

◇ Increase or decrease of liquidity in the economy.
◇ Inflation potential of price levels.
◇ Economic activities and demand for capital.

Only a detailed and careful analysis of all factors permits interpretation of the future course of interest rates. It does not suffice to consider the status of interest rates isolated from all other factors. A stock market prognosis based on the various monetary factors is certainly not infallible. However, it would mean paying dearly for the experience if one were to disregard them. Successful investments require the observation of the course of interest rates and money supply, of the state of liquidity of banks and industry, of the technical state of the market, and a correct evaluation of all psychological factors. As Baron Rothschild said at one time: "Give me power over monetary circulation (and thus over interest rates) and you can pass as many laws as you want." [Schweizer Wirtschafts Revue Bilanz, *Hauptsache die Zinsen fallen,* March 3, 1978.]

Other Political Influences

Wage Policy

In a free enterprise economy such as ours, only part of the economic responsibility lies on the shoulders of the government and the Federal Reserve. The government has no specific control over wage policy, which is a highly important factor in the overall economic picture. Wages and income are exclusively negotiated by management and labor. Wages can influence stock prices directly, not just indirectly via the GNP. The attraction of stocks can diminish considerably compared to other types of investment if there is a rapid growth in the rate of wages at the expense of earnings. Wage-intensive industries naturally are more heavily influenced by any factors concerning the wage policy than highest capital-intensive industries. This, too, contributes to the various shifts of stock prices. And finally, if the domestic wage policy differs from foreign wage policy, the ratio of yields in inland and foreign investments is affected.

For all these reasons, the investor should carefully observe wage policy. If, however, he wanted to project future stock prices, he first would have to be able to anticipate the results of future wage negotiations. Here the methodological difficulties are the same as

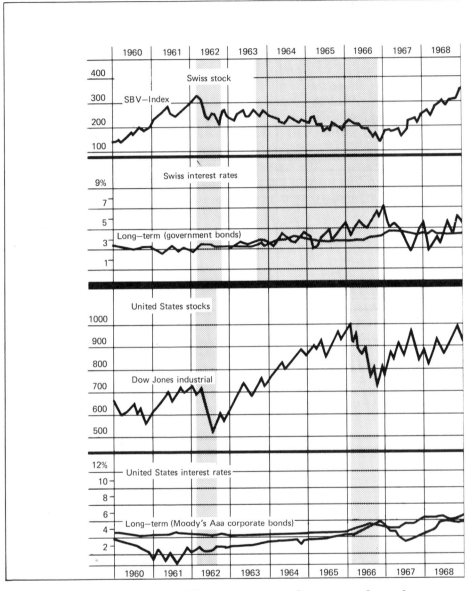

Figure 7 Comparison of the American and Swiss stock market and interest rates, 1960–1978. (Schweizer Wirtschafts Revue, March 1978.)

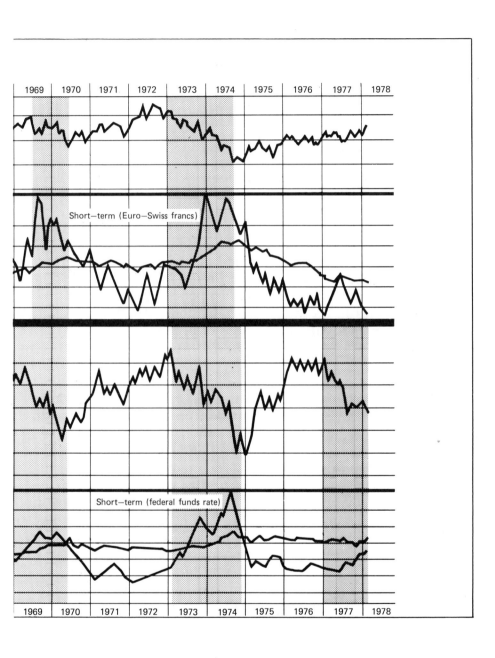

| 1969 | 1970 | 1971 | 1972 | 1973 | 1974 | 1975 | 1976 | 1977 | 1978 |

Short—term (Euro—Swiss francs)

Short—term (federal funds rate)

| 1969 | 1970 | 1971 | 1972 | 1973 | 1974 | 1975 | 1976 | 1977 | 1978 |

47

with the GNP: the indicator that is supposed to help him establish a price forecast, is itself predictable only to a limited extent. Even if one were to apply the whole spectrum of overall economic indicators, there will always be an element of doubt and uncertainty because the stock market anticipates the economy.

Tax and Social Security Laws

Overall economic developments happen within an intricate framework of social, technological, cultural, and legal conditions, all of which have a definite impact on the economy. Therefore, it is also very important to note whether there are any changes in these individual conditions. In Germany, for example, the reform of the corporate tax law and the joint management laws are the most prominent examples of such changes in recent years. The yield of stock investments is affected by the corporate tax reform and the investor now has to decide whether this form of investment still compares favorably with other modes of investment.

Conclusion

The reader may feel that although all these overall economic conditions and influences on the stock market are extremely important, they are also very difficult to predict and therefore hardly suitable for an analysis. Especially with respect to the GNP, it would seem hard to contradict this assumption. The prediction of business cycles is of importance to all investors, to all industry, the Federal Reserve, and to governments. But even research institutes reach somewhat inaccurate conclusions in their economic forecasts and rarely agree in their figures. In view of this, it seems rather unfair to expect the investor as a layman to achieve more dependable results. However, the investor who declines to tackle this task runs the danger of not recognizing important business cycles. The importance of the interactions between stock prices, changes in interest rates, money supply, business cycles, and the like cannot be stressed enough. Even the smallest effort made to penetrate these relationships ultimately benefits the investor.

The real problem in using these indicators for practical purposes of analysis lies in the fact that these connections cannot be pinned down accurately. This leaves a lot of room for interpretation and

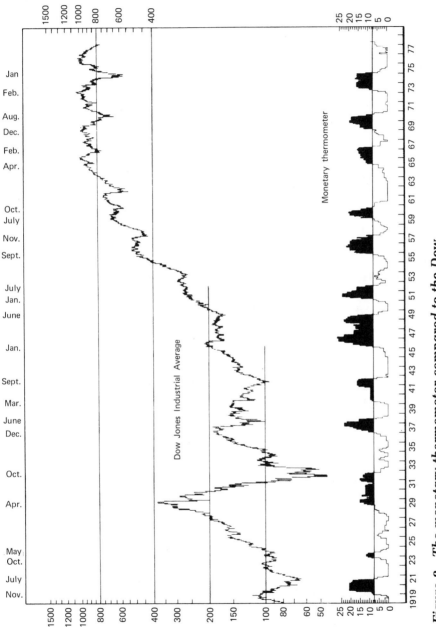

Figure 8   The monetary thermometer compared to the Dow Jones Industrial Average 1919–1977. (The Bank Credit Analyst, Montreal, Canada.)

49

makes a direct application as a means for price forecasting rather troublesome. However, the monetary thermometer of the Bank Credit Analyst (Figure 8) shows that such efforts can, in fact, bring quite favorable results. This demonstrates how an aid for price forecasting can be constructed if a multitude of monetary factors are taken into account. The results achieved by these analytical tools can be traced from 1919 to 1977. Under this system, values above 7 are negative and those under 7 positive. For the long-term-oriented investor, this is a much better tool for analyzing the overall situation of the market than merely watching the separate monetary data. The investors who in the past have used this analytic tool for making buying and selling decisions participated in most upwaard trends and were in general saved from the effects of downward movements.

The favorable results achieved with the help of such models apply only to forecasts of the general stock market. They offer very few indications as to how separate stocks will perform—unless one assumes that a rise in the market will also cause all stocks to go up or vice versa. Therefore, to work successfully with stocks and options, a variety of individual analytic tools have to be applied.

TECHNICAL ANALYSIS OF THE STOCK MARKET

The evaluation of all those data the stock market itself supplies is called "technical analysis." A large number of relationships of all kinds are used for forecasting, among them volume, price movements, most active stocks, short sales, cash reserves of funds, and investors. Several possibilities for analysis are described in the following sections.

Measurement of Market Variation Using the Advance/Decline Line

A comparison of the movements of the Dow Jones with that of separate stocks shows that although they predominantly move together, these movements vary considerably with regard to their extent and magnitude. During the first phase of a bull market, the high quality values of the Dow Jones and similar issues are frequently favored. It is only months later, when the trust in continuing favorable economic and political news is firmly established, that the investors begin to concentrate more and more on speculative stocks and secondary securities. When the blue chips have surpassed their peak and the first doubts in a long-lasting upswing of the economy begin to spread, investors frequently turn to low-priced stocks. Stocks priced at $10.00 to $30.00 suddenly become the focus of attention, and often there is a large percentage increase one never finds with the blue chips. The volume very often can go above 100,000 shares per day. These distinctions in trends within the individual market segments and industrial groups (interest sensitive, energy, technology, consumption, etc.) can be seen in every market phase. It is therefore important for the profit-minded investor to discover which stock groups are favored and also which of the stocks within those groups are the best movers.

One of the oldest methods for measuring price trends is to collect and analyze the data, published daily, of advancing/declining stocks. These figures reflect the movement of all stocks and present a much clearer picture of the market than the Dow Jones alone, which contains only 30 stocks out of more than 1800 traded on the New York Stock Exchange. (Among the Dow Jones stocks, however, are most of the important United States industrial giants.) To arrive at the advance/decline line, one adds up daily (weekly) the number of stocks that have gone up. The number of stocks that have declined during that day or week are then subtracted from that sum, and these figures are accumulated. The result is the advance/decline index. The individual numbers achieved that way have by themselves no explanatory value. But, as Figure 9 shows, the favorable or unfavorable trend of this line has a good predictive value for the entire market structure, because it indicates the predominant trend of all stocks.

In the middle of a bull market, nearly all stock groups move in the same direction. The analytic value of the advance/decline line is of particular importance if there are divergences with respect to the Dow. If the Dow is still rising while the advance/decline line starts pointing downward, it is usually a warning signal that the Dow, too, will soon follow this downward trend. The bearish divergence (the Dow rises, the advance/decline line falls) simply means that the overall market has already changed direction

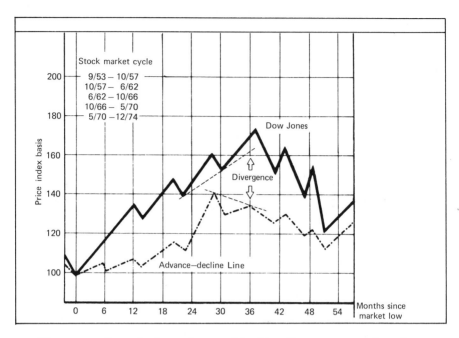

Figure 9 Cumulative advance/decline line compared to the typical stock market cycle. (Michael Hays, The Dow Jones Irwin Guide, Homewood, Ill., 1977.)

while the Dow Jones issues or comparable blue chips still retain their presumed position as favorites. If divergences occur, one should be wary of the movements of the Dow Jones Averages.

On the New York Stock Exchange approximately 1800 stocks are traded. Figures on all the transactions can be obtained daily from the exchange, the news media, and brokers. The absolute fluctuation of rising or falling stocks compared to the total number of the 1800 stocks traded can be established by means of a 10-week moving average. (The method of computation differs only slightly from that used in statistics; therefore, one cannot really speak of a true moving average.) If, for example, 1000 out of those 1800 stocks go down, 400 have risen and 400 remained unchanged, the absolute margin of difference between the stocks that have risen and those that have declined amounts to 600. If one puts the 600 in relation to the total number of 1800, one achieves a rate of 33%. As long as the moving average fluctuates between 20 and 30%, the short-term market fluctuation can be considered to be normal. In recent years, a rise of the indicator up to more than 40% has always been a fairly certain indication that the lowest point of a market had been reached. Only a disproportionately strong selling pressure, a selling climax, can cause this high figure.

Volume

The interpretation of changes in the volume traded daily creates more confusion than any other market factor. Too often the generalization is made that increasing volume together with a market increase is bullish (favorable), whereas falling volume and a declining market are signs for a bearish (unfavorable) situation.

According to Joseph E. Granville (*A Strategy of Daily Stock Market Timing for Maximum Profit*, Prentice-Hall, Englewood Cliffs, N. J., 1960), a change in volume signifies the following:

◇ If the quality of market leadership deteriorates on an upswing in the Dow Jones Industrial Average, it is pretty reliable evidence that a near-term decline is in the making.

◇ If the quality of market leadership deteriorates on a downswing in the Dow, it is pretty reliable evidence that a good near-term advance is in the making.

◇ If the quality of market leadership improves on a downswing in the Dow, it indicates that the market decline is likely to continue.

◇ If the quality of market leadership improves on an upswing in the Dow, it indicates that the market advance is likely to continue.

In the early phase of a bear market the volume usually is small, because the public believes that this is just a normal price correction. Investors tend to buy more stocks at a favorable, that is, lower price, rather than sell. If, however, the price decline continues, the odd-lotters get scared, too. Profit taking, steadily growing short sales, and finally panic sales speed up the downward trend. In the end there is a selling climax with which investors gripped by panic want to save the small remainder of their original stake. As soon as the market has shaken out the last seller, the overall market has regained its power for a long-term upswing.

New Highs—New Lows

The analysis of the figures provided by new highs and new lows is another method by which the general conditions of the stock market can be measured. For this, the 1800 stocks of the New York Stock Exchange serve as a basis. The method works on the principle that a favored (i.e., technically strong) stock will continue to achieve new highs. A new peak in the index and a decline in the number of new highs point toward a deterioration of the market. There are, in this case, fewer stocks in great demand, leading to variations with the index movements. On the other hand, if the index declines, the number of new lows will show a rising trend. If both the index and the number of new lows decrease, a reversal in trend of the overall market can be anticipated. The investor can recognize at what point the total value changes its positive or negative direction if he combines the declining and rising stocks in a moving average. Figure 10 shows the divergences between the new highs–new lows with the Dow and how an indicator for forecasting market trends can be deduced from these data.

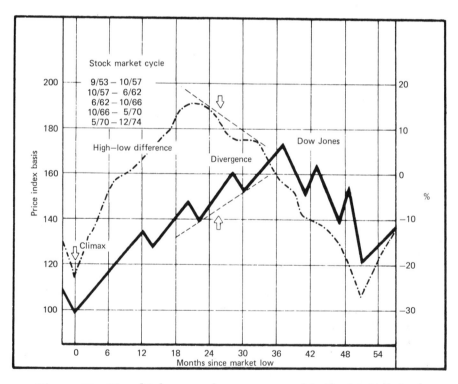

*Figure 10   New highs–new lows compared to the typical stock market cycle. (Michael Hays, **The Dow Jones Irwin Guide**, Homewood, Ill., 1977.)*

ANALYSIS OF INVESTORS' BEHAVIOR (OPTIMISM/PESSIMISM)

Stock prices in a functioning market are determined by a constant adjustment of supply and demand. Every factor that changes either the supply or the demand will thus automatically be reflected in the prices of stocks.

Sources for the supply of stocks are, among others:

⋄ Corporations that offer new shares.

⋄ Investors who are dissatisfied with their holdings and therefore sell.

⋄ Profit taking.

⋄ Investors who want to limit their losses and therefore sell.

⋄ Investors who are engaged in short-selling.

The demand for stocks is influenced by the following factors among others:

⋄ A rise in prices that is expected because the overall economy seems favorable.

⋄ Investors who have the opportunity to buy on credit from brokers and banks.

⋄ The free liquidity of the big funds and institutions.

⋄ The necessity to cover the short positions, that is, to buy back when prices have risen too much.

The constant adjustment of supply and demand in many cases reflects certain kinds of investors' behavior. A few examples follow.

Cash Reserves of Investors in Brokerage Accounts

Every month the New York Stock Exchange reports the outstanding free credit balances held by brokers in their customers' accounts. These assets, which remain untouched for a fixed time, have been deposited in advance for future stock purchases or have been left in the account after stocks have been sold. They can be very valuable indicators for the market. Credit balances are highest in the early phase of a bull market. When prices go up and optimism grows, these credit balances slowly diminish. Consequently, these balances are at their lowest when the overall market has reached its peak. The fluctuations of the free credit balances can therefore be considered valuable contrary opinion indicators. These figures also give an idea of how the public feels with respect to the future market—is the mood predominantly optimistic or pessimistic?

Cash Reserves of Funds

In 1977, the equity capital of 5000 United States joint stock corporations amounted to approximately $900 billion. The actions of institutions have gained extraordinary importance to price movements, because 60 to 70% of all transactions involve them. For this reason, the free cash reserves the funds have at their disposal are an important indicator for future price trends since the accumulated cash reserves represent a potential increase in demand. An examination of the funds' results has shown that their performance was no better than that of the layman. Of course, the funds' managers have to submit to a number of restrictions. But even so, the published figures show that the funds almost always were wrong in their evaluation of timing (i.e., the moment when one should be either fully invested or have a large amount of cash reserves). The ideal procedure for the investor would be to become invested fully when the market is low or to sell when the market has reached its peak. Since the data on the free cash positions of the big funds are available each month, another contrary opinion indicator can thus be established.

Figure 11 shows that the managers of the big funds behave no better or wiser than the small investor. Cash reserves are very high when the market is depressed. For that reason, no selling pressure is fed into the market at those times. The funds' statutes require that they normally be fully invested. Under these circumstances, they can, at a time like that, only make purchases. Consequently, when the market is topping out, the cash reserves are sharply reduced, and the funds can no longer apply buying pressure. On the contrary, they can only operate from the buyers' side in such a situation. Obviously, not even the professional funds follow the golden rule of engaging in counter-cyclical investments to ensure success. When prices have peaked, investors bubble over with optimism; they give in to bleak pessimism when the market touches rock bottom.

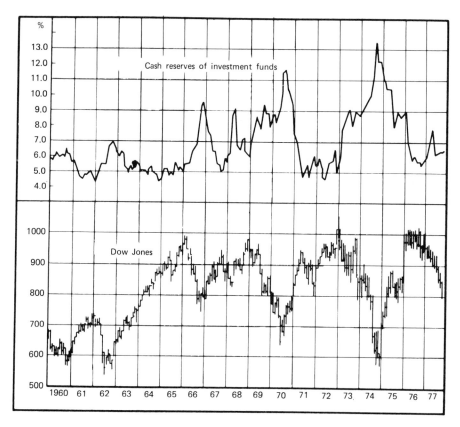

Figure 11 Funds cash reserves compared to the Dow Jones Industrial Average, 1960–1977. (Jerome B. Cohen et al., Investment Analysis and Portfolio Management, 3rd ed., Dow Jones, Irwin Inc., Homewood, Ill., 1977.)

Recommendations of American Stock Market Advisory Letters

Not only do the changes in daily prices serve—individually and collectively—as criteria for price forecasting, but the recommendations of market letters are at least of equal interest. A study of market letters conducted from 1962 to 1975 showed that overall their recommendations would have produced poor results. When the market is at the bottom, the mood of these professionals is singularly pessimistic, but they become elated when the market is nearing a top. It seems safe to assume that these professionals, too, simply follow their emotions. Obviously, they do not base their recommendations on proper analysis but merely adjust to the general market and thus plainly support the small investor in his irrational opinions (optimism/pessimism).

Figure 12 shows the correlation between the recommendations of market letters and the changes in the Dow Jones Industrial Average. Whenever pessimism prevailed, the Dow clearly moved upwards: when the Dow had reached its peak, optimism was also at its highest.

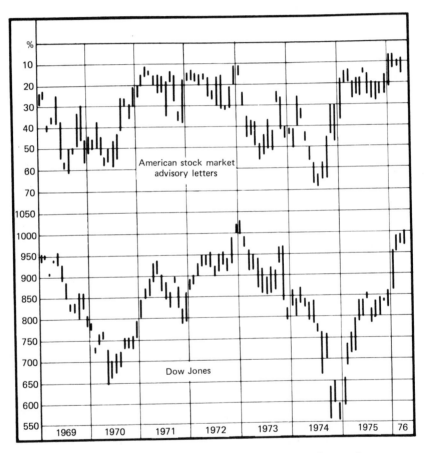

Figure 12   Recommendations of American stock market advisory letters compared to the Dow Jones Industrial Average, 1969–1976. (Investors Intelligence, Inc., Larchmont, New York, 1977.)

Short Sales of Odd-Lotters, Members, and Specialists

Another indicator for measuring the investors' behavior is contained in evaluating short positions. Investors who expect falling prices engage in short sales. Since short sales always have to be covered at some time by rebuying stocks, this practice automatically creates a future buying demand. In practice, the short interest ratio is of more interest than the sum of short sales. This ratio is computed by dividing the monthly total of short positions by the daily average volume of the same month.

As Figure 13 shows, the ratio of all stocks traded on the NYSE in general moved from 1960–1977 between 1.0 and 2.0. When the

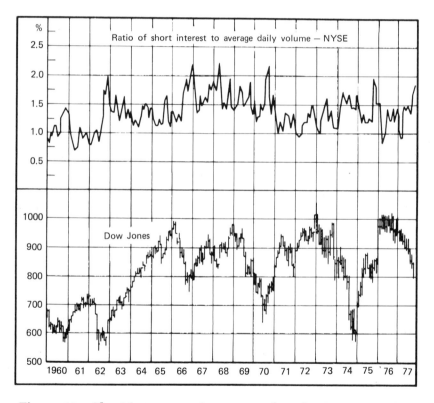

Figure 13   Short-interest ratio compared to the Dow Jones In-dustrial Average, 1960–1977. (Jerome B. Cohen et al., Invest-ment Analysis and Portfolio Management, *3rd ed., Dow Jones Irwin, Inc., Homewood, Ill., 1977.)*

ratio rose above 2.0, that meant, as a rule, a significant low of the market. With an increase in the short interest ratio, the number of investors who must cover sooner or later grows steadily. Even a small event will finally induce investors to cover these positions. This in turn causes a strong up-trend in the market because of the strong demand for replacement of the borrowed shares.

Just as an analysis can be conducted with the short interest ratio, in which all short figures are combined, the short figures of the odd-lotters can be used as an analytical tool as well. (An odd-lotter is an investor who deals in fewer than 100 shares per trade.) It has gener-

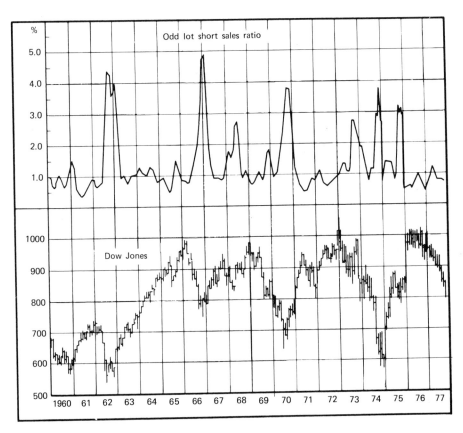

Figure 14   Odd-lot short sales ratio compared to the Dow Jones Industrial Average, 1960–1977. (Jerome B. Cohen et al., Investment Analysis and Portfolio Management, 3rd ed., Dow Jones Irwin, Inc., Homewood, Ill., 1977.)

ally been thought that this group of investors represents the portion of the public that usually makes the wrong investment decisions, and therefore the short figures of this investors' group are analyzed. (Incidentally, although this opinion was valid in the 1960s, it could no longer be as significant in the 1970s.) As Figure 14 shows, the market moved in conjunction with the extremes of these short sale indicators. Whenever the ratio rose to approximately 4%, the market had reached a low.

The behavior of specialists can also be measured by analyzing the short figures. Specialists are among the few who have suc-

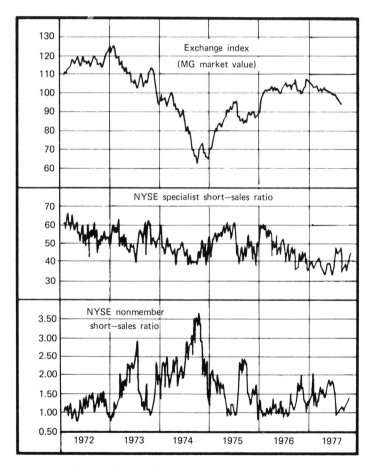

Figure 15   Short sales indicators. (*The M/G* **Financial Weekly,** *October 1977.*)

ceeded in making above-average profits over a long period of time, since they are in a position to evaluate and apply the knowledge they have gained from incoming orders. The short figures of these specialists are also published and can therefore be evaluated as well. For that purpose, the short figures are converted into percentages of the total. If the short figures of specialists during one week amount to $1.5 million and the total short figures together amount to $3 million, the percentage is 50%. Generally speaking, the market trend would be considered favorable if this figure falls below 40%. An increase to more than 60% signals an unfavorable market trend. The specialists' short sales can not be considered a contrary opinion indicator, as are the short interest ratio and the short sales of odd-lotters. Figure 15 shows the extent of the difference between the short sales of specialists and those of nonmembers of the exchange.

INTERIM CONCLUSIONS

So far, various means for judging the medium- and long-term condition of the stock market have been discussed. Although each indicator in itself possesses a certain predictive ability, a more extensive application of other indicators would greatly heighten the chances for a successful analysis. Figure 16 gives an example of such a process of analysis as well as the conclusions that may be drawn from it.

Economic and Fundamental Indicators

The first indicator, the GNP, clearly illustrates that the stock market anticipates the economy—nearly without exception. Any investor who in 1970, 1973, and 1974 had waited for a turn in business conditions before making an investment decision, certainly had missed the boat—both getting on and getting off. Investors, however, seem unable to get it into their heads that the market can hit rock bottom in the middle of an economic boom. However, the

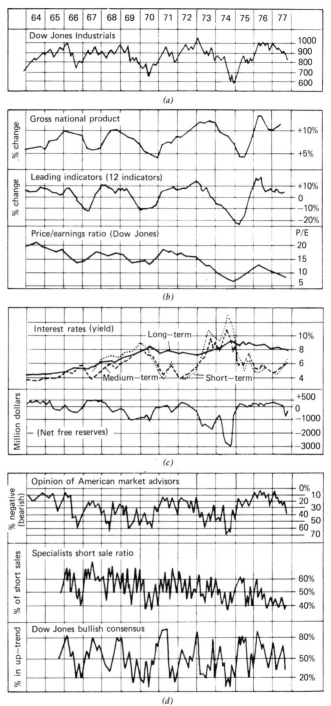

| 64 | 65 | 66 | 67 | 68 | 69 | 70 | 71 | 72 | 73 | 74 | 75 | 76 | 77 | |

Dow Jones Industrials
—1000
—900
—800
—700
—600

(a)

Gross national product
% change
+10%
+5%

Leading indicators (12 indicators)
% change
+10%
0
−10%
−20%

Price/earnings ratio (Dow Jones)
P/E
20
15
10
5

(b)

Interest rates (yield)   Long—term
10%
8
6
Medium—term   Short—term
4

Million dollars
+500
0
−1000
(Net free reserves)
−2000
−3000

(c)

Opinion of American market advisors
% negative (bearish)
0%
10
20
30
40
50
60
70

Specialists short sale ratio
% of short sales
60%
50%
40%

Dow Jones bullish consensus
% in up—trend
80%
50%
20%

(d)

Figure 16   Dow Jones Industrial Average 1964–1977. (a) *Stock exchange index.* (b) *Economy indicators.* (c) *Monetary indicators.* (d) *Technical and psychological indicators.* (Schweizer Wirtschafts Revue, *November 1977.*)

63

truth is that there is no direct connection between economic news and the current state of the market. Many of the figures published on the economy refer to conditions that have long since changed. The figures of the GNP, for example, are only published every quarter.

The second indicator—the leading indicators—shows a much better and more favorable correlation with the Dow than the GNP. These figures are published monthly and therefore possess a relatively small time lag. If this indicator falls continuously for several months, the outlook for a bull market is not good.

The *third indicator*, the price-earnings ratio, is said to be the favorite analytic tool of the fundamentalists. As it turns out, however, hardly any tangible connections can be established between the price-earnings ratio and the level of the market.

It is important to remember that the economic news, wars and crises, earnings reports, or any other daily news have no direct influence on the market. The important factor is the reaction of millions of investors to this "news." This is the secret why the market reacts to identical news favorably once and then again totally unfavorably, given a different cycle.

Monetary Indicators

Monetarists believe they have found the key to success in the evaluation of money supply, liquidity, interest rates, and the policy of the Federal Reserve. Even today, many people share the opinion that interest rates are an absolutely dependable indicator for the market. Increasing interest rates have to serve as the scapegoat if the market goes down.

The fourth indicator, which represents the development of interest rates in the United States during the past 14 years, parallels the stock price movement over the same period. In the beginning of 1970 and in the middle of 1974, short-term interest rates showed a tendency for a strong decline, and the market followed suit. But in 1972 the market rose, while interest rates, too, went up. This is the trap the investor is liable to overlook when he relies on a single indicator and gives it too much weight. The same can happen to the analyst who becomes the slave of his charts.

The fifth indicator, the bank liquidity—like the changes in the discount rate—is a much better indicator than the interest rate itself. As the textbooks pronounce gravely, "liquidity is the driving power of the economy and the stock market." This rather dependable indicator says: buy when the index rises above +$100 million; sell, if it falls below −$200 million.

Events in the past have proved that the analysis of monetary factors leads to much better timing than the fundamental analysis. The London Exchange performed the impressive feat—in a time span of 15 months—of rising from 145 points in January 1975 to 420 points in May 1976 (Financial Times Index). This increase was achieved despite an ailing economy, galloping inflation, a battered currency, and an enormous tax load. But the monetary indicators were all favorable. Stocks were stalwart values, the short-term interest rate tumbled from 15% to nearly 5%, the balance of payments improved remarkably, and the money and capital market were liquid.

Technical and Psychological Indicators

Many analysts have reached the conclusion that the market itself would probably be its own best indicator, since the sum of all knowledge and all expectations for the future were already embedded in the prices. After all, is not the movement of the market determined by the subjective behavior of all investors, that is, by supply and demand? Accordingly, these analysts have set up a whole catalog of inquiries the investor should make: how extensive is the trust or mistrust of the public in the market? Is the public inclined to be pessimistic or optimistic? What are the various groups of investors doing, the conservatives, the speculators, the odd-lotters and the professionals? If all these questions were answered correctly, the investment decisions would improve considerably. For that purpose, the most actives are analyzed, trading scrutinized, short sale figures analyzed, the cash reserves of various investors' groups are sorted out, and supply and demand are measured. By means of divergences, extremes, changes in trends, and ratios, empirical values and laws are determined and given their meaning as buying and selling signals. When a certain extreme has been reached, the probability of a break or even a change in trend becomes more and more likely.

The *sixth indicator* shows the mood of the United States market advisors. The investor has a good chance for profit if he adds to his portfolio when 60% of all United States market letters advise against buying stocks. As soon as the mood becomes too optimistic, however (as was the case in January 1977 when only 5% expected a bad market year) it is advisable to get out—and fast!

The seventh indicator shows short sales of specialists. For a long time, this was an excellent indicator. When it rose above 60%, it meant selling; when it fell below 40%, it was a buying signal. This was true until 1976. Since then, the investors' behavior has changed once more. The reasons for that could be the boom in the options market or defensive tactics, such as hedging.

The eighth indicator measures the Dow-Jones stocks in their upward trend. As soon as the market has reached an extreme, it turns around. High tide follows low.

The indicators mentioned above can be arbitrarily extended. Considered separately, not one of them is an absolutely safe tool for forecasting. Taken together, however, they represent a good thermometer for measuring the overall state of the market. Their purpose is also to protect the investor from quick and unreflected actions. This way, precedence will be given to a rational evaluation of the market, and the purely subjective and emotional reactions will recede into the background. The evaluation of the state of the market, however, does not answer the question of which stocks the investor should concentrate on and which industries or groups should be selected. However, the investor buys stocks, not the market, and therefore some aspects of technical analysis that help to choose suitable stocks will be described in the following. Particularly with options, the choice of appropriate companies is of special importance because the investor has to select his stocks under a short-term point of view, because of the limits set by expiration dates.

ANALYSIS OF INDIVIDUAL INDUSTRIAL GROUPS

Analysis of Technological and Sociological Developments

The investor who wants to predict changes in the economic position of corporations and changes in industries should concentrate on two questions:

◇ What social changes will occur in society? What needs will manifest themselves on that basis that will have an impact on the economy?

◇ What new technologies will be developed in the future and which of them will be successful commercially? (For example, the development of the video recorder and the video disk have created a new market segment for the electronics industry.)

If we take the overall market situation into account, these two questions will naturally have to be asked the other way around as well, namely, which of the industrial branches will reach a saturation point with their products in the near future? And which techniques will have no future at all? These are the kind of questions management of the various industries must ask itself. In essence, the long-term investor should have the same qualities as a successful manager: namely, managerial foresight. Investors like J. P. Morgan and Flick who made fortunes in the market all possessed these qualities, which their less successful rivals lacked. After analyzing the overall market, the investor should check out the expected growth of an industry with the help of technical analytic tools or fundamental analysis before he starts selecting individual stocks.

Measuring the Relative Strength of Individual Industrial Groups

Any stock purchase should be preceded by a rough market selection. A possible subject heading might be, for example:

◇ Growth stocks
◇ Energy stocks
◇ Stocks sensitive to interest rates
◇ Consumer goods stocks

or:

◇ Blue chip stocks
◇ Secondary stocks
◇ High-priced stocks
◇ Low-priced stocks

Certain industrial groups are either favored or injured by changes in the interest rates, a new energy program, or an overall reduction of taxes. According to the level of information or methods of analysis, a preselection for purchase can thus be made.

On a purely technical basis, an even more differentiated division can be made by employing the method of "relative strength." For that, the changes of stocks, or industry groups, among themselves are measured and put into a ranking. The concept of "relative strength" was investigated by *Levy* on the basis of price movements of 200 stocks on the New York Stock Exchange from 1960 to 1965. He came to the conclusion that there is little sense in using this method if one wishes to achieve an accurate price forecast for individual stocks. However, it proved a relatively useful tool for forecasting the movements of an entire industrial group or index. The following hypothetical example will serve to explain the concept in detail.

Example: Within four weeks, the prices of stocks *A* and *B* moved as follows compared to the weekly closing prices:

		Week		
Stock	1	2	3	4
A	$10	$12	$10	$11
B	$10	$15	$14	$18

Measuring the changes of stocks *A* and *B* in dollars from week to week, one arrives at the following result:

		Week	
Stock	1–2	2–3	3–4
A	+$2	−$2	+$1
B	+$5	−$1	+$4

The changes in dollar value of the stocks within these four weeks have very little forecasting value seen by themselves. It is remarkable, however, that stock *B* in all three weeks behaved relatively stronger than stock *A*. The percentage changes of the stocks per week are as follows:

		Week	
Stock	1–2	2–3	3–4
A	+20%	−16%	+10%
B	+50%	−6.7%	+28%

The example shows that stock B during the three weeks behaved relatively stronger than stock A. However, the analysis of percentage changes can now only be done by computer, since the number of industries and individual stocks has become so great that it cannot be calculated in any other way.

Dean Witter Reynolds has established a "compare system" which divides 3500 stocks traded on different exchanges into 115 industrial groups. The relative changes of the individual industrial groups against each other are measured with the help of a 10-week moving average. A ranking of 1 to 100 is then introduced. Rank 1 represents the strongest industrial group; the weakest occupies rank 100. These changes are calculated and published every week.

Figure 17 shows that the industrial group "steel" on August 19, 1977, held rank 100 with a relative change of −14.96% in the 10-week moving average compared to other industrial groups. The retail discount industrial groups held rank 1 with a percentage change of +10.38%.

The movements of individual industrial groups can be followed and evaluated by the weekly observation of this ranking. A listing of changes in the industrial group "mobile homes" disclosed the following ranking:

Mobile Homes	
1977	Rank
August 19	80
August 26	73
September 2	67
September 9	59
September 16	49
September 23	42
September 30	42
October 7	38
October 14	30
October 21	18
October 28	12
November 4	9

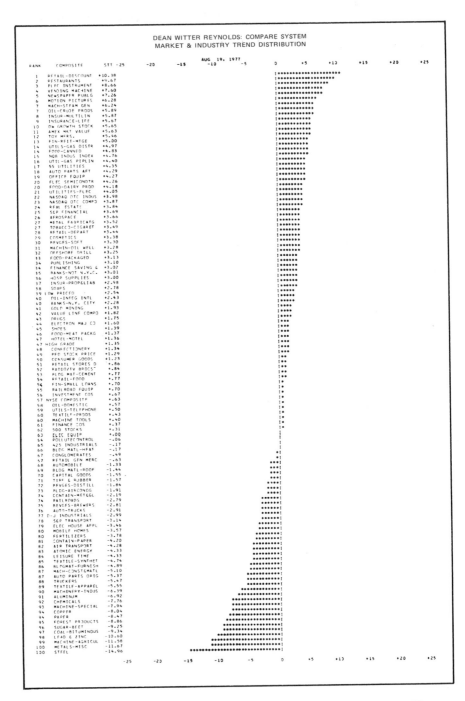

Figure 17 *Market and industry trend distribution. (Dean Witter Reynolds, Inc., New York, Düsseldorf.)*

This example shows how the development of an industry can be checked. If it improves steadily over the weeks, it can offer clues for a good selection. On average, with stocks in the mobile homes group, investors achieved a profit of approximately 30% during the period from August 19 to November 11, 1977. The next step, after a trend within an industrial group has been recognized, is to look for the stocks within this group that show the highest price appreciation potential. How this can be done is discussed next.

ANALYSIS OF INDIVIDUAL PRICE MOVEMENTS

Fundamental Analysis

Fundamental analysis attempts to deduce the price of a stock from the condition of the company that issues those shares. Roughly, the fundamentalists say: if a corporation is in good health, stock prices will go up, and vice versa. The starting points for price forecasting according to this method are changes in turnover, dividends, earnings, and the price-earnings-ratio.

With this form of analysis, attention focuses on predicting the earnings capacity of a corporation. Since profits of shareholders from dividends and/or increase in prices are much more likely to be good if the earnings capacity of a company is fairly sizable, the relation between earnings capacity and investment aims of the individual investor can be established. Aside from the quantitative data from the past, (earnings, inventory, turnover, rate of indebtedness, etc.) the qualitative aspects, such as management structure, production line and research expenditures, are taken into account.

In his article "The Trouble with Earnings" [*Financial Analysts Journal*, Vol. 28, No. 5, pp. 41–46 (September–October 1972)] Treynor pointed out how difficult it is to predict future earnings. Malkiel found out that the analysts' earnings estimates on the average are no more precise than the extrapolation of earnings on the basis of figures available from the past years. He compared the actual earnings of 115 companies with the earnings forecasts made for those companies by analysts of five big banks. The divergences in the individual forecasts were extreme and, in combination with the results of other studies, permit the conclusion that estimated future earnings of companies can hardly be of any help in forecasting price changes. [John G. Cragg and Burton G. Malkiel, "The Consensus and Accuracy of Some Predictions of the Growth of Corporate Earnings," *The Journal of Finance*, pp. 67–84 (March 1968).] In other words, any investor can achieve profit estimates of the same quality if he takes the published earnings from the past as a basis for his profits forecast. The famous "Higgledy Piggledy Growth Study" by Little [Institute of Statistics, Oxford, Vol. 24, No. 4, (November, 1962)] proved that the predicted profits had no connection whatsoever with those finally achieved. Clearly this means that earnings of individual corporations behave just like a random walk and permit no future forecasting. Companies with above-average profit earnings one year can have a considerable decrease in the following year. The same applies to forecasts by analysts. There will always be analysts who can boast of a good performance in this area. It is highly improbable, however, that good estimates of profits and earnings are sufficient for price forecasting. Price forecasts on the basis of profit estimates and the growth potential of a company have their limitations, as the following example shows.

In 1970 IBM's earnings after taxes amounted to approximately 1 billion dollars. In many of the preceding years, IBM had registered earnings growth of about 18% per year. If this earning growth were to continue up to the year 1995, the yearly earnings after taxes would come to approximately 63 billion dollars that year. If, during that same period, all company earnings after taxes in the United States would rise by 3.6%, the combined corporate profits in the United States would only come to approximately 100 billion dollar by 1995. Although the possibility that this rate of growth for IBM will materialize is theoretically possible, every analyst shies away from contemplating such a possibility and flatly refuses to include such profit forecasts in his considerations. Somehow, analysts manage to reduce automatically the rate of growth of IBM in their minds. This problem has been extensively discussed by David Durand in his article, "Growth Stocks and the Petersburg Paradoxon," *Journal of Finance*, Vol. 12, No. 3, pp. 348–363 (September 1957).

Studies have shown that the prognosis of the P/E ratio does not bring solid results either. It seems, rather, that psychological factors that are not measurable have an important influence on price movements, at least on a short-term basis. If there are enough investors who believe that an increase of the P/E ratio from 10 to 20 or more is justified because of the company's growth, the price will go up, no matter what the analysts proclaim in their price forecasts. A number of examples for this kind of behavior could be found in the 1960s.

Polaroid had a monopoly position for the production of instant photograph cameras. A nearly unlimited demand clashed with a limited supply. (At that time, there was a great number of these growth stocks around!) A P/E of 40-50-60 proved the child-like trust and starry-eyed expectations the investors had in the further growth of this company. But by 1977, the investors' behavior had changed profoundly. Stocks with a high P/E were no longer in demand. Suddenly, investors were no longer interested in the growth of a company but concentrated their attention on the yield. The change of the P/E is exemplarily demonstrated by Polaroid.

Example: Polaroid

Year	Earnings/share	Breadth of price (in $)	P/E ratio
1967	1.81	127– 77	70–43
1968	1.86	134– 88	72–47
1969	1.90	146–102	77–54
1970	1.86	131– 51	70–27
1971	1.86	117– 76	60–41
1972	1.30	150– 86	100–66
1973	1.58	143– 65	100–75
1974	0.86	88– 14	100–16
1975	1.91	41– 15	38–12
1976	2.43	44– 32	22–15
1977	2.64	39– 25	17– 9

The reasons analysts encounter such difficulties when trying to predict earnings, growth potential, or the P/E are mainly that

◇ Corporate releases rarely give complete insight into the actual conditions of the company. In some cases, the statements are deliberately falsified.

◇ Many analysts are incapable of interpreting correct figures correctly; that is, they are unable to extract the right answer from the real material.

◇ Many analysts—and some of the best among them—try to get managerial positions with big funds or institutions.

Chart Analysis

Since the beginning of this century, analysts have tried to extract profits from the market by using chart analysis. The starting point for this method is the conviction that all factors that influence pricing (economic, psychological, political, etc.)—no matter how accurately they can be determined—finally appear in prices via supply and demand. Earnings, dividends, economic changes, and so forth do not come into play, since all of them are already embedded in the price. Chartists try to recognize with the aid of charts at what time a change in the constellation can be expected and what effects it will have. They try to deduce the future price development solely on the basis of price patterns.

Some time ago, the autobiography of Konrad Adenauer, first German chancellor after World War II, was published, and one anecdote gave rise to a small but animated discussion: Adenauer had maintained that he had seen a shell coming directly at him and that he was able to watch its progress. Assuming that this really could be done, one could describe the difference between a chartist and a fundamentalist—a bit facetiously, maybe—as follows.

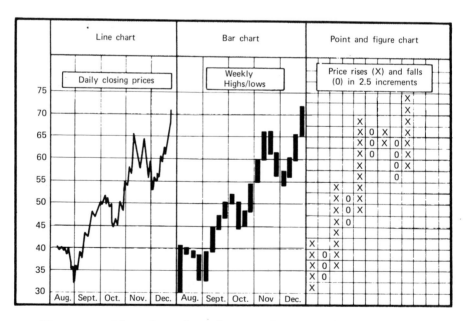

Figure 18   Line chart, bar chart, and point and figure chart.

Had Konrad Adenauer been a fundamentalist while he was watching the said shell hurtling toward himself, he would have had to reason as follows: We are at war, the Americans have arrived at the Rhine river, they are our enemies, they will bombard their enemies, they will also shoot at me since I am one of their enemies. They will have brought the necessary implements for firing a murderous object, and this object may hit me because of all those circumstances. It is therefore advisable to seek cover immediately. As a technician or chartist he would have had to argue this way: There comes a shell, I am standing exactly in its line of flight. If it continues like that—and everything points that way—it will hit me. Therefore, it is advisable to get out of its way quickly and seek cover.

Chart analysis is described explicitly and vividly in the textbooks by Magee and Granville. Therefore, we give a general summary and point out briefly the advantages and disadvantages of this method. For the chartist, only the price changes that are pinpointed in the charts such as the line chart, the daily bar chart, or the point and figure chart are important. (See Figure 18.)

The chartist tries to put price movements into a pattern by using the following aids, among others:

◇ Trend channels
◇ Rectangles
◇ Triangles
◇ Flags
◇ Diamonds
◇ Head-shoulder formations
◇ Support lines
◇ M and W formations
◇ Resistance lines

A certain investor's behavior is attributed to each of these formations. This can clearly be demonstrated with the rectangle formation (see Figure 19).

The basic assumption with the rectangle formation is that two equally strong contestants face each other. While one of them has fixed point A as a selling limit, the other continues to add to position at point B. This fluctuation between supply and demand causes prices to jump up and down between point A and point B until either one of the groups can no longer keep up the pace (i.e., they

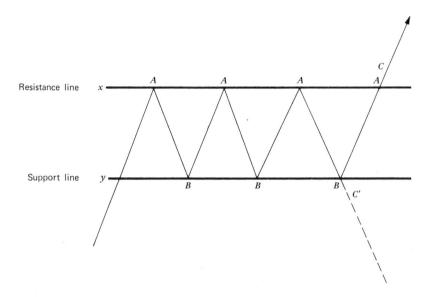

Figure 19   Resistance line and support line.

have run out of stocks or money) or until a new investor's group barges in and disturbs the relative equilibrium with additional purchases or sales. Only at that point will the price break through the resistance line X or the support line Y at either point C or C'. According to the chartists' rules, the investor has to wait until an unequivocal formation has been completed with a so-called break-out before he can make his investment decision.

Only at that point is the probability of rising or falling prices considered to be sufficiently certain. No professional chartist is so supremely confident, that he would claim the observation of formations will result in a precise forecast for the future price of a stock. He only tries (a) to determine the direction of a trend and (b) to stay with a trend as long as possible.

Since it can never be predetermined how long a trend will continue, the investor has to take care that his positions are safeguarded against failures. This can be done, for example, by stop-loss orders, where a limit is set according to certain criteria, such as the 3% rule. Similarly, the investor can determine in advance when he wants to take profits. The position automatically ends when those points are reached—unless the trend continues.

The problems of chart analysis can be summarized as follows:

◇ To follow the rules of chart analysis consistently can mean that a great number of trial runs are necessary before one gets hold of a strong trend. Numerous small losses incurred until that time, or high commissions, can dampen the investors' enthusiasm in this system.

◇ In many cases, the criteria of chart analysis are too confused and the investor has no clearly defined rules to grasp. Quite often, it is left to the investor to decide whether a certain movement is strong enough to be considered a signal.

◇ Consistent adherence to charts prevents the investor from taking advantage of a large share of the profits that would theoretically be possible. In the rectangle formation, it would obviously—in hindsight—have been best to buy at point B, assuming there had been a movement at C. The chartist is, however, expected to buy only when point C is reached. At that point the relative possibility for a continuing trend would be really good.

Frequently, the investor does not have the discipline to wait for the breakout but tries to "guess" at the price movement of a stock and consequently buys much too early. The surprise is great when prices then do not move in direction C but in the opposite direction C' and losses come tumbling in instead of the expected profits. Any rational strategy, by the way, is destroyed by this kind of "maybe—should I?—yes, I could" thinking!

Most investors neglect the relatively objective criteria of chart analysis for psychological reasons. For instance, if the press reports unfavorable earnings of a company, the investor pays scant heed even to unmistakeable buying signals concerning the shares of that company. When in doubt, the investor believes more in the newspaper or market letters than in a chart. However, if the investor wants to use this system successfully, he will have to follow the signals, even when nobody believes in them and all publications recommend the opposite.

Chart analysis has both its advantages and disadvantages. Still, it is a valid aid for making decisions, provided the investor follows the rules strictly. The investor cannot improve the system by constantly trying to substitute the objective criteria of chart analysis with his own emotional ideas. An imperfect system is always better than no system at all. Such excuses as "Just once won't hurt! Maybe there will be a rally? And the others aren't any better either!" are the first steps on the road to total failure and frustration. The big advantage of chart analysis is its homogenous system which presents relatively clear and useful clues for making decisions on individual stocks and also on groups or stock indices. The temptation of price forecasting on the basis of formations or trend lines is great, since the application of chart analysis seems so easy. This, however, can really backfire and prove to be a total fallacy. The person who tries to follow simplified chart rules without previous relevant experience in this area will hardly be successful in making profits. Afterward, it is always obvious how a formation came about, and the investor can hardly believe his own stupidity. He wonders how on earth he could have missed the signs for a movement. However, the inference that the next formation can be predicted on the basis of past information (here: formation) simply is wrong.

Even if chart analysis had predictive value, it would lose its usefulness because of its wide dissemination if everybody acted accordingly. (Incidentally, this applies to all methods of forecasting!) The forecast made on the basis of the chart would in this case simply confirm itself and thus rob the investor of his basis for a successful speculation. The prediction that a rise in prices is due would cause purchases, and they in turn would trigger an increase in prices. A pessimistic forecast would also create sales and thus lead to a slump in prices. The prognosis would be correct, true, but only because it confirms itself once it has been created and distributed. However, this would not be of any help, since nobody could make proper use of it by the appropriate actions. In practice, however, the different experiences with chart analysis, psychological factors, lack of time, different character traits, and the like never permit investors to come to the same decisions, no matter how plainly the chart points urge them on toward certain decisions. Even if the investor does not agree with the interpretation of the technicians the charts still offer a good visual summary of stock movement over the past years. Inferences can still be drawn whether a stock is over- or undervalued, and the charts also supplement in the best possible way the "risk and opportunity" method, developed by Thomas (*Risk and Opportunity*, Dow Jones Irwin Inc., Homewood, Illinois 60430, 1974). This method is dealt with in Chapter 3.

Every investor would welcome analytic tools that would offer him a realistic chance for making a profit. These tools should also eliminate the flexibility of buying and selling signals contained in chart analysis and instead offer a fixed point for investment decisions which can be determined objectively. Such a tool would automatically restrain the investor from vacillating between the ever-gnawing doubts "Should I now? Later? What or when or how?" He may find a remedy for those doubts if he turns to moving averages.

Moving Averages

The ultimate aim of any stock analysis is the elimination of subjective and emotional decisions and the establishment of criteria that guarantee the most accurate results possible. The method of moving averages is an aid in judging individual stock price changes. The moving average is not a forecasting method in the literal sense, but rather a trend-following method. The method of moving averages is used to set up criteria that enable the investor to recognize whether a trend is still intact. On a purely mathematical basis, lines can be computed for short-, medium-, and long-term strategies as an interesting and helpful supplement to any investment strategy. A moving average can be calculated individually by any investor. In its simplest form it consists of the sum of past stock prices divided by the number of stock prices observed. The following example shows how a 5-day moving average is calculated:

Price trading day	Moving total		Moving average
1st day 50			
2nd day 52			
3rd day 54			
4th day 53			
5th day 55	264 1.–5. day	: 5 =	52,8
6th day 56	270 2.–6. day	: 5 =	54
7th day 54	272 3.–7. day	: 5 =	54,2
8th day 52	270 4.–8. day	: 5 =	54

The most commonly utilized averages for stock analysis are the 200-day moving average (30 weeks) and the 10- or 5-week average. For a really short-term analysis, the 10-day average can be used as well. Figure 20 shows Dow Chemical in a bar chart which also depicts the weekly high-low closing data and the 10-week average

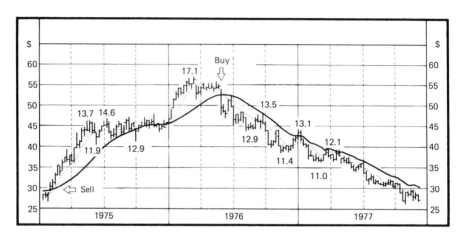

Figure 20   Dow Chemical, 1975–1977. (The Mansfield Stock Chart Service, Jersey City, N. J.)

(200-day moving line), respectively, for the period of 1975 to 1977. (These charts can be purchased from Mansfield Chart Service, 26 Journal Square, Jersey City, New Jersey 07306.)

200-Day Line (30-Week Moving Average)

In general, it can be said that the moving average becomes more and more insensitive to short-term fluctuations of stock prices the further the moving total is extended. Therefore, the 200-day moving line is of real importance for determining long-term trends. The following rules should help the investor apply the 200-day moving line:

◇ If the 200-day average line flattens out following a previous decline or is advancing and the price of the stock penetrates that average line on the upside, this is a major buying signal.

◇ If the price of the stock falls below the 200-day moving average price line while the average is still rising, this also is considered to be a buying opportunity.

◇ If the stock price is above the 200-day line and is declining toward that line but fails to go through and starts to turn up again, this is a buying signal.

◇ If the price falls too fast under the declining 200-day average line, it is entitled to an advance back toward the average line, and the stock can be bought for this short-term technical rise.

◇ If the 200-day average line flattens out following a previous rise or is declining and the price of the stock penetrates that line on the downside, this comprises a major selling signal.

◇ If the price of the stock rises above the 200-day moving average price line while the average line is still falling, this also is considered a selling opportunity.

◇ If the price is below the 200-day line and is advancing toward that line but fails to go through and starts to turn down again, this is a selling signal.

◇ If the price advances too fast above the advancing 200-day average line, it is entitled to a reaction back toward the average line, and the stock can be sold for this short-term technical reaction.

If the investor had used only the 200-day average line in combination with the stock price, Dow Chemical would have been purchased in January 1975 at a price of $30. At that point, the price of the stock penetrated the average line on the upside. The position would have closed only when the stock price had penetrated the average line on the downside at $52 in June of 1976. Since the moving average showed a falling tendency until the end of 1977, no new buying signals occurred.

10-Week Moving Average

The 10-week moving average is a way to define more clearly short- and medium-term price trends. This average is much more sensitive to short-term changes in prices and should therefore be considered when taking speculative positions. Attention should be paid not only to the question of whether the moving average continues to rise or fall but also to the question of how big the change in that average is.

Short-term selling is advisable when prices fall below the 10-week average. An opportunity for buying is indicated if prices rise above the average. The rather close adherence of the average to prices smoothes over many short-term fluctuations. This saves the short-term investor a lot of anxiety since he does not have to worry unduly when a countermovement becomes visible. However, the closer the moving average is to the prices, the more frequently buying and selling signals occur, if the trend of the stock does not remain stable. The high commissions involved in religiously following those signals can, however, really turn the investor away from total dependence on short-term moving averages.

Combination of 10-Week Moving Average and 200-Day-Line (30-Week Moving Average)

Another strategy with moving averages would be to watch the penetration points of the stock price with a moving average and also those points where the lines of various averages cross each other. It could, for example, be quite profitable to buy or sell at the point where the 10-week average penetrates the 200-day line.

The advantage would be that the investor need not worry about his stocks if the price falls below the 200-day line for just a short period. As long as the 10-week moving average stays above the 200-day line, he does not have to sell. The same goes for the opposite situation: he should refrain from buying as long as the price stays below the 200-day line.

Figure 20 shows that on September 30, 1975 and on December 15, 1975, the stock Dow Chemical fell noticeably below the 200-day line. The investor would probably have sold out at that point if the 10-week moving average had not served as an additional aid for decision making. However, since the 10-week moving average still held above the 200-day line, the investor could stay with it and continue to profit as it rose to $52 in June 1976. On the other hand, no buying signal was given on January 13, 1977, when the price penetrated the 200-day moving line at $44 on the upside, because the 10-week moving average continued below the 200-day moving line.

Shadow Line

In 1972, Larry Williams published a simple medium-term "trading strategy" which apparently produced profitable signals in the majority of cases. He employed a standard 10-week moving average. Parallel to this line, a second line was drawn which showed the 10-week moving average projected one week ahead. This line represents the "shadow line." A buying signal is generated when the 10-week moving average crosses from below to above its shadow line, a selling signal if the 10-week average crosses from above to below the shadow line. The results have been excellent, especially considering the fact that this is a purely automatic system. The sole

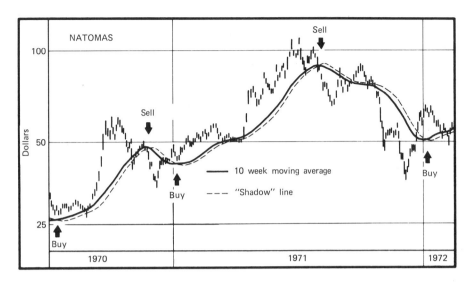

Figure 21   Natomas, 1970–1972. (Gerald Apple, Winning Market Systems, Signalent Corp., Great Neck, N. Y., 1974.)

criterion for buying and selling decisions is the penetration points of the two averages. It is understandable that the buying or selling signals can never occur at the extreme high or low point. This simple system works best with strongly trended stocks and avoids the whipsawing that plagues other moving average systems. Figure 21 uses Natomas as an example to show how the shadow line functions.

Advantages and disadvantages of moving averages can be summarized as follows:

◇ Investment decisions that are made on the basis of moving averages have the advantage that they provide unmistakable buying and selling signals.

◇ As long as the trend of a stock is stable, no further decisions have to be made.

◇ Short-, medium-, or long-term decisions can be worked out with the help of 5-10-20-week moving averages or with the 200-day moving average line, depending on risk preferences.

◇ This method can be learned very quickly. Other than with chart analysis, no formations are created that might leave room for interpretation.

◇ Within this system, individual stocks, industries, and stock indices can be analyzed and coordinated. If a group index rises, the investor should be on the lookout for the stock within that group whose moving average is also going up and vice versa.

◇ Economic data and the fundamental positions of a company do not have to be taken into account any more. The investor now only has to watch for the price or the moving average to change. Why this is happening is of no interest.

◇ The disadvantage of the moving averages is that tops or bottoms can never be achieved. Also, if the application is too short or if a sidewise movement occurs, the investor can be sure that he will have to pay large commissions.

◇ Finally, although the system is extremely transparent and clear, it should be remembered that by using it, the investor consciously rejects all other information that might prove helpful in making correct investment decisions.

"AT Börsenbarometer" (*AT Stockmarket Barometer*)

So far, only indicators and systems using American examples have been discussed. That does not mean, however, that these tools can only be applied to American stocks and the American stock market. An example for the German stock market is shown in Figure 22 which is based on the AT stock market barometer. Nobody is

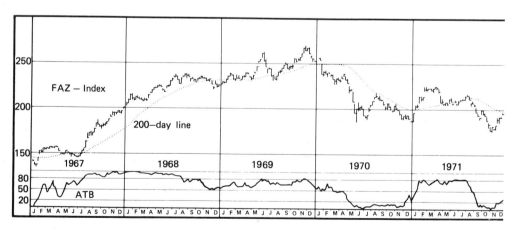

Figure 22   German stockmarket trend thermometer (ATB).
(Bad Honnef, No. 51/52, 1977.)

perfect—and neither is this system. However, between 1967 and 1977, the long-term investor was able to achieve a return of 13.5 to 19% per annum, depending on the conditions of his investment schedule. This may not sound overwhelming, if measured by the type of newspaper advertisement that promises fabulous fortunes on low stakes within a short period of time. Compared to the performance of the big funds, however, this really is a good performance.

First, the most important facts about the AT stockmarket barometer: it is calculated weekly. It fluctuates between 0 and 100, and remains within one of four main ranges at the given time. The basis for the calculation are the 200-day moving averages of—at present—76 German institutional stocks. It indicates, to begin with, the percentage of averages that have risen. A value of 80 therefore means that 80% of the averages included are rising. It is assumed that stocks with a rising 200-day moving average are in an upward trend. It is further assumed that a bull market exists as long as more than 50% of the stocks are going up; and, of course, the stronger the bull market is, the greater the number of stocks participating. If, however, less than 50% of the stocks go up a bear market is indicated which grows stronger and progresses in relation to the declining percentage.

On the basis of experience and calculations that have been con-

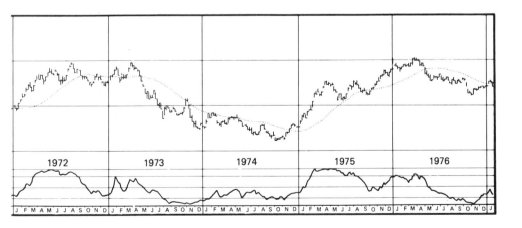

ducted over the years, certain rules have been established for the use of this indicator. The most important ones are:

◇ It is a bullish signal if the ATB rises above 20 after having remained in the 0–20 range for a longish period.

◇ A further rise above 50 and then to 80 confirms the bullish signal.

◇ The bull market can be considered a certainty as long as the ATB remains in the range 80–100; the higher the better.

◇ It is a bearish signal if the ATB falls below 80.

◇ A confirmation of that signal is given if the ATB falls below approximately 65. If it falls below 50, the final signal for a bearish market is triggered.

◇ A new and lasting rise can only be expected when the ATB has reached the range 0–20 again and has remained within that range for several months.

From this, one very important conclusion can be drawn: the most favorable range for buying is the 0–20 range, the most favorable one for selling 80–100. The investor who acts accordingly really follows the ideal of anticyclical investment, which is so often called for and so rarely realized. He "buys cheap and sells dear." On that basis, we shall develop a very simple but effective system. The rules are as follows:

◇ Of a certain cash reserve, 50% is invested as soon as the ATB falls below 20; the remaining 50% is invested as soon as it rises above 20.

◇ The portfolio will be held until 80–100 is reached.

◇ As soon as it falls below 80, 50% of the portfolio is sold; the remainder will be sold when it falls below 65.

◇ The return will be invested in treasuries or bonds. When the ATB again reaches 0–20, the investor again buys stocks. Then the whole process starts afresh from the beginning.

The investor who adopts this system only has to check the ATB condition every Saturday; if a decisive point has been reached, he will act immediately. If not, he will wait for the following week. The amount of time the investor would have to allot to this is negligible. And yet, the result would definitely be worth the time and effort. In order to keep the example simple, we will assume that the FAZ* Index is bought and sold; a portfolio of 10 stocks out of different industry groups however, would probably bring the same result.

If the returns achieved had been re-invested as indicated above each time, a total gain of 233 index points between 1967 and 1977 would have resulted. That corresponds to approximately 149% profit compared to the starting point of 150. Excluded are the dividend payments and the possible returns from investing liquid assets at favorable interest rates. For about 67 months, the capital was not invested in stocks, and if the investor had invested only the starting capital of 150 at a 6% average, 50 more index points would have accrued. If one assumes a 4% return on stocks, one would have to add another 40 index points in dividends. All in all, this would have amounted to a profit of 223+50+40 points which would come to about 220% total and a yearly average of 19%.

If one had not used the index but had followed all signals only with Siemens stock, a starting capital of DM 10,000 would have increased to DM 49,000 during that time. This would mean 396% total profit and a plus of 36% on the average per year (provided the liquid assets had been reinvested at 6%).

CONCLUSION

Success, money, fortune—those are words that appeal to anybody. And there are hundreds of books that aim to lure the unwary into the treasure hunt on the market. These sugary traps carry catchy titles like: "The Road to Wealth," "Just a Little Bit of Money, My System and Your Fortune is Made," "I Survived 45 Years on Wall Street," "Everybody can Make a Million." Fairytales about making a fortune in the market are rampant—the alchemists' goals and promises were peanuts compared to that game. The credulous and the innocent (but nevertheless greedy) investors all fall into the same trap, the promise of the fast buck. Philanthrophists publish (oh so disinterestedly) the magic formulas—money back guaranteed, of course. They make up new proverbs and checklists that are supposed to help avoid making mistakes. Investment strategies are indeed plentiful, but not one of them could even faintly be called a

* *Frankfurter Allgemeine Zeitung*, a large German daily newspaper.

dead certainty. Certainly, a number of them can be extremely useful. But, the better the strategy, the more time has to be spent on the job.

There are nearly as many forecasting methods as there are investors and advisors. However, there is no single method, and there will be no method, that will permanently guarantee profits. Ahy such strategy, if it were to become generally known and used, would lead to the disintegration of the market. Whoever has a really functioning, successful system would be well advised to jealously guard it from prying eyes, else it will lose its value, since everybody could put his fingers into that pie. Still, any system, and be it ever so simple and faulty, is better than no system at all. It is enough if the sum of the decisions is favorable, even if some of the individual choices did not work out. Only thus would it be possible—up to a certain point, anyway—to overcome the indecision and insecurity that come naturally with any individual choice because of the investor's emotions, intuition, or even hot tips.

In the past decades, stock market analysts have formed schools according to the variety of theories and disciplines, and each one swears by his own method. The most important of these systems have been explained at length in the preceding pages. It became clear then, that the individual procedures are not alternatives that exclude each other, but rather methods that deal with the same problem from different aspects.

◇ The nonbelievers among the investors cling to the random walk theory. According to that, everything is haphazard, and a blind monkey throwing darts at the Wall Street Journal would be just as successful in choosing stocks as the best analyst.

◇ For the monetarists, the money supply is the sole criterion for making an investment decision. They attempt to make timing decisions for the overall market simply by analyzing monetary factors.

◇ The fundamentalists concentrate on the fundamental data of business cycles, inventory turnover, earnings, and so on of individual corporations. On the basis of those data, they conclude whether a stock is over- or undervalued.

◇ The chartists believe that all factors that influence pricing can be deduced from the charts, and they put their faith into the interpretation of formations, support and resistance lines. The chartist is not interested in the reasons for a price movement. For him, it is purely a question of *if* and *when* there is going to be a lasting change in prices.

◇ During the past few years, people have shown more and more interest in the methods of market technicians. Contrary to the pure chartists, who restrict themselves to the interpretation of chart formations, the range of analytic tools used by the technicians is much wider and more comprehensive. As Figure 16 shows, the analysis begins with economic, monetary and fundamental data. With the help of these and numerous other indicators, the market technicians try to establish the structure of the overall market with respect to the present and future supply and demand. It is only after this part of the analysis has been executed that individual industries branches are studied. Finally, individual stocks are chosen on that basis. Charts, moving averages, changes in volume of most actives, block trades, short sales, insider transactions, the relative strength, weekly range, price-earnings-ratio, and so on all are aids for accomplishing the analysis.

None of these analytical methods is so good that it would solve all problems of forecasting. However, a lot can be said for not simply concentrating on a single stock when one is looking for an investment. If the system is enlarged to include the industrial group concerned and the overall market, the chances for more profitable investment decisions definitely improve substantially. However, it leads to problems if the investor follows the suggestion to compromise by combining several systems, namely, to give them equal weight. This would be the case, if one were to choose a stock according to fundamental criteria, but then make the timing dependent on a chart signal. One might conceivably agree with this compromise, if one were to use the fundamental analysis only to make a preselection of stocks according to qualitative points of view, such as statements of condition, earnings, growth, or management. It would become difficult if one were to push the fundamental analysis so far that a specific price would be considered the ideal buying price (undervalued or properly valued), because the chart might look unfavorable when the purchase price is analyzed according to fundamental principles. There is no logical solution to this quandary. The investor would be confronted by two equally valid but still contradictory recommendations, and again he would have to make his decision on a purely arbitrary basis. If the investor limits the use of fundamental analysis to making a preselection of stocks according to certain qualitative requirements, the consideration of chart formations in these stocks could possibly lead to a better timing when buying or short-selling.

Next to the best possible selection of analytic tools, the discipline of the investor is an extremely important aspect in an investment strategy—maybe even the most important one. Discipline means that the investor has to stick with a rational purchase, sale, or short-sale decision once made, and not go back on it as soon as there are positive or negative reactions from the outside. It is of utmost importance to know who has voiced the diverging opinions and for what reasons. The investor should not be satisfied with the knowledge that these opinions originated with a newspaper, a market letter, a bank, or brokerage house. Even if optimism spreads more and more, that is no certain indication for a change in trend of the market or a single stock, as the figures already shown make clear. Only the investor who has the necessary self-discipline to follow an established system, and who prefers reasonable decisions based on facts to emotions, intuition, or tips can hope for continuous and lasting success on the market.

The investors' mentality, too, is of great importance. Naturally, everybody hopes to make money in the market, but how this can be accomplished is a constant bone of contention among them. The avid investor, who runs after his profit, also has to be willing to take a big risk. Nobody has a real chance to make a large profit on a small and meager stake—neither in the market nor anywhere else. The situation becomes even more problematical if the investor is influenced by newspaper advertisements and pressure salesmen, promising outstanding performances, to choose a form of investment with which he is totally unfamiliar. "Confidence is fine, supervision is better" is a maxim that holds true for the stock market as well. Even if full powers for the deployment of capital have been given to a third party, the investor should not only insist on a monthly statement of the account on the basis of current prices, but also check his portfolio regularly in order to understand the risk he is undertaking with the individual securities. Ignorance is never an excuse when possible losses are involved.

Even the best and most refined method cannot eliminate all risks. Any rational investment strategy therefore has to include the methodical treatment of that risk, next to the well-founded price projection. Both the risk per se and the attitude of the various investors toward that risk have to be measured. How this can be done is discussed in the next chapter.

3 *THE ROLE OF RISK IN INVESTMENT PLANNING*

RISK AND RISK PREFERENCE

The most intricate and complicated method of forecasting and the best sources of information give no guarantee for a correct prognosis of the stock market or of price movements of individual stocks. Qualified methods of prognosis can help reduce the investment risk but can never totally eliminate it. This risk is, therefore, an important factor that must be taken into account when choosing an investment strategy.

The Concept of Risk

The concept of risk tends to create quite a bit of confusion. For example, there is no principal risk with treasury bills, for which the rate of return is guaranteed for the length of maturity unless the nation declares bankruptcy. The investor can be assured that he will receive the specified rate of interest until the final maturity date. Quite often, however, the investor is not satisfied with the return from government issues. An alternative, then, is to invest in stocks. If the expected return of a stock that included profits plus dividends was not any higher than that of a bond and yet was plagued with the uncertainty of price fluctuations and possible losses, then nobody would buy stocks. Contrary to bonds, a definite **91** return in stocks can never be guaranteed; it is the intrinsic risk of this form of investment. Price changes can either be favorable (with gains) or unfavorable (losses). In daily usage, added gains are called "reward" and possible losses "risk." In the scientific concept of risk in capital market theory, both the reward and the risk are composed of "variability" or "standard deviation." The theory is based on the assumption that reward and risk are symmetrically divided. The concept of variability as used in some of the following models encompasses the whole range of reward and risk (from maximum profit to maximum loss for each situation), whereas risk—according to everyday usage—is defined as half of the variability or as possible loss.

Methods for Estimating Risk

The investor who is eager for an above-average reward has to be willing to undergo above-average risk. The investor who is looking for a relatively safe, low-risk investment, however, will have to be satisfied with smaller gains. The extent of reward or risk of a capital investment can be predetermined with the help of the beta factor, developed by Sharpe, or according to the risk/reward method developed by Thomas, as is shown later on. In general, one could say that stocks with wide price fluctuations offer both high risks and high rewards. Stocks with relatively low price fluctuations tend to be low-risk investments. Here, however, the low risk is accompanied by equally small rewards.

Investors' Attitude Toward Risk (Risk Preference)

To choose rationally amongst the various investment alternatives, the investor has to know exactly how great a risk he is willing to accept. The risk structure of the individual investment form has to be taken into account, but it is at least as important to know the individual and personal attitude toward risk and how much the investor is willing and able to take on. Significant elements include financial resources, the knowledge the investor has of the individual form of investment, and the investment horizon envisaged. It is unlikely that a speculator who is more than willing to assume risks and who has profound knowledge of the market and a conservative investor who has more thought for security would be interested in the same investment for the same time period; it goes against the basic attitude or objectives of the investors. This becomes more than obvious if one compares the investment strategies practiced in the recent past, and which are discussed next.

DIVERSIFICATION AND CONCENTRATION

Diversification by means of purchasing stocks of different industrial groups had become more and more neglected in the second half of the 1960s while the new concept "concentration" had become increasingly popular. Concentration means investing in a few select stocks that promise high returns. Investors hope for profits from price gains rather than from dividend payments. The disadvantage with concentration is that it functions only as long as the strong growth trend of the selected industrial branches continues. Dreams of the "instant fortune" make many investors forget the fundamental principles of investment strategy—the importance of diversification. Concentration became merely another expression for more risky investments.

So far, the concept of concentration has never been fully and satisfactorily defined. The old timer on the exchange who has extensive knowledge of companies at his fingertips and automatically considers them when making a decision will have a different notion of concentration than the amateur who seeks quick dollars by concentrating on fashionable stocks such as Xerox or Polaroid. The results of the concentration idea, which were propagated by experts, are known well enough. The go-go funds from the 1960s aimed mainly at concentration. All of them suffered such huge losses that they disappeared as fast as they had turned up. The number of investors who lost their entire fortune because of this concentration fad will probably remain unknown. However, the fortunes gambled away are probably many times bigger than the capital lost by the concentration funds. Only the funds and investors who stuck to the principles of diversification have survived.

With diversification, rewards may be smaller, but they are safer. The investor who still talks of concentration and turns up his nose at diversification as a way of investing belongs to the group of incurable optimists who never learn from the past. Concentration presupposes good selection and exact timing. Very few investors, however, really have mastered the art of timing, and therefore losses are practically inherent in their selection. The investor who has concentrated in a few stocks—watching over them constantly—and has found to his chagrin that things have not gone as he had planned will suffer extreme anxiety. If he tries to apply the same method to the options trade, he will meet with an even worse fate.

STATIC ANALYSIS: DIVERSIFICATION *WITHOUT* TIMING

When setting up a portfolio, there are two kinds of decisions that have to be made:

◇ The investor has to decide which stocks to buy or sell and in what combination (selection).

◇ He has to decide the timing for entering into these transactions.

The investor who concentrates on selection, trying to determine the optimum combination of a portfolio at a given time, is engaged in static analysis. Timing as representing a degree of freedom in making a decision is disregarded. Most of the investment models discussed in literature are static in that sense. We first begin with a discussion of results of static analysis. The various risks, which have their origin in the combination of different securities, can be made particularly transparent with the help of these models.

Distributable and Nondistributable Risks

Every experienced investor knows that the risk of a portfolio can be minimized if the capital is distributed among several stocks and not concentrated in a single security. *Markowitz* was the first to study the results of diversification using statistical methods. He separated the function of the analyst who has merely to calculate an estimate on returns from that of the portfolio manager whose task it is to balance return and risk. A hypothetical example helps illustrate this process.

Let us suppose there are only two companies operating on an island. One of them has both a concession and manufacturing operation for open air sports, such as tennis, horseback riding, and golf; the other produces only umbrellas. With respect to their returns, both companies are entirely dependent on the weather. During the summer, the company operating and supplying open air sports facilities lives in the full swing of prosperity, and only very few umbrellas are sold. During fall and winter, it is the other way around. The following table shows the assumed returns of the two companies:

	Umbrella factory	Open air sports facilities
Rainy season	+50%	−25%
Summer	−25%	+50%

Suppose it rains half the year and the sun shines for the other half. The investor who purchased only one of the two stocks has set a return of 12.5% on his investment. The risk becomes substantially greater if the rainy and the summer season are not equally divided. The investor who holds only stocks in the sports enterprise during a year with a great amount of rain will take a sizable loss as the unavoidable consequence. If the investor were to buy not just the stocks of one company but invest in both of them equally, he would still achieve a return of only 12.5% per year. He has, however, the advantage that he will *always* get a return of 12.5% because of the offsetting risk which makes the combined investment independent of the weather. With respect to this example, the investor has cut the risk to zero. This is only possible because the two companies are influenced by the weather in exactly the opposite degree. Only under that kind of circumstances can a risk be totally eliminated.

In the stock market there is no possible way to totally eliminate investment risk. Individual stocks are dependent on such factors as overall economy of the country and the movement of the market taken as a whole (the Dow Jones Index, etc.); they do not move contrary to each other, but rather with equal steps—even though with varied strength. The attempt to minimize the risk of investments by diversification, therefore, is strictly limited. The following division of risk makes this unmistakably clear. As Figure 23 shows,

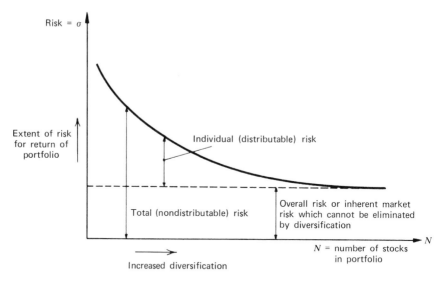

Figure 23 Relationship of risk to diversification.

the risk of capital investment, that is, the probability of loss, can be divided into

◇ The individual (distributable) stock risks that can be eliminated by diversification.

◇ The overall (nondistributable) risk or inherent market risk which simply cannot be overcome by diversification (the only remedy for this is good timing).

If the investor keeps adding stocks to his portfolio, individual risks can be cut down to the minimum risk which is part of the market, but no further. The investor simply has to live with the market risk. Lorie and Fisher have combined stocks of several companies of different industrial groups at equal parts in one portfolio. They found that if the number of companies represented in that portfolio was increasing the risk was reduced as follows [James H. Lorie and Lawrence Fisher, "Some Studies of Variability of Returns on Investment in Common Stocks," *Journal of Business* (April 1970)]:

Number of companies represented in the portfolio in the Lorie–Fisher study	Relative risk with respect to the number of companies represented in the portfolio (%)
1	100
2	81
8	64
16	60
32	59
128	57
510	57

This study shows quite plainly that diversification into eight companies within the portfolio represents the most significant improvement. Beyond that, however, hardly any reduction in risk is achieved. The question is: can the overall risk (intrinsic market risk) be measured? If this were possible, the investor would have a good auxiliary aid for adjusting the degree of the risk taken within his portfolio to his own individual risk preference.

Methods of Optimum Portfolio Diversification

The Basics of Risk Analysis

Markowitz was the first seriously to study and formulate the systematic basics of treating opportunities and risks in a portfolio that is comprised of stocks of various companies. He based his work on the fact that the price movement of each stock can be represented by a probability distribution. The relative frequency (probability) with which prices have changed in the past can be determined for each separate stock so that if a stock had been traded three times at $120 when trucked through 20 price changes, we have a relative frequency of 3/20 or 15% for this price. It should be noted that when applied to long time intervals, the frequency distribution must be inflated or deflated by the direction of the long-term trend.

Stocks with extreme fluctuations between the highest and lowest prices within a specific time period are represented by probability distributions of a wide spectrum. Each price within the range has a relatively low-frequency density because the span from highest and lowest is of such a great distance. Stocks with a small range of fluctuation or a long-term constant development of prices have a narrow probability distribution which includes only a few prices with a comparatively high-frequency density. For instance, trading ranges from $100 to $300 are suited more to the speculator; the conservative investor would be more interested in stocks with a restricted range, say $100 to $150.

Figure 24 is the ideal representation of a stock with a steady price (A) and a volatile price (B). To simplify the concept, the probability distributions are shown as continuous lines (also called a frequency distribution or Gaussian distribution) rather than a main cluster of data points (scatter diagram).

The two distributions are distinguished from each other by an expected (mean) value of E_A and E_B, and also by a standard deviation of $\sigma_{(A)}$ and $\sigma_{(B)}$. The expected value determines the orientation of the distribution and can be interpreted as a measure of the normal price of the stock. If, for example, the price of stock had been studied at 100, 160, and 200 in the past, and if the highest and the lowest prices were each quoted twice, while the middle price was quoted four times, the expected value is computed as the weighted average:

$$E = (2 \times 100 + 4 \times 160 + 2 \times 200) \div 8 = 155$$

The expected value is computed by weighing the individual prices according to their frequency density and by then adding them up.

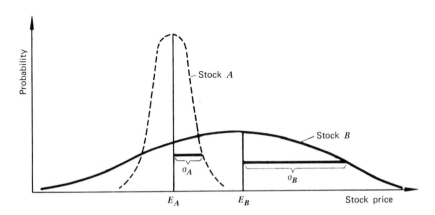

Figure 24   Distribution of prices for volatile (a) and nonvolatile (b) stocks.

The standard deviation measures the range of variability of possible stock prices and describes the risks and opportunities within its price development. Markowitz designates, with the help of the expected value and standard deviation, the future price development of stocks studied. He assumes that the past is representative for the future. As with a single stock, a portfolio composed of a variety of securities can be represented by a probability distribution. To do this, however, it is necessary to consider the possible interdependencies between the price movements of the various stocks. Markowitz has solved this problem by using statistical correlation, and thus opens up the possibility of representing each portfolio by the extent of its expected return (E) and its relative risk (σ). In that way portfolios can be directly compared by means of quantitative coefficients, and a rational decision can be made as to whether a change in the composition of the portfolio would result in an improvement in returns.

In the Markowitz method, each portfolio is represented by two coefficients. In a comparative evaluation, one of these coefficients remains unchanged, and improvement is indicated when

◇ The expected return (E) for a given risk (σ) has increased
◇ or the risk (σ) for a given expected return (E) has decreased.

This can be seen in Figure 25 which shows three different portfolios, A, B, and C, for a combination of different values of E and σ.

For portfolio B, the optimum selection has not yet been achieved. It can be improved in either of two directions: by changing the composition of securities, to portfolio A with the original expected return and reduced risk or to portfolio C with the original risk and higher expected return. A change beyond point A and C, however, is not possible. Portfolios A and C are on the efficient frontier. A portfolio cannot move into the range above this efficient frontier, since expected return and risk do not allow arbitrary variations. If the composition of a portfolio is altered, a multitude of possibilities offer themselves below the efficient frontier. This, however, does not lead to optimum solutions. A movement on the efficient frontier itself, such as the exchange of portfolio A with portfolio C, would simply mean replacing one portfolio that is diversified to a maximum extent with another, similarly diversified portfolio, with changed parameters. Whether such a switch is beneficial can only be decided by consulting the risk preference of the investor. If the

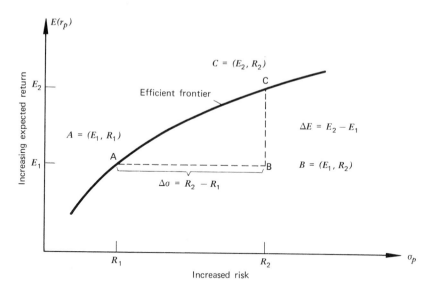

Figure 25   Expected return as a function of risk for an individual stock.

investor changes from A to C, for example, one must assume that he is willing to accept a risk increased by $\Delta\sigma$, provided he thereby receives an increase in expected returns by ΔE. The curve of the efficient frontier clearly shows that an increase in the expected re turn always entails a disproportionate increase in risk. Investor₂ who are adverse to risk will therefore prefer to move toward the left area of the efficient frontier, whereas investors willing to take high risks will try to realize efficient combinations of E and σ toward the upper right part of the curve. It is interesting to note that the efficient frontier demonstrates the need for the individual investor to determine his personal risk preference.

An important aspect of Markowitz's theory is that the investor automatically limits the maximum expected return to the point fixed by the efficient frontier by choosing his maximum acceptable risk. On the other hand, the determination of a return automatically fixes the point of the smallest risk on the efficient frontier. Therefore, no portfolio manager can be expected to achieve a high return with a very low risk. The investor can only indicate one of the two parameters—risk or return—as his preference.

Markowitz includes the advantages of diversification in his model. He states that one can calculate the risk of a portfolio by evaluating the variability of the individual securities and combining the results with the correlation of the securities with each other. This, however, requires an extensive mathematical process which is not realistic in practice for an individual investor.

A Practical Approach to Measuring Risk

In 1963, Sharpe published a model that considerably reduced the high mathematical requirements of the Markowitz model. He eliminated the necessity of measuring the risk of a portfolio using the correlation coefficients of all stocks with respect to each other. Instead of comparing returns of all the stocks to each other, the returns of a portfolio are measured against the appreciation of the NYSE index, the Dow-Jones Industrial Average, or Standard & Poors Index. The Markowitz model requires about 500,000 computations per 1000 shares, but Sharpe's model requires only about 3000.

In this way the measuring of risk has been essentially simplified. The "beta factor," a result of Sharpe's model, serves as a new measure of risk. This beta factor takes into account the variability in expected returns of the generalized market portfolio (index), the variability of the individual portfolio, and the correlation between the returns from the market portfolio with that of the individual portfolio. The formula describing this relationship is:

$$\beta = \frac{\text{cov}\,(r_m, r_p)}{\sigma^2\,(r_m)}$$

where

    beta factor (β) = risk measurement for the overall (market) risk
co-variance (cov) = rate of dependency of two expected returns
        r_m = return of the overall market (based on an index)
        r_p = return of the individual portfolio
variance $\sigma^2\,(r_m)$ = measurement of variability of market returns

In the formula for calculating the beta factor, the numerator, cov (r_m, r_p) = 1 when the selected portfolio (r_p) performs exactly the same as the overall market (r_m). Since the variability of the overall market is defined as 1, the denominator $\sigma^2 (r_m) = 1$ and beta $= 1$.

The Practical Application of Risk Measurement

When judging the practical meaning of beta coefficients, one has to remember that they are parts of a static analysis. Through them, the optimum combination of portfolio contents can be determined with regard to the risk at a certain time. The question of maximizing returns by forecasting future price movements cannot be answered by them. The beta factors show the investor the extent to which the risk of a portfolio, as planned by him, deviates from the risk of the market portfolio in either a favorable or unfavorable way. Thus the beta factor enables him to select a portfolio that corresponds to his personal risk preference. Using the beta factor of an entire portfolio, the investor can see that an increase in diversification (the number of unique stocks in the portfolio) results in the beta factor approaching 1, indicative of greater stability and usefulness. Compared to that, the beta factor of a single stock is very unstable and consequently not very useful [Jerome I. Valentine, Investment Analysis and Capital Market Theory, Paper no. 1, *The Financial Analyst*, Research Foundation, S. 33 (1975)].

If beta moves close to zero, the returns of the portfolio is not related to the performance of the overall market. As beta approaches 1, changes in the market returns correspond exactly to changes in the returns of the portfolio. For values of beta greater than 1 there is a magnified or exaggerated effect of changes in market returns to changes in the returns of the portfolio; for example, a beta factor of 1.5 represents a market return of 10% and a portfolio return of 15% (50% greater). If the beta factor is 0.5, the portfolio return will be only 5%, while the market return is expected to be 10%. It can be said that if the beta factor is smaller than 1.0, it is a defensive investment, and if the beta factor is greater than 1, it is an aggressive investment. This relationship is now illustrated with three portfolios that are based on actual stock prices.

Examples: At the end of July 1977, the Dow was at approximately 920, and in December 1977 at approximately 800. On the basis of Standard & Poors Option Guide, three portfolios, each including eight different corporations and the same number of stocks, were set up. The beta factors of the three portfolios were approximately 0.5, 1.0, and 1.5. As previously discussed, the reason for taking eight stocks into each portfolio is that the advantages of diversification are most significant with up to eight stocks if various industrial branches are included. The calculation of the beta factors is based on the price fluctuations of the separate stocks during the past 52 weeks.

*Portfolio 1 (**high-risk investor**)*—An investor who is willing to take high risks will tend to choose stocks for his portfolio that rise or fall more than the overall market. According to the beta theory, these securities must have a beta factor greater than 1.0. The securities selected possessed a beta factor of approximately 1.5 which means that the return of the portfolio is expected to be 50% greater than the generalized market returns.

| Stocks | Prices in dollars | | Beta factor July 1977 |
	July 1977	December 1977	
Hewlett Packard	85	70	1.89
Honeywell	54	45	1.50
Motorola	48	35	1.75
North West Airlines	26	22	1.51
Penzoil	35	28	1.57
Reynolds Metals	39	30	1.91
Texas Instruments	93	72	1.64
Zenith Radio	21	14	1.64
Total	401	316	1.68

From July to December 1977, these stocks showed an average price loss of approximately 27%. During the same period, the Dow lost only about 15%. The selection of speculative stocks with a high beta factor of 1.68 thus had a very bad effect on the portfolio return. If, however, the overall market value had increased during that period, the investor would have profited from a comparably exaggerated return compared to the general market return.

*Portfolio 2 (**average investor**)*—The second portfolio was composed of securities with a beta factor of approximately 1.0. As a rule, the investor can depend on a nearly parallel development of the portfolio returns with market movement under those circumstances. The following table shows the development of this portfolio:

	Prices in dollars		Beta factor
Stock	July 1977	December 1977	July 1977
Allied Chemical	49	43	1.08
American Broadcasting Corp.	44	40	0.99
Exxon	52	46	0.97
Goodyear	22	19	1.02
Household Finance	20	18	1.05
Int. Tel. & Tel.	34	30	1.03
Owens Illinois	26	23	1.03
Woolworth	21	18	1.04
Total	268	237	1.14

With a price loss in the Dow of approximately 15%, the value of the selected portfolio was reduced by about 13%. The beta factor of 1.14 thus was a pretty good indication that the risk of the portfolio would parallel the general (representative) market returns.

Portfolio 3 (conservative investor)—The risk-averse investor should acquire stocks whose price fluctuations are less than those of the overall market. In a bull market, he will get a smaller return on those stocks, but in a bear market he will have fewer losses than the development of the overall market promises. The following table shows the development of a portfolio that has been selected according to the criterion of a conservative beta factor of approximately 0.5%.

	Price in dollars		Beta factor
Stock	July 1977	December 1977	July 1977
American Tel. & Tel.	63	60	0.47
Consolidated Edison	33	31	0.44
Grace	29	26	0.56
Homestake Mining	44	39	0.46
Int. Minerals & Chemicals	40	40	0.56
Middle South Utility	17.5	16.5	0.59
Rockwell Int.	32	29.5	0.44
Union Oil of California	55	51	0.56
Total	313.5	292.5	0.51

It can be seen that the Dow-Jones Industrials fell by 15% during the 6-month period from July through December 1977, but this portfolio only suffered a loss of approximately 7.5%. This result was anticipated, since the beta factor was 0.51.

Summary

The results of the three portfolios show how important the beta factor is for measuring the risk of a portfolio. Under static criteria (i.e., setting aside the question of timing), the investor thus has an auxiliary aid which can be of considerable help in determining the risk of the portfolio he intends to establish. Studies by Sharpe show that the beta factor is very unsteady and unreliable for judging individual stocks. However, the effectiveness of the beta factor increases when a larger number of stocks is represented in a portfolio. The beta factor provided a fairly exact measure of risk with the three sample portfolios. However, it should be remembered that changes in returns may also be due to an anticyclical behavior of a stock. An alteration in the fundamental factors can be responsible for a rising stock price, even while the market is falling. The investor must also know that the beta factors published by the different market services may vary to some extent because they use different methods of calculation. Therefore, the investor should consistently use the same market service and should consider only those beta values given out by his "personal" service in his portfolio strategy. The beta factor is also limited in its use, since it does not give information about the current status of a stock. It is important to recognize whether the stock price is at a high or a low when it is bought. This question will be discussed in the chapter on *dynamic analysis*.

Risk Spreading by a Combination of Stock Investment and Treasuries

Markowitz and Sharpe have tried to construct the most favorable models in their theories. Although Markowitz's studies have provided the theoretical basis for all present theories of risk variation, they are practically useless for everyday purposes. Sharpe was able to give the investor and portfolio manager the first practical help by determining the beta factor and simplifying the Markowitz model. The *capital asset pricing theory* intends to define the optimum relationship between risk and return by studying combinations of fixed-income securities and stocks.

Example: The investor who puts his money exclusively into treasuries behaves like a person who stands on the shore of a lake and puts on a life-belt without going into the water. His risk of drowning is reduced to zero, but so is the pleasure received from the use of the lake. He could, of course, throw away the lifebelt, jump into a dilapidated sailboat, and go for a ride. It might give him great pleasure, but it would be a precarious situation with considerable danger instead of security. This is similar to the action of the investor who holds only stocks in his portfolio incurring risk with no offsetting security. The two methods of investment could be combined as proposed by the *capital asset pricing theory*. This would still be similar to going for a sail in that rickety boat, but wearing a lifebelt. The pleasure may be smaller, but it would still be more exciting than standing rooted to the spot on a lonely beach with a lifebelt on.

Figure 26 explains the capital asset pricing theory. It is presumed that the market return of stocks is higher than that of treasuries. This figure, which indicates the return on the vertical axis and the risk on the horizontal axis, contains:

◇ The efficient frontier established by Markowitz represents his theory that portfolios with optimum diversification (i.e., combinations of stocks with highest expected returns at a certain risk) are placed on the efficient frontier line. The theory has been supported by Sharpe.

◇ Sharpe's market line is constructed by drawing a tangent to the efficient frontier line starting at point R_F (R_F = treasuries return). Each point on the vertical axis between R_F and R_M denotes the returns of a combination of stock portfolio and treasuries investment where treasuries are considered to have no risk.

An investment of the entire available capital in treasuries would result in a return (without risk) at point R_F. According to Sharpe, point M represents the maximum diversification of a stock portfolio, maximum in the sense that the return/risk ratio is optimized. This so-called market portfolio has a stock market return R_M with market risk σ_M. If the investor puts his resources partially into treasury bills and partially into the market portfolio, his return will be higher than the one he would be able to realize through treasuries alone, but his risk would be lower than the stock market risk.

If the capital is divided equally between treasuries and a market portfolio, the return that can be expected is placed exactly in the middle between R_M and R_F. The combination of treasuries and stocks is, therefore, the best possible form of investment for all *conservative* investors who want to achieve a higher return than is possible with treasuries, but do not want to shoulder the entire risk

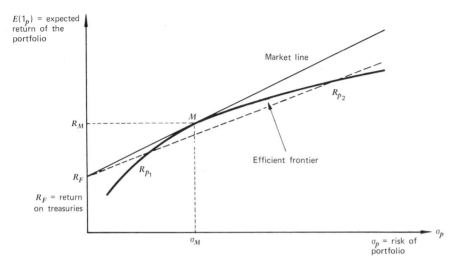

Figure 26   Expected return for a portfolio which includes treasuries.

intrinsic to the market portfolio. The desired higher returns of *speculative* investors lead to points on Markowitz' efficient frontier line that are farther to the right of M. The investor can only afford to remain on the $R_F R_M$ line beyond point M if he can borrow capital under treasury terms—which is unrealistic—and then re-invest this capital in a market portfolio.

Sharpe's analysis proves that the investor can optimize his investment by combining treasuries with a stock market portfolio. In that case, he could select returns on the line from R_F to M. If the investor combines treasuries with stocks that are selected so as *not* to pass through point M, the risk-return ratio can change to the points R_{P1} or R_{P2}. With such a strategy, the chance of a higher expected return with a smaller risk is simply gambled away. These interrelations become clearer if one looks at the formula by which the market line is defined:

$$E(R_P) = R_F + (E(R_M) - R_F) \cdot \gamma$$

where $E(R_P)$ = expected return of the portfolio
R_F = interest rate for treasury bills
$E(R_M)$ = market return
γ = the portion of the total portfolio which is invested in stocks

The formula shows that the investor can gradually increase his expected return from the treasury bill interest rate R_F to the optimal market return $E(R_M)$ if he replaces treasuries in his portfolio by stocks. To do this, the factor moves from 0 to 1.

Example: If the treasuries without risk yield $R_F = 8\%$, the expected market return $[E(R_M)]$ is 10%, and γ has been fixed at 0.5, then the expected return on the portfolio becomes

$$E(R_P) = R_F + \gamma[E(R_M - R_F)]$$
$$= .08 + 0.5(0.10 - .08)$$
$$= .08 + 0.5(0.02)$$
$$= .09 \text{ or } 9\%$$

With the figures given, the investor can count on an expected return of 9% from the combined portfolio. Because of the combination of treasuries and stock, the expected rate of return is considerably higher than the 8% that treasuries alone have yielded, but below the expected market return of 10%. If the treasuries are replaced by stocks, the risk of the portfolio increases correspondingly. The risk of a mixed portfolio σP can be measured as a percentage of the market risk; this is achieved by multiplying the market risk σM with the relative portion of the stock investment (γ) to the total size of the portfolio:

$$\sigma_P = \gamma \cdot \sigma_M$$

This formula, as well as all others, has presupposed that the treasury bill investment is combined with a diversified stock investment. This stock portfolio, representing only part of the entire capital investment, must remain representative of the overall market portfolio. This requirement is extremely limiting, since the market portfolio represents only one point on the efficient frontier line, and one could choose among a variety of alternative rational investment strategies, depending on risk of preference. Indeed, the portfolio that is constructed according to the ideal of the market portfolio is a rare exception in practice. We must consider how the expected return $E(R_P)$ and σ_P risk of a mixed portfolio are determined when the combination of tresuries and stocks differs from that of the market portfolio, that is, the resulting combination does not lie on the efficient frontier line.

The risk of a combined portfolio that differs from that of the stock market portfolio can be measured by its beta factor. The risk of a portfolio that combines treasury bills can be measured by multiplying the risk of the stock portfolio by the beta factor and γ, which measures the portion of stocks in the total portfolio:

$$\sigma_P = \gamma \cdot \beta \cdot \sigma_M$$

γ serves to reduce the risk of the combined portfolio based on the proportional use of stocks, and the beta factor adjusts the overall risk of the two media taken together.

Conclusion

After this excursion into the intricate and complicated realm of the capital asset pricing theory, we are faced with the question: is it really worthwhile to combine treasury bills with stocks?

For the *conservative* investor with enough capital to hold a portfolio that comes very close to the maximum diversified portfolio (stock market portfolio), the answer is definitely *yes!* It is the only possible way to reduce the basic market risk, which cannot be eliminated with a portfolio that is made up exclusively of stocks. At the same time, it offers the opportunity of a higher return than can be realized with treasuries alone. Most of the large, conservatively administered portfolios contain both treasuries and stocks. The capital asset pricing theory provides the reasoning behind this successful strategy.

For the *speculative* investor with a portfolio containing only a few stocks or the investor who consciously rejects the efficient stock portfolio or who does not want a combination of treasuries and stocks, the answer is definitely *no!* Any combinations of treasuries and stocks that does not correspond to the market portfolio results in a higher return. This carries a risk that is equal or greater than that of the market portfolio for achieving the desired return. Any conservative investor should vary his risk by diversification to the extent that he approaches the market risk as closely as possible. Any strategy that is different contains a risk that cannot be measured. Still, many investors consciously look for those types of investments.

DYNAMIC ANALYSIS: DIVERSIFICATION WITH TIMING

The studies of the SEC, which claimed that the risk of stocks cannot be measured exactly, are in strong contrast to the hypothesis of the risk and reward methods that are intended to overcome these difficulties. Risk and reward are measured by taking the current stock price as a starting point—and we immediately find a weak point in the beta theory, which disregards the current price level of stocks. According to the beta theory, the investor who establishes his portfolio at peak market prices assumes the same risk as the investor who buys his stocks when the market is at its lowest. The beta theory gives no indication of *when* to buy. It only says: "If the market condition is like this, the stock will behave like that." For the investor who wants to have the option of changing between a stock investment and an investment in treasuries, the timing of his investment is of paramount importance for measuring the risk. To him, it is obvious that the risk of a stock increases with rising prices; the higher prices become, the higher the volatility and the closer they get to a major reversal or correction and hence the increased risk in taking new positions.

This is true for the entire portfolio, not just for the individual stocks. Any valid measuring of the risk can therefore only be carried out within the framework of a dynamic analysis; one that takes into account the current price level and gives the proper recommendation depending on the rising or falling stock price. A measurement of risk that considers current price movement as well as timing must combine the range of variation of prices with the current price as a factor. According to Thomas, it can be constructed as follows.

Example: We will consider a stock whose price fluctuated during the past years between $100 and $40. The range of the stock, which is the difference between the highest and lowest price of a stock in a period of time, came to

$$\text{Range} = \text{high} - \text{low}$$
$$= 100 - 40$$
$$= 60$$

The formula for the range variability includes the average price of the stock:

$$\text{Range variability, } RV = \frac{H - L}{(H + L)/2} = \frac{100 - 40}{(100 + 40)/2} = \frac{60}{70} = 0.86\%$$

The range variability of 0.86% means that the price of a stock that has been bought exactly at the average price of $70 can fluctuate 43% over or 43% below the average price; since 43% of $70 equals $30, the range variability has a high of $100 and a low of $40.

The investor can rarely buy a stock at exactly the average price because the stock usually trades either above or below that price; therefore, the current price has to be taken into consideration. If the stock is traded above average price, the risk becomes greater and the reward smaller. If a stock is traded below average price the reverse is true. The following formula accounts for the current price:

$$\text{Current price factor, } CPF = \frac{\text{current price} - \text{average price}}{\text{average price}} = \%$$

We take a stock whose current price of $80 is $10 above average price:

$$CPF = \frac{80 - 70}{70} = \frac{10}{70} = 14.5\% \text{ above average price}$$

If the stock is traded at $60, or $10 below average price, we have

$$CPF = \frac{60 - 70}{70} = -\frac{10}{70} = -14.5\% \text{ below average price}$$

To calculate the resulting CPF in dollars, we multiply the percentage variation by the average price. Only if the price is exactly the same as the average price will risk = reward = range variability.

Risk and reward move in opposite directions and fluctuate between 0 and range variability. This maxim is true for all stocks and

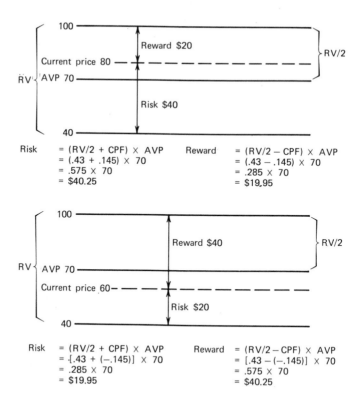

Risk   = (RV/2 + CPF) × AVP   Reward   = (RV/2 − CPF) × AVP
         = (.43 + .145) × 70   = (.43 − .145) × 70
         = .575 × 70   = .285 × 70
         = $40.25   = $19.95

Risk   = (RV/2 + CPF) × AVP   Reward   = (RV/2 − CPF) × AVP
         = [.43 + (−.145)] × 70   = [.43 − (−.145)] × 70
         = .285 × 70   = .575 × 70
         = $19.95   = $40.25

Figure 27   Variations in risk and reward.

shows why stocks with a high volatility relative to its price level carry the biggest risk and the greatest reward. With the help of these findings, the risk factor for each stock in the portfolio can be calculated and compared with others. The advantage of this simple method is that it supplies a well-defined measurement. In this way, the main disadvantage of the beta factor—that is, that the various information services work with different beta factors—is overcome. Beyond that, these risk-reward methods also include the current stock prices in their calculations, information which is of no concern in the beta theory. Further, this provides a measurement that indicates whether and how strongly a stock could be over- or undervalued.

The risk and reward factors can be calculated for a single index in the same way as a single stock. Therefore, it presents no difficulties to relate the risk factor of a single stock with the risk factor of an entire portfolio index. The problem of the market risk that had not been solved in the beta theory seems solved. Since stock prices are constantly forming new highs and new lows, the calculation of risk and reward presented above can easily be extended to include other formulas. Changes in fundamental data, such as dividends and earnings, can be included in an extended formula. The interval which includes the highs and lows, included in the evaluation, can be individually changed. In this way, one can tabulate entire port- folios and control them by constantly checking the figures with respect to changes in the individual stocks.

As opposed to the beta theory, the method described above can pinpoint more accurately the time when stocks should be bought or sold. But it is still static in an essential area: the assumption is that the average price and the highs and lows are fixed and price fluctu- ations are recorded on that basis. It must lead to misinformation if the parameters themselves fluctuate. We can illustrate this process with a simple example.

Let us assume that a company has been on the market with an outdated product for years, but has lately developed a completely new product which is clearly superior to any comparable products its competitors are offering. After the new product has been put on the market, the market shares of our company increase and with that the earnings improve considerably. The higher earnings and the stock price increase which result from the company's better situation have a decisive influence on both the average price, which had remained unchanged for years, and on the highs and lows.

If one were to interpret the timing tools described before schematically, the sale of the stocks would be indicated as soon as the actual prices reach or surpass the high that had been valid so far, and if the calculations point toward risk while the expected reward has dropped to zero. However, this impression is mislead- ing and is due to the fact that the method cannot distinguish the accidental fluctuations of a constant average price from systematic variations of the entire process. So, in order to avoid misinforma- tion, the method has to be made more dynamic.

This can be done in several ways. A first step could be to proceed from moving averages instead of using a constant average price, when calculating the range variability RV and the current price factor (CPF). This would guarantee that real changes in the stock price development will be reflected in corresponding variations of the calculation basis "average price"—if only with a certain delay which is caused by the method. The degree of averaging out the moving average can be determined individually by the length of the moving average. Assuming at the same time that there are constant distances between the average price and the high or low of a stock, a fast succession of buying or selling signals is avoided when there are systematic structural changes. The extremes that are used for calculating risk and reward follow the actual price development.

An argument against this method would be that it is neither realistic nor logical to assume a constant or unvarying distance between highs and lows. If one accepts that the medium average price can be subject to systematic changes, one also has to agree that the range between high and low prices changes systematically.

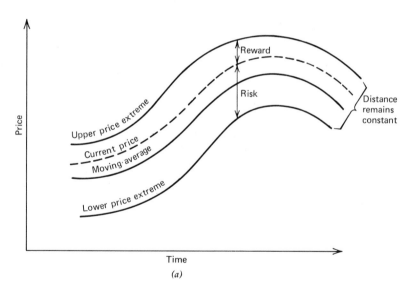

Figure 28(a)   Moving average with fixed volatility.

Methodically, changes of this kind can be approached in various ways. The easiest would be to recalculate the variable "range" on a regular basis for those time intervals on which the calculations for the moving averages are based and thus bring them up to date automatically. This can be done, e.g., by adding the current price when calculating the moving average and eliminating the first entry. The "range" has to be adjusted every day: the current highs and lows are included and the highs and lows of the first entry are scratched. If one goes one step beyond that, one could include in the analysis an empirical connection between current price or average price and volatility or range. P. Kaufman has used this idea in his book (*Technical Analysis in Commodities*, New York, John Wiley, 1979). Kaufman proceeds from the movements of commodity prices, but one could draw the parallel and assume that the variability of the stock price increases with rising prices and vice versa. Hypotheses of such a kind, however, require careful substantiation and statistical proof. Even if this were successful, the question remains whether such a procedure with its extremely sophisticated

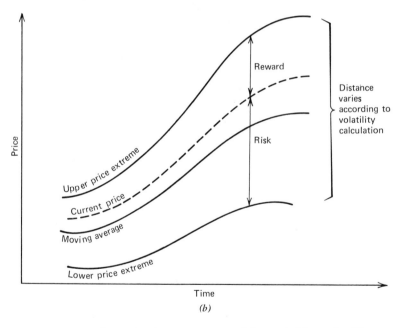

Figure 28(b)   Moving average with variable volatility.

theoretical requirements really is superior to a relatively simple method, such as the moving range calculation described above. The quality and effectiveness of a timing strategy does not necessarily increase proportionally with the complexity of the mathematical formulas used, nor with the size of the computer necessary for carrying out the calculations.

CONCLUSION

There is no such thing as certain success. Therefore, each investment in the stock market carries a certain risk. But not all investments contain the same degree of risk. If one wants to set up the optimum portfolio for an investor, it is necessary to know the risk of various securities and also the readiness of the individual investor to take on risk. The risk inherent in the purchase of stocks can be generally defined as danger of loss of capital. The extent of the risk is determined by the size of the possible capital loss and its probability of realization. The range of variability of a stock price over some past interval is a way of measuring the risk. The greater the variability of the range, the greater the probability of capital loss.

Large price fluctuations always contain the possibility that the price will move unfavorably, but at the same time offers the chance of a favorable development in prices. Therefore, fluctuations also offer indications for the rewards of a stock investment. Risk and reward are closely related: whoever wants to realize a higher return has to accept the higher risk involved. The investor who insists on playing it safe, has to be satisfied with smaller returns. Therefore, it is the individual risk preference of the investor that finally determines the choice of maximum risk or optimum reward of a portfolio (as seen by the efficient frontier).

With this in mind, we have debated the merits of diversification and concentration, considering which of the two would be the better investment strategy. Without doubt, a widely diversified portfolio would be the optimum form of investment for the risk-averse investor. The speculator who is willing to take more risks will naturally be more inclined to put everything on one play. The fate of the concentration funds in the 1960s demonstrated that an increase in opportunities with the help of the concentration strategy is an integral part of higher risks. The investor who puts his capital exclusively into stocks can reduce the risk by means of wide diversification, since stock prices at no time move in the same direction with the same inequitude. There is, however, a natural limit to the reduction of risk through diversification. The minimum risk attainable without timing decisions, the so-called overall or market risk, has been reached when a portfolio contains all stocks comprising the market in the same proportion as they exist in the market—that is, when it corresponds exactly to the market portfolio. The literature concerned with risk analysis on a theoretical basis concludes that the market risk cannot be eliminated. This, however, is the result of a static interpretation. If one allows for the possibility of an interchange between stock analysis and market risk that is oriented toward the development of the entire stock market, then there is indeed a chance to eliminate the market risk. The prerequisite for that would, however, be a timing strategy that works.

The first studies of combinations of securities with varying risk factors were made by Markowitz. His model for determining a portfolio with optimum diversification makes it plain that either the maximum risk or the minimum expected return has to be fixed when looking for the best possible diversification of securities. The optimum portfolio would be the one with the optimum expected return at a given risk limit or with the minimum risk at a given return. It is not possible to increase the expected return to a maximum while simultaneously decreasing the risk to a minimum. Although Markowitz's model is theoretically brilliant, its practicability is questionable. There is an enormous amount of work involved in calculating all possible risks for all stocks in the portfolios. Sharpe's beta theory strongly simplifies Markowitz's model and makes it possible to use it in practice. His basic idea is that instead of comparing all stocks with each other, the stocks should be compared separately with a common risk factor established as the market portfolio. The measurement of risk for a stock or portfolio is expressed by the beta coefficient, indicating to what extent the price of a stock or the value of a specific portfolio changes when the value of the general market portfolio changes. The general market portfolio itself has a beta factor of 1.0; a beta factor higher than 1.0 indicates an increase in risk; below 1.0 it means a reduced risk. The beta factors—which can be obtained from market services—only carry limited significance with respect to the individual stock, but are a valuable aid for analyzing the risk of a complete portfolio.

An additional possibility for reducing the investment risk is the combination of stocks and treasury bills. The capital asset pricing theory concerns itself with the theoretical aspects of this strategy. With the help of this theory, it can be shown that a combination of stocks and treasuries is preferable to exclusive investment in stocks. The optimum ratio between stocks and treasuries, however, is determined by the investors' risk preferences. According to the capital asset pricing theory, the investor who combines stocks with treasuries should structure his stock investments to correspond to the selected market portfolio.

A successful stock investment is not only based on the selection of stocks represented in a portfolio; the investor must be just as careful of the timing of his decisions. The risk, therefore, has to be analyzed both from a static (analytic) and a dynamic (market executions) point of view. The risk-reward method developed by C. W. *Thomas* tries to take into account the dependency of the risk on timing by correcting the variability of stock prices by means of a current price factor. According to this method, the risk increases as the price of a stock increases. On the other hand, the reward also increases as prices go up. Thomas's risk-reward method is a valuable supplement to the beta theory. Like any attempt to quantify the risk, it must be based on a questionable assumption: viz. that price movement in the past contains information (patterns or trends) that allow predictions about future price developments. Whoever denies the possibility of recognizable connections between the past and the future denies at the same time the possibility of any rational capital investment on the stock market.

The importance of price forecasting and risk analysis grows as the risk increases. If the investor decides to put his capital into treasuries, he can practically do without any analytical tools. However, any investor who refuses to use an efficient risk analysis when dealing with high risk investments acts with a dangerous foolhardiness. In Chapter 4, we investigate to what extent the analytic tools and methods that have been discussed so far can be applied to options; the "digression" into the stock analysis proves itself to have been worth the time spent: to develop an intelligent options strategy requires a knowledge of the conditions, opportunities, and dangers of the stock market.

4 *THE OPTIONS TRADE: PROBLEMS AND STRATEGIES*

Numerous different subjects have been covered so far. The entire preparation is intended to create a basis for understanding the options market. The reader who thinks that he can skip all the information and details about the stock market really is mistaken and will, sooner or later, find himself going back to it. Stock prices are the starting point for the movement of option prices. The choice of the exercise price and the expiration date for individual options really is a secondary decision. But the person who cannot properly judge a stock should stay away from the option belonging to that underlying security because:

◇ In addition to the intricacies of stock pricing, the investor has to cope with the pitfalls of options premiums.

◇ He not only has to analyze the overall market, the industrial groups, and the individual stocks, but the premiums as well.

◇ The range of risk and opportunity of options is much wider than that of stocks.

Many advertisements and pamphlets claim that investments in options are practically synonymous with big and quick profits. However, this shows either complete ignorance of the options trading or a conscious attempt to take advantage of the investors' credulity. A disclosure of the fact that an increase in opportunities always car- **119** ries with it an increase in risk is neglected to a nearly criminal degree. Any investor interested in option investing in the United States or the European Option Exchange (EOE) in Amsterdam would be well advised to spend some time to really study, and not just leaf through, the official prospectus of the Options Clearing Corporation. The key point is made right on the first page:

> Both the purchase and writing of Options involve a high degree of risk and are not suitable for many investors. Such transactions should be entered into only by investors who have read and understood this prospectus and, in particular, who understand the nature and extent of their rights and obligations and are aware of the risks involved. An investor should not purchase an Option unless he is able to sustain a total loss of the premium and transaction costs of purchasing the Option, and should not write an Option unless he is able to sustain substantial financial losses, or unless, in the case of a Call, he owns the underlying security.

This prospectus is available to all investors and can be obtained from any brokerage house. Joseph Sullivan, former president of the Chicago Board Options Exchange (CBOE) has described the peculiar risks inherent in options as follows:

> The claim that options are purely for the speculator is just as true or false as the assertion that alcohol is made exclusively for alcoholics. It is absolutely true that options are used in a very speculative way, and that alcohol is the main element of liquor. But alcohol is also used in the production of gasoline, cosmetics and medicine. And in the same way options can be used for various purposes—especially to limit and control the risks of an investment.

It is therefore wrong for the German legislature and leading banks to categorically disqualify options because of high risk. As will be seen later on, options can offer less risk than is possible with stock investments alone. However, if this reticence to recommend options springs from the fear that the investor will balk at the expertise and discipline that is required from him to a great degree, one should think better of it. Many investors are ready and eager to acquire the knowledge that will open the door to another promising form of investment. On the European Options Exchange in Amsterdam, European securities are traded the same way as in Chicago. It has therefore become of paramount importance to point out explicitly and in great detail the opportunities and risks with which the investor is faced when he employs various options strategies.

The investor who is interested in options should not allow himself to be intimidated by the many strategies described in the following pages. The main thing is to have a solid grasp of the basics and the possibilities that are opened up by the purchase or sale of a call or a put. All other combinations are auxiliary strategies that, depending on the market situation, the investor's mentality, or the diversification of a portfolio, might take on special importance. We will therefore discuss the basics of options in detail before delving into and weighing the merits of the various other forms of investment possible with options.

INSTITUTIONS OF THE OPTIONS TRADE

The Options Exchanges

With the opening of the Chicago Board Options Exchange (CBOE) in 1973, and later on the American Stock Exchange (ASE), the Philadelphia Stock Exchange (PHE), the Midwest Stock Exchange (MWE), and the Pacific Coast Stock Exchange (PSE), the way was open for an options business that allowed for exchange traded calls and puts in an organized format. As a rule, this market has the necessary depth, continuity, and liquidity needed for an exchange to function in an orderly way. The key to the success of the options exchanges lies in their structure, which combines two different kinds of transactions in a single process:

◇ The creation of an option by writer and purchaser.

◇ The "secondary market," which gives the investor the opportunity to liquidate his positions by cancelling transactions via the exchange.

The Options Clearing Corporation

The Chicago Board Options Exchange Clearing Corporation, whose function is to guarantee a uniform exchange options trade, was established in 1972. This organization bears the responsibility for an efficient processing of options transactions even given heavy volume. It is independent of the individual stock exchanges. The price of the exchange traded options is not negotiated individually between writer and purchaser, but is determined through supply and demand on the exchange. The options exchanges, therefore, have a clearing corporation that serves as an accounting office and intermediary between the writer and the buyer of an option. The Option Clearing Corporation is the issuer of individual options; for the purchaser it takes a position as the writer, and for the writer it acts as the buyer. It thus guarantees the financial stability of options transactions and makes certain that the writer of a call always fulfills his obligation to deliver the securities if the buyer of a call exercises the option. There is a similar guarantee that the writer of a put purchases the securities offered if the option is exercised.

The members of the Options Clearing Corporation are, as a rule, the brokerage houses, and they are accountable to the Clearing Corporation for the smooth processing of options transactions. If a buyer of a call wants to exercise his option, he notifies his broker, who in turn informs the Options Clearing Corporation. The OCC then chooses a broker at random with whom the corresponding option has been written. Because there has to be a writer for each buyer and the number of all buyers and writers is registered with the Clearing Corporation, it is relatively easy to find out which brokerage house acts for the customer who has written those calls. The brokerage house selected by the Clearing Corporation will assign the exercise notice to a customer who, as the writer of the call, must deliver the securities. OCC members may use a random selection, FIFO (first in, first out), or some other method in assigning notices to customers.

FACTORS INFLUENCING THE OPTIONS TRADE

Legal Requirements Involving Options

With a call or a put, the buyer receives certain rights and the writer accepts certain obligations to buy or to sell:

◇ A security represented by the option contract.

◇ At an exercise price that has been determined before the contract is agreed upon.

◇ Within a fixed time period.

◇ Under the conditions prescribed by the options exchanges.

In the following the term *options premium* (options price) is the sum of the intrinsic value plus the "net" premium.

The Call

With the payment of the options premium, the buyer of a call purchases the right to buy the underlying securities (1 option = 100 shares) at a fixed exercise price within a fixed time period. The buyer has no obligation to exercise the option, and he can let the right to exercise the option expire. The writer of the call is obligated to make delivery at the exercise price agreed upon in the options contract when the securities are called (exercised) by the purchaser. If the investor does not have the securities to be delivered in his portfolio, he must buy them and deliver them at the exercise price. The buyer of a call pays the options premium at the time the contract is entered, and the writer receives the options premium into his account immediately in compensation for the obligation undertaken.

The Put

The buyer of a put purchases, by payment of the options premium, the right to sell the underlying securities of an option at the fixed exercise price within a fixed time period. If the buyer of a put exercises his option, he may buy the securities at the market and deliver them to the writer at the exercise price, or he may sell these securities if they are already in his own portfolio. The writer of a put has accepted the obligation to buy the underlying securities at the exercise price whenever the buyer exercises his option and delivers the securities. The writer of a put therefore must pay the exercise price at any given time for the securities delivered, that is, he must have the necessary funds at his disposal at all times.

Although the writer can be a covered writer [either in securities (call) or money (put)], he does not have to remain in that position. He can, at any time, avoid the obligation to make delivery (call) or purchase the securities (put) by entering the opposite transaction on the exchange. The rights and duties of the participants in the different options transactions are outlined in Figure 29.

Participant	Options transactions	Call	Put
Buyer	Rights	Purchase of a security at exercise price	Sale of a security at exercise price
Buyer	Obligation	Payment of the options premium	Payment of the options premium
Writer	Rights	Claim on the options premium	Claim on the options premium
Writer	Obligation	Sale of the security at exercise price	Purchase of security at exercise price

Figure 29

Components and Conditions of the Options Contract

The Expiration Date

To facilitate trading options on the exchange in the same manner as stocks, the expiration months (the term of the options contract) have been standardized. Three cycles of expiration months are available for options trading, which permit a maximum of 9 months for the life of the option.

At first, the CBOE permitted three months for trading using the expiration months January, April, July, and October, but then additional options were introduced when the volume increased and new securities were accepted. Today there are three different expiration cycles, depending on the securities:

1st	2nd	3rd
January	February	March
April	May	June
July	August	September
October	November	December

Exercise Price or Striking Price

All securities admitted by the Options Exchange possess an exercise price that is fixed by the Options Clearing Corporation and valid for the individual expiration months. When the exercise price is standardized, it is set in a round dollar sum. The exercise price is standardized according to the following pattern.

When the stock price is less than $50, the exercise prices are 5 points apart. With a price of $50 to $200, the exercise prices are 10 points apart and when above $200, they are 20 points apart. Exceptions such as an exercise price of $55 are possible, but infrequent. Exercise prices that are not one of the standard variations can be traded during the life of the option in the event of a stock split or stock dividend. In 1976, Digital Equipment split 3 for 1; consequently the previous exercise price of 160 was reduced to 53⅓. Cash dividends do not have to be considered because there are no contract adjustments for such exchange traded options. Only the number of the underlying securities is adjusted according to changes caused by stock dividends or stock splits.

Size of Contract

Every options contract with exchange traded calls or puts represents 100 shares. (Exceptions are possible with stock splits or stock dividends.)

The Options Premium (Option Price)

The options buyer pays the options premium for the right to exercise the option at exercise price within a time period determined by the expiration date. The premium is determined by supply and demand by means of the option exchanges. The investor can react in many ways to expected price movements by choosing among various exercise prices and expiration dates.

Example: Assume that with the stock XYZ at $60, a call with exercise price 60 has a premium of $6, and the put has an option price of $5. A change in the stock price can result in the option prices shown in Figure 30.

Stock Price	Call Price	Put Price
66	10	2
64	9	3
62	8	4
60	6	5
58	5	7
56	4	8
54	2	9

Figure 30

The premium of the calls and puts is determined by:

◇ **The intrinsic value of the option.** The intrinsic value of an option is the difference between the current stock price and the lower exercise price (call) or the higher exercise price (put).

◇ **The "net" premium.** The "net" premium is the difference between the premium and the intrinsic value of the option. If there is no intrinsic value, the "net" premium is the same as the premium.

Example for a call: In the preceding example, the stock XYZ was traded at $60, and the corresponding call at $6. The "net" premium is then $6, since there is no intrinsic value (no difference between stock price and exercise price.) A call has intrinsic value only when the exercise price of the option is below the current market price of the stock. All exercise prices above the stock price trade on "net" premium. If the options price is $10, with a stock price of $66, then we can see the following relationships:

Intrinsic value	+	"Net" premium	=	Premium
Option 66 − 60	+	10 − 6	=	10
6	+	4	=	10

Figure 31

Example for a put: In the previous example, the call was purchased at $6 when the stock price was $60. Under the same circumstances, the value of a put might be $5. Experience with the Over-The-Counter-Market (OTC) has shown that as a rule the put is normally valued slightly lower than the call. This does not always have to be true, however. In this case, because there is no difference between the stock price and the exercise price, the net premium for the put is $5. The put has an intrinsic value only if an exercise price is chosen that is higher than the stock price when the put is bought or sold. All exercise prices below the stock price trade with a "net" premium. An options price of $9, with a stock price of $54, results in:

Intrinsic value	+	"Net" premium	=	Premium
Option 60 – 54	+	9 – 6	=	9
6	+	3	=	9

Figure 32

It is important to remember that the intrinsic value of a call increases as the stock price goes up, whereas the intrinsic value of a put increases when the stock goes down. When a call has an exercise price above the stock price, and a put has an exercise price below the stock price, the option is said to be "out of the money." If, however, a call has an exercise price below the stock price, or a put has an exercise price above the stock price, then the option is called "in the money." Figure 33 shows how the relationship of intrinsic value and "net" premium to premium changes when the exercise prices for puts and calls are different.

Options transactions / Premium	Call	Put
Exercise price far below stock price	High intrinsic value / Small "net" premium	Small "net" premium / *No* intrinsic value
Exercise price equals stock price	High "net" premium / *No* intrinsic value	High "net" premium / *No* intrinsic value
Exercise far above stock price	Small "net" premium / *No* intrinsic value	High intrinsic value / Small "net" premium

Figure 33

BASIC REQUIREMENTS FOR WORKING WITH OPTIONS

What Are the Differences Between Stocks and Options?

In contrast to stocks, warrants, convertible bonds, and the like, which are issued in fixed amounts and numbers by individual corporations and can be changed only by those corporations, the amount of exchange traded options is determined by purchasers and buyers themselves (i.e., supply and demand). Therefore, there is no predetermined number of options for a certain security. Certificates, which serve as proof of ownership for stocks, are not issued for options. To show the position of purchases and sales, the brokerage house prints statements and sends them to the customer as verification that his order has been executed. Because of this simplified clearing system, the efficiency of options transaction is considerably increased while commissions are kept relatively low. Another major difference between stocks and options is in the limitations of duration of ownership. Whereas an investor can hold a stock indefinitely, the life of an options contract is predetermined by the expiration date. A stock can be a long-term investment; an option, on the other hand, becomes worthless on the expiration day.

The leverage available through options is another key difference, that is, a small change in the stock price may result in a larger percentage change in the option. The investor who knows how to employ this leverage effect to his advantage can hardly find a better form of investment than options. However, the person who does not have the knack of correctly judging the dangers connected with the leverage effect, undertakes risks that frequently lead to rapid and total loss of the capital set aside for investment purposes. The following example explains the leverage effect.

Example:
 Price of the stock XYZ in September—$60
 Options price call in October—$2
 Exercise price—$60

The investor has the choice of paying $6000 for 100 shares of stock XYZ or of buying an October call with an exercise price of 60 for $2 (=$200). (Alternative expiration months and exercise prices are not included in this example.)

1st Case: If the stock XYZ rises above $62 prior to the October expiration date, the options purchaser will always realize a profit. At $66, the option will be traded at least at $6 because this represents the intrinsic value of the call (the difference between the stock price and the exercise price). In this case, the investor who bought 100 shares for $6000, will realize a profit of 10% or $600 while the options buyer with an investment of $200 will make at least $400, that is, a 200% profit. It is important to note that the investor who chooses options achieves nearly the same actual dollar profit using only $200 as the investor who buys $6000 worth of shares.

2nd Case: If the price of stock XYZ remains unchanged until October or even falls to slightly below $60, there will be little or no effect on the investment in shares. The buyer of the option, on the other hand, will realize a total loss of $200 on the expiration date unless he sells the option at its residual value before the expiration day.

These simple examples plainly show the risks and opportunities of investment in options compared to that in stocks. The investor in options has a great opportunity to make a profit but only if he can correctly predict the trend of the stock prices. Depending on his risk preference, he can vary the amount of his investment by varying the expiration months, exercise prices, or option contracts. But an investor who puts his capital into stocks will rarely lose his entire capital in such a short time as the investor who puts the $6000 into options. If the options buyer makes the wrong decision about a short-term price trend, he will hardly be able to keep track of his fast-dwindling capital.

On the other hand, the conservative investor who cannot determine the current direction of prices and wants to watch that movement quietly before committing himself to buy $6000 worth of the stocks can secure the option on the stocks for an outlay of only $200 when the stock price is $60. If the stock has fallen to $50 by October, his decision would have been correct; he would have incurred a loss of 16% had he bought the stock whereas the loss of $200 on premium would have been only 3% of the stock value. If the stock recovers after the expiration date, of course, he no longer benefits from the upswing because the option will have expired.

Options with a high exercise price and a near expiration date offer the investor a particularly good chance to realize a very high, but speculative return. These options can be purchased at a very low price per unit, and the opportunity to multiply the investment is greater than with an option that was a low exercise price and therefore a high market price. The greater the chance to profit, however, the lower will be the probability to realize that profit and the greater the danger of incurring big losses. Frequently the speculative investor only has an eye for profit and does not stop to consider the possibility of actually realizing it. Quite unconsciously, he often values the chance of making a killing—which is extremely unlikely—much more than the chance for a more modest profit, even though the latter would be far more realistic. People still dream of making a $5000 profit in a very short time with a capital of only $500 and think little of making $750 with a $500 investment. They simply do not stop to think that the probability of realizing such a large profit is infinitesmally small compared to the more modest return, while the risk is disproportionately great. They might just as well turn the old proverb around and have two birds in the bush rather than the one in hand.

Unlike the speculator, the conservative investor can retain the same chances to make a profit by purchasing calls instead of stocks; furthermore, by doing this he reduces his risk considerably. The "correct" procedure for selecting exercise prices and expiration dates, the exact calculation of opportunities and risks with options, and the "proper" ratio of stocks and options are discussed in detail in Chapter 6.

Chicago Options Table

Option & price	Vol.	Last — Apr —	Vol.	Last — Jul —	Vol.	Last — Oct —	Close
All R	60	5 1-16	a	a	b	b	45¾
Avon	40	28 4⅜	a	d	2	5⅜	44⅝
Avon p	40	13 ⅜	76	13-16	94	1 3-16	44⅝
Avon	45	287 1⅛	292	2 1-16	31	2 13-16	44⅝
Avon p	45	36 1⅛	45	2¾	28	3	44⅝
Avon	50	148 3-16	84	½	77	1	44⅝
Avon p	50	39 6	17	6⅛	a	a	44⅝
BankAm	25	11 3-16	8	⅜	25	⅝	21⅞
Beth S	15	14 7⅛	a	a	b	b	22⅛
Beth S	20	166 2 7-16	139	3⅛	42	3⅜	22⅛
BethS	25	321 ⅜	183	½	301	1⅛	22⅛
Beth S	30	1 1-16	b	b	b	b	22⅛
Bruns	10	20 3⅛	15	4	a	a	13⅜
Bruns	15	369 ⅜	201	1	14	1⅛	13⅜
Burl N	40	96 1 1-16	16	2⅛	20	3	40⅜
Burl N	45	132 ¼	7	⅝	21	1	40⅜
Burrgh	60	159 4⅜	67	6⅛	1	8½	63⅛
Burrgh	70	381 ¾	197	2¼	27	3⅜	63⅛
Citicp	20	190 ⅞	86	1 9-16	206	1 13-16	19¾
Citicp	25	758 1-16	50	¼	302	½	19¾
Delta	35	19 4½	4	5⅛	8	6	39
Delta	40	57 1 5-16	50	2 5-16	4⁹	3⅛	39
Dig Eq	40	960 1 13-16	449	3	123	4⅛	40
Dig Eq	45	702 ½	507	1¼	1444	2 1-16	40
Dig Eq	50	319 1-16	295	½	160	15-16	40
Disney o 34½	40	1½	a	b	b		33¾
Disney o 39⅜	a	a	20	13-16	b	b	33¾
Disney	30	16 4⅜	a	a	a	a	33¾
Disney	35	36 1 1-16	35	2⅜	7	3⅜	33¾
Disney	40	2 3-16	30	¾	a	a	33¾
DowCh	25	218 ⅞	110	1 7-16	204	1⅞	24⅛
Dow Ch	30	289 ⅛	188	5-16	221	⅞	24½
Dow Ch	35	1 1-16	b	b	b	b	24⅛
du Pnt	100	174 8¼	21	10½	2	11¾	106⅜
du Pnt	110	325 2-16	24	4½	16	6¼	106⅜
du Pnt	120	228 ½	78	1⅞	16	2 11-16	106⅜
Eas Kd	45	671 1 15-16	250	3	113	3¾	45
Eas Kd p	45	515 2	176	2 11-16	32	3⅛	45
Eas Kd	50	799 7-16	461	1¼	158	1 15-16	45
Aas Kd p	50	522 5½	81	5¾	2	5⅝	45
Eas Kd	60	157 1-16	400	3-16	592	½	45
Eas Kd p	60	192 15⅛	7	15	a	a	45
Eas Kd	70	36 1-16	b	b	b	b	45
Exxon	40	122 5⅛	20	5½	9	5¼	44⅝
Exxon	45	512 1¼	166	1¾	142	2¼	44⅝
Exxon	50	277 ⅛	91	7-16	60	11-16	44⅝
F N M	15	117 11-16	20	⅞	12	1	15⅜
F N M	20	a a	a	a	5	⅛	15⅜
Fluor	30	133 3½	a	a	7	4¾	33⅛
Fluor	35	25 ¾	30	1⅝	12	2¼	33⅛
Fluor	40	5 3-16	1	5-16	b	b	33⅛
Ford	40	144 2⅛	5	2 13-16	10	3⅛	41⅝
Ford	45	122 5-16	91	¾	8	1⅛	41⅝
Gen El	45	43 2⅝	68	3¼	20	4¼	46⅞
GenEl	50	173 7-16	72	1	34	1½	46⅞
GenEl	55	2 ⅛	1	¼	b	b	46⅞
GM	50	56 8⅜	21	8¾	23	8⅜	58⅜
G M p	50	8 3-16	51	11-16	94	⅞	58⅜
G M	60	559 1	130	1 11-16	108	2¼	583
G M p	60	360 3⅜	9	4⅜	16	5¼	58⅜
G M	70	115 1-16	8	¼	a	a	58⅜
G M p	70	49 12⅝	4	13	a	a	58⅜
Gt Wst	15	10 4¼	a	a	a	a	19⅛
Gt Wst	20	9 ⅝	28	1¼	7	1½	19⅛
Gt Wst	25	11 1-16	a	a	a	a	19⅛
GlfWn	10	17 1½	12	1 13-16	8	2	19⅛
Glf Wn	15	128 1-16	45	⅛	82	5-16	11⅜
Halbtn	50	42 10	6	13¾	a	a	59¼
IHalbtn	60	44 2⅛	37	3⅜	a	a	59¼
Halbtn	70	7 ¼	a	a	b	b	59¼
Homstk	35	121 2¼	104	3⅜	42	3¾	35⅞
Homstk	40	380 9-16	96	1 5-16	36	2	35⅞
Homstk	45	3 ⅝	14	7-16	116	¾	35⅞
Hou OM	25	218 4½	35	5½	34	6⅜	28¼
Hou OM	30	587 1 11-16	193	2 13-16	11	3⅜	28¼
Hou OM	35	635 ½	326	1¼	118	2⅛	28¼
Hou OM	40	22 3-16	b	b	b	b	28¼
Hou OM	45	36 1-16	b	b	b	b	28¼
I N A	35	a a	1	2⅞	a	a	36⅛
I B M	240	1818 21⅜	206	24	60	26⅝	258⅝
I B M	240	1408 ⅞	119	2 7-16	68	37⅜	258⅝
I B M	260	3950 6¾	224	10½	111	13⅜	258⅝
I B M p	260	2155 6¼	185	9¼	87	11⅜	258⅝
I B M	280	3037 1¼	602	3⅝	265	5⅞	258⅝
Tln Har	25	33 3⅞	1	4⅛	a	a	28⅞
In Har	30	117 ½	182	⅞	6	1 5-16	28⅞
InMin	35	12 4¾	a	a	a	a	39⅝
In Min	40	14 ¾	12	1⅛	a	a	39⅝
In Pcp	35	a a	2	5¼	b	b	39
InPa⊃	40	66 1¼	53	2⅛	15	3	39
InPc⊃	45	57 3-16	77	11-16	10	1 3-16	39
I T T	25	1 4⅜	11	4¼	70	4⅜	29¼
IT T	35	108 1-16	34	3-16	33	5-16	29¼
John J	60	31 10½	b	b	b	b	70½
John J	70	25 2¼	10	3¾	a	a	70½
John J	80	a a	1	13-16	5	1½	70½
K mart	25	138 ⅞	36	1½	233	2	24⅝
K mart	30	145 ⅛	52	7-16	27	¾	24⅝
Kenn C	20	35 4	18	4½	a	a	23½
Kenn C	25	54 ⅞	52	1 11-16	38	2⅛	23½
KennC	30	54 ⅛	a	a	5	¾	23½
Kerr M	45	143 11-16	55	2	9	3	43¼
Kerr M	50	64 3-16	75	15-16	43	1⅜	43¼
KerrM	60	7 1-16	16	¼	b	b	43¼
Loews	30	19 4⅜	4	4	6	4½	34
Loews	35	98 ¾	15	1½	40	2	34
Mc Don	40	177 5¾	28	6⅝	b	b	45½
Mc Don	45	153 2 5-16	23	3⅜	32	4⅜	45½
McDon	50	221 ½	173	1¾	20	2⅛	45½
Merck	50	17 6	87	7	a	a	55¾
Merck	60	10 ⅝	58	1⅜	25	2⅛	55¾
Merril	15	2 ⅜	14	⅞	30	1¼	13¾
Merril	20	4 1-16	200	⅛	a	a	13¾
M M M	45	52 2¾	5	3¾	a	a	47¼
Monsan	50	61 1¾	8	3	a	a	50
Monsan	60	3 ⅛	57	½	9	15-16	50
N C R	35	55 5⅜	6	6⅜	20	7⅜	40½
N C R	40	295 2	148	3⅛	59	4⅛	40½
N C R	45	342 ½	85	1 3-16	b	b	40½
Nw Air	15	2 2	9	a	b	b	24
NwAir	20	57 4	3	4¾	7	5⅝	24
Nw Air	25	64 ¾	33	1 11-16	11	2 1-16	24
Pennz	25	73 5	10	5	5	7	29⅝
Pennz	30	325 ⅞	102	1 5-16	a	a	29⅝
Pennz	35	4 1-16	b	b	b	b	29⅝
Pepsi	20	a a	b	b	b	b	25⅞
Pepsi	25	9 1½	15	2⅛	12	2¾	25⅞
Pepsi	30	1 1-16	49	½	12	11-16	25⅞
Polar	20	214 4⅞	25	5⅜	a	a	25⅛
Polar	25	244 1⅛	289	1¾	453	2¾	25⅛
Polar	30	266 3-16	315	½	272	⅞	25⅛
Polar	35	7 1-16	b	b	b	b	25⅛
R C A	30	73 1⅛	36	⅜	b	b	25
Sears	25	139 1⅛	107	1¾	28	2½	25⅜
Sears	30	122 3-16	47	7-16	73	11-16	25⅜
Sears	35	122 3-16	47	7-16	73	11-16	25⅜
Sperry	30	13 4	1	4¾	a	a	33⅞
Sperry	35	57 1	21	1 13-16	9	2 5-16	33⅞
Sperry	40	57 1-16	12	5-16	183	¾	33⅞
Syntex	15	a a	5	6⅜	a	a	20¾
Syntex	20	247 1 9-16	103	2⅜	29	2¾	20¾
Tandy	20	6 13⅜	b	b	b	b	33
Tandy	25	8 8⅜	5	8¾	b	b	33
Tandy	30	65 4	7	5	a	a	33
Teldyn	45	44 1½	a	a	1	27⅛	67
Teldyn	50	180 17½	9	18¾	b	b	67
Teldyn	55	165 12⅝	8	14¼	14	16⅛	67
Teldyn	60	805 8⅝	48	10⅜	20	12½	67
Teldyn	70	1361 2 9-16	199	5	129	6⅞	67
Tesoro	10	24 ⅝	54	5-16	24	9-16	77⅛
Tex In	70	582 2¾	166	4¾	97	6¼	6½
Tex In	80	1617 ⅜	681	1⅜	141	2⅜	69½
Tex In	90	219 1-16	99	½	b	b	69½
Upjohn	30	14 4¾	a	a	a	a	34⅜
Upjohn	35	162 1	19	1 11-16	19	2 3-16	34⅜
Upjohn	40	a a	10	⅜	35	1½	34⅜
Weyerh	20	a a	a	a	21	4⅞	23¾
Weyerh	25	18 ⅝	12	1¼	37	1 11-16	23¾
Weyerh	30	a a	a	a	22	⅝	23¾
Weyerh	35	5 1-16	b	b	b	b	23¾
Xerox	40	90 5¼	5	6	16	7⅛	44¼
Xerox	45	246 1 13-16	172	3	20	3¾	44¼
Xerox	50	123 ⅜	198	1 3-16	40	1 15-16	44¼

Total volume 77,113   Open Interest 1,506,819

a—Not traded. b—No option offered. p—Put.
Sales in 100s. Last is premium (purchase price).

Figure 34   *Chicago Options Table.*

131

How To Read the Options Table

Many papers, such as the *International Herald Tribune* and the *Wall Street Journal*, regularly print all options prices of the United States options exchanges. Figure 34 is taken from the *Herald Tribune*:

The symbols signify the following:

Option: Designation of the stock. The individual stocks are abbreviated:

Atl R = Atlantic Richfield
Avon = Avon Products
Beth. S. = Bethlehem Steel

Any broker will provide a list of all abbreviations in use on request.

Price: Price at which the option may be exercised. Atl R 60, for example, means that Atlantic Richfield has an exercise price 60.

Vol. (= volume): Number of options contracts traded on that particular day. Every options contract is normally 100 shares.

Last: Closing prices of the options for that day. The options prices are traded in fractions of $1, with a minimum move of $1/16$ of a dollar. Therefore it is possible that after the dollar amounts, quotations appear of $1/16$, $1/8$, $3/16$, $1/4$, $5/16$, $3/8$, $7/16$, $1/2$, $9/16$, $5/8$, $11/16$, $3/4$, $13/16$, $7/8$, and $15/16$. Each $1/16$ = $6.25 per 100 shares.

April-July-Oct.: Expiration months for the options traded.

a: An option can be traded but there was no supply or demand on that day.

b: No options are traded in this exercise price and expiration month because they have not yet been opened for options trading by the exchanges.

Close: Closing price of the stock.

p: Put option.

Total volume: Total volume of the options exchange for that day.

Open interest: Number of open options contracts (explained in detail later).

The Underlying Securities for Options Traded in August 1979

S&P	Stock	Symbol	Option Exch.	Cycle
A−	AMF Inc.	AMF	ASE	FMAN
—	ASA Ltd. (p)	ASA	ASE	FMAN
A	Abbott Laboratories	ABT	PBW	FMAN
—	Aetna Life & Casualty (p)	AET	ASE	JAJO
A−	Allied Chemical	ACD	PBW	JAJO
B+	Allis-Chalmers (p)	AH	PBW	JAJO
B+	Aluminum Co. of Amer.	AA	CBOE	JAJO
B+	Amerada Hess (p)	AHC	PBW	FMAN
A−	Amer. Broadcasting (p)	ABC	PSE	FMAN
A	Amer. Cyanamid Co.	ACY	ASE	JAJO
A−	Amer. Electric Pwr. Inc.	AEP	CBOE	FMAN
—	Amer. Express	AXP	CBOE,ASE,MWE	JAJO
A+	Amer. Home Products	AHP	ASE	JAJO
A+	Amer. Hospital Supply	AHS	CBOE	FMAN
A+	Amer. Tel. & Tel.	T	CBOE	JAJO
A	AMP Inc.	AMP	CBOE	FMAN
B	ASARCO Inc.	AR	ASE	MJSD
A	Ashland Oil	ASH	PBW	JAJO
A	Atlantic Richfield	ARC	CBOE	JAJO
A−	Avnet Inc.	AVT	ASE	FMAN
A	Avon Products Inc. (p)	AVP	CBOE	JAJO
A	Baker Intl. Corp.	BKO	PSE	MJSD
B+	Bally Mfg.	BLY	CBOE,ASE	FMAN
—	BankAmerica Corp.	BAM	CBOE	JAJO
A+	Baxter Travenol Labs.	BAX	CBOE	FMAN
A+	Beatrice Foods	BRY	ASE	MJSD
B	Bethlehem Steel	BS	CBOE	JAJO
A+	Black & Decker Mfg. Co.	BDK	CBOE	FMAN
A	Blue Bell Inc.	BBL	PBW	JAJO
A	Boeing Co.	BA	CBOE	FMAN
B+	Boise Cascade	BCC	CBOE	FMAN
B+	Braniff Int'l. Corp.	BNF	PBW	FMAN
A+	Bristol-Meyers Co.	BMY	MWE	MJSD
B+	Brunswick Corp.	BC	CBOE	MJSD
A−	Burlington Northern Inc.	BNI	CBOE	JAJO
A+	Burroughs Corp.	BGH	CBOE,ASE	JAJO
A+	CBS Inc.	CBS	CBOE	FMAN
A	Caterpillar Tractor Co.	CAT	ASE	FMAN
A−	Champion Int'l. Corp.	CHA	MWE	MJSD
—	Chase Manhattan	CMB	ASE	MJSD
—	Citicorp	FNC	CBOE	JAJO
—	City Investing Co.	CNV	PBW	JAJO
A−	Clorox Co.	CLX	PBW	JAJO
NR	Coastal States Gas Corp.	CGP	ASE,MWE	MJSD
A+	Coca-Cola Co.	KO	CBOE	FMAN

S&P	Stock	Symbol	Option Exch.	Cycle
A+	Colgate-Palmolive Co.	CL	CBOE	FMAN
A	Combustion Engrng. Inc.	CSP	PSE	MJSD
A−	Commonwealth Edison	CWE	CBOE	FMAN
A−	Communication Satellite	CQ	PBW	JAJO
A	Conoco (p)	CLL	PBW	JAJO
B+	Consol. Ed. Co. NY Inc.	ED	ASE	FMAN
A−	Continental Tel. Corp.	CTC	ASE	JAJO
B	Control Data Corp. Del.	CDA	CBOE	FMAN
A−	Corning Glass Works (p)	GLW	MWE	MJSD
A+	Deere & Co.	DE	ASE	MJSD
A	Delta Air Lines Inc. Del.	DAL	CBOE	JAJO
A−	Diamond Shamrock Corp.	DIA	PSE	JAJO
A−	Digital Equipment Corp.	DEC	CBOE,ASE	JAJO
A+	Disney (Walt) Prdctns	DIS	CBOE,ASE,PSE	JAJO
A	Dr. Pepper Co.	DOC	ASE	FMAN
A	Dow Chemical Co.	DOW	CBOE	MJSD
A−	Dresser Industries Inc.	DI	PBW	JAJO
A−	DuPont (EI) De Nemours	DD	CBOE,ASE	JAJO
A−	Duke Power Co.	DUK	PBW	JAJO
B+	Eastern Gas & Fuel	EFU	PBW	JAJO
A+	Eastman Kodak Co. (p)	EK	CBOE	JAJO
B+	El Paso Co.	ELG	ASE	FMAN
A	Engelhard Mins. & Chems.	ENG	PBW	JAJO
B+	Evans Products Co.	EVY	MWE	MJSD
A+	Exxon Corp.	XON	CBOE	JAJO
—	Federal Nat'l. Mtge.	FNM	CBOE	JAJO
A+	Federated Dept. Stores	FDS	PSE	FMAN
B+	Firestone Tire & Rubber	FIR	PBW	FMAN
—	First Charter Fin'l. Corp.	FCF	ASE	JAJO
B+	Fleetwood Enterpr. Inc.	FLE	ASE	FMAN
B+	Fluor Corp.	FLR	CBOE	JAJO
A−	Ford Motor Co.	F	CBOE	MJSD
B+	Freeport Minerals Co.	FT	MWE	MJSD
B+	GAF Corp.	GAF	PBW	JAJO
B+	General Dynamics Corp.	GD	CBOE	FMAN
A+	General Electric Co.	GE	CBOE	MJSD
A	General Foods Corp.	GF	CBOE	FMAN
A−	General Motors Corp. (p)	GM	CBOE	MJSD
A	General Tel. & Elec.	GTE	ASE	MJSD
A	Georgia Pacific Corp.	GP	PBW	JAJO
A−	Gillette Co.	GS	ASE	MJSD
A−	Goodyear Tire & Rubber	GT	ASE	JAJO
A−	Grace, (W.R.) & Co.	GRA	ASE	FMAN
—	Great Western Fin'l.	GWF	CBOE	JAJO

134

S&P	Stock	Symbol	Option Exch.	Cycle
B+	Greyhound Corp.	G	ASE	JAJO
A−	Gulf & Western Inds.	GW	CBOE	MJSD
A−	Gulf Oil Corp.	GO	ASE	JAJO
A+	Halliburton Co.	HAL	CBOE	JAJO
B+	Hercules, Inc.	HPC	ASE	MJSD
A	Heublein Inc. (p)	HBL	PSE	FMAN
A+	Hewlett-Packard Co.	HWP	CBOE	FMAN
A−	Hilton Hotels Corp.	HLT	PSE	FMAN
A−	Holiday Inns Inc.	HIA	CBOE	FMAN
B+	Homestake Mining Co.	HM	CBOE	JAJO
A	Honeywell, Inc. (p)	HON	CBOE	FMAN
A−	Household Finance Corp.	HFC	ASE	JAJO
B+	Houston Oil & Minerals	HOI	CBOE,PSE	JAJO
A	Howard Johnson Co.	HJ	PBW	JAJO
B+	Hughes Tool (p)	HT	MWE	MJSD
—	INA Corp.	INA	CBOE	JAJO
B	Inexco Oil Co. (p)	INX	PBW	FMAN
A+	Int'l. Bus. Machines (p)	IBM	CBOE	JAJO
A	Int'l. Flavors & Fragrance	IFF	CBOE	FMAN
B+	Int'l. Harvester Co.	HR	CBOE	JAJO
B+	Int'l. Minerals & Chem.	IGL	CBOE	JAJO
B+	Int'l. Paper Co.	IP	CBOE	JAJO
A−	Int'l. Tel. & Tel. Corp.	ITT	CBOE	MJSD
B	Itel Corp.	I	PSE	JAJO
A−	Johns-Manville Corp.	JM	CBOE	FMAN
A+	Johnson & Johnson	JNJ	CBOE	JAJO
B+	Joy Mfg. Co.	JOY	PBW	FMAN
A+	K Mart Corp.	KM	CBOE	MJSD
B−	Kennecott Copper Corp.	KN	CBOE	MJSD
A	Kerr-McGee Corp.	KMG	CBOE	JAJO
A	Levi Strauss Co. (p)	LVI	PSE	JAJO
A+	Lilly (Eli) & Co.	LLY	ASE	JAJO
B−	Litton Indus. Inc.	LIT	MWE	MJSD
B	Lockheed Corp.	LK	PSE	MJSD
A	Louisiana Land & Expl.	LLX	PBW	FMAN
B+	Louisiana Pacific Corp.	LPX	ASE	FMAN
A+	Lucky Stores Inc.	LKS	PSE	MJSD
—	MGIC Investment Corp.	MGI	CBOE,ASE	FMAN
A	MAPCO Inc.	MDA	PSE	JAJO
B+	Marriott Corp.	MHS	PBW	JAJO
B+	McDermott (I. Ray)	MDE	CBOE	MJSD
A−	McDonald's Corp.	MCD	CBOE	MJSD
B+	McDonnell Douglas	MD	PSE	FMAN
A+	Merck & Co. Inc.	MRK	CBOE	JAJO
—	Merrill Lynch & Co., Inc.	MER	CBOE,ASE	JAJO

135

S&P	Stock	Symbol	Option Exch.	Cycle
B+	Mesa Petroleum Co. (p)	MSA	ASE	JAJO
A	Middle South Util. Inc.	MSU	MWE	MJSD
A+	Minnesota Mining & Mfg.	MMM	CBOE	JAJO
A+	Mobil Corp.	MOB	CBOE	FMAN
A−	Monsanto Co.	MTC	CBOE	JAJO
A−	Motorola Inc.	MOT	ASE	JAJO
B+	NCR Corp.	NCR	CBOE	MJSD
B+	NL Industries Inc.	NL	PBW	FMAN
B+	Nat'l. Distillers & Chems.	DR	ASE	FMAN
B	Nat'l. Semiconductor	NSM	CBOE,ASE	FMAN
B+	Northwest Airlines Inc.	NWA	CBOE	JAJO
B+	Northwest Industries (p)	NWT	MWE	MJSD
B+	Norton Simon Inc.	NSI	ASE	FMAN
B	Occidental Petroleum	OXY	CBOE	FMAN
A	Owens-Illinois Inc.	OI	MWE	MJSD
A	PPG Industries Inc.	PPG	PBW	FMAN
A	Penney (J. C.) Inc.	JCP	ASE	FMAN
A−	Pennzoil Co.	PZL	CBOE	JAJO
A+	Pepsico Inc.	PEP	CBOE	JAJO
A−	Perkin-Elmer Corp.	PKN	PSE	MJSD
A+	Pfizer, Inc.	PFE	ASE	MJSD
B	Phelps Dodge Corp.	PD	ASE	JAJO
A+	Philip Morris Inc.	MO	ASE	MJSD
A	Phillips Petroleum Co.	P	ASE	FMAN
B+	Pitney-Bowes Inc.	PBI	ASE	JAJO
B+	Pittston Co. (o)	PCO	PBW	FMAN
B+	Polaroid Corp.	PRD	CBOE,PSE	JAJO
A+	Procter & Gamble Co.	PG	ASE	JAJO
A−	RCA Corp.	RCA	CBOE	MJSD
A+	Ralston Purina Co.	RAL	MWE	MJSD
A	Raytheon Co.	RTN	CBOE	FMAN
B+	Reserve Oil & Gas (p)	RVO	ASE	FMAN
A+	Revlon, Inc. (p)	REV	MWE	MJSD
A+	Reynolds (R. J.) Indus.	RJR	CBOE	FMAN
B	Reynolds Metals Co.	RLM	PSE	FMAN
A−	Rite Aid Corp.	RAD	ASE	JAJO
A	Rockwell Int'l. Corp.	ROK	MWE	MJSD
A−	Safeway Stores Inc.	SA	MWE	MJSD
B+	Sambo's Restaurants	SRI	PSE	JAJO
A	Santa Fe Int'l Corp. (p)	SAF	PSE	JAJO
A+	Schering-Plough (p)	SGP	PSE	FMAN
A+	Schlumberger Ltd.	SLB	CBOE	FMAN
B+	Scott Paper Co.	SPP	PBW	JAJO
B+	Seaboard Coast Line Ind.	SCI	PBW	JAJO
A−	Searle (G.D.) & Co	SRL	ASE	FMAN
A+	Sears, Roebuck & Co.	S	CBOE	MJSD

S&P	Stock	Symbol	Option Exch.	Cycle
B+	Signal Companies Inc.	SGN	PSE	FMAN
B+	Simplicity Pattern Inc.	SYP	ASE	FMAN
B	Skyline Corp.	SKY	CBOE	FMAN
B+	Southern Co.	SO	CBOE	FMAN
A+	Sperry Rand Corp.	SY	CBOE	JAJO
A+	Squibb Corp.	SQB	CBOE	JAJO
A+	Standard Oil Co. Calif.	SD	ASE	MJSD
A+	Standard Oil Co. Indiana	SN	CBOE	FMAN
A+	Sterling Drug Inc.	STY	ASE	FMAN
B+	Storage Technology Corp.	STK	CBOE	JAJO
A	Sun Inc.	SUN	PBW	FMAN
A−	Syntex Corp.	SYN	CBOE	MJSD
A	TRW Inc.	TRW	ASE	JAJO
B+	Tandy Corp.	TAN	CBOE,ASE	JAJO
B+	Teledyne Inc.	TDY	CBOE,PSE	JAJO
A	Tenneco, Inc.	TGT	ASE	FMAN
A−	Texaco, Inc.	TX	ASE	JAJO
A	Texas Instruments Inc.	TXN	CBOE	JAJO
B	Texasgulf, Inc.	TG	CBOE	FMAN
B+	Tiger Int'l. Inc.	TGR	ASE	FMAN
—	Transamerica Corp.	TA	PBW	FMAN
—	Travelers Corp.	TIC	PSE	FMAN
B	UAL Inc.	UAL	CBOE	FMAN
A−	Union Carbide Corp.	UK	ASE	JAJO
A	Union Oil of Calif.	UCL	PSE	JAJO
A+	Union Pacific Corp.	UNP	PBW	FMAN
B+	United States Steel Corp.	X	ASE	JAJO
A	United Technologies	UTX	CBOE	FMAN
—	United Tech 2.55 Pfd.	UTXD	MWE	MJSD
A	Upjohn Co.	UPJ	CBOE	JAJO
A−	Virginia Elec. & Power	VEL	PBW	JAJO
A+	Walter, Jim Corp.	JWC	CBOE	FMAN
A+	Warner-Lambert Co.	WLA	ASE	JAJO
B+	Western Union Corp.	WU	PBW	JAJO
B+	Westinghouse Elec. (p)	WX	ASE	JAJO
A−	Weyerhaeuser Co.	WY	CBOE	JAJO
B+	Williams Companies	WMB	CBOE	FMAN
A−	Woolworth (F.W.) Co.	Z	PBW	FMAN
A+	Xerox Corp.	XRX	CBOE,PSE	JAJO
B	Zenith Radio Corp.	ZE	ASE	FMAN

(p) Listed Put Options available.

137

When and Why Options are Suspended from Trading (Restricted Options)

Options suspended from trading may create confusion in initiating new transactions; that is, the purchase of options and the sale of uncovered options are prohibited when the premium is less than $.50 and when the exercise price is more than $5 away from the current stock price. This means that these transactions are prohibited if the closing price of the stock on the preceding day was more than $5 below the exercise price and the closing price of the call option is less than $.50. The same rules are true for puts: they are restricted if they are traded at less than $.50 while the current stock price is more than $5 above the exercise price. Options that are restricted are announced daily by the options exchanges.

Example: Stock XYZ closes on a certain trading day at $44⁷/₈ and on the same day, the XYZ 50 call closes at $⁷/₁₆. In this case, the option will be restricted the next day because both conditions are fulfilled. As long as the option is traded at $.50 or more it is always open for trading. The same is true, of course, if the difference between the stock price and the exercise price is less than $5, and the option is traded at less than $.50.

Options are *not* restricted for:

◇ Liquidation or closing transactions made with calls and puts, that is, if an option that has been previously bought is sold again or an option that had first been sold is repurchased.

◇ Opening covered transactions (initiating a position), that is, if the options contract is covered by a stock position in the portfolio, as is the case with covered call writing transactions.

◇ Spreads that are entered.

—At the same time.
—In the same class of options.
—At different exercise prices.
—As purchases and sales in the same or in various expiration months.

Trading options at $.50 may seem ridiculous at first glance; in this way, however, the aggressive speculator can achieve extraordinary leverage with minimal capital investment, and the covered writer can realize an additional return on his stock portfolio with little risk. The sale of 10 options at the price of $\$5/16$ against 1000 shares in the portfolio still yields a net amount of $260. Sometimes this return can be realized within only a few days of the expiration date.

How Many Options Can the Individual Investor Hold?

The exchanges have limited the number of options contracts that the individual investor is allowed to hold. Any investor, whether he works solely for himself or administers money for numerous customers, cannot control more than 1000 options contracts in one stock on the same side of the market (equivalent to 100,000 shares). Since calls purchased and uncovered puts sold profit by an upward trend, they are considered to be on the same side of the market and may not exceed 1000 contracts taken together. The same situation exists for puts purchased and calls sold, since both these options profit by a decline in price.

A position with 1000 long calls and 1000 long puts (i.e. a spread position) is permitted in the same stock, since they profit from counter movements of prices. This is also true for 1000 calls sold and 1000 puts sold. In this case a total of 1000 option contracts is permitted.

At What Point Does the Option Buyer Exercise the Option?

If on the expiration day of the option the stock price is above the exercise price of the call (or below the exercise price of the put), the option writer must be prepared for the possibility that the options buyer will exercise his option and that he will have to deliver (call) or buy (put) the stocks. This is usually true if the stock is quoted about $\$1/2$ above call or below put the exercise price. A typical example is the case of the Houston Oil & Mineral stock, whose call of January 30, 1978, with a stock price of $\$30\frac{1}{2}$ was quoted at $\$1/2$ of the expiration day. The investor very often has no advantage in exercising the option at a price of $\$1/2$, since the commission for the transaction may be considerably higher than the return of $\$1/2$ realized through the sale of the option. Such a transaction is reversed for arbitragers or members of the exchange, who often profit by paying no commissions. During the life of an option, the writer of a call or a put has to be prepared for the possibility that the option will be assigned and that he will have to deliver stocks (call) or take delivery (put) at the exercise price. The premium decreases as the expiration date approaches until it finally reaches zero. If the option is traded *without* any premium before the expiration date, the writer has to be prepared for the contingency that the buyer will exercise his option even before the expiration date.

Example:

Call option	Put option
Stock price XYZ $256	Stock price XYZ $256
Exercise price $240	Exercise price $280
Options premium call $15½	Options premium put $13½

As a rule, the option premium consists of (1) the intrinsic value of the option (the difference between the exercise price and the stock price) and (2) a net premium. In the example just cited, this means that the market price of the call would have to be at least 256 − 240 or $16 (put option 280 − 256 = $14). This is logical, since each time the market price of the call or put is traded at a discount—that is, below its intrinsic value—market participants who do not have to pay commission, such as floor-member firms or specialists, can be certain of arbitrage operations without risk.

These discount option prices can be caused by an oversupply from options writers who sell their options "at the market" shortly before the expiration date to save a small portion of their investment. Frequently, brokers and brokerage houses buy these options at discount for arbitrage transactions. Simultaneous with the purchase of the options, the option is exercised and the stock is sold short on the market. A 100% arbitrage profit of approximately $½ is not to be disdained if a large number of shares is involved. These arbitrage operations with calls cause a constant sales pressure on the stocks that levels off only when the stocks are traded below the exercise price and the options thus lose all value. Arbitrage operations in puts cause a permanent buying pressure that pushes the stock price up toward the higher exercise price.

Because most exchange-traded American companies go ex-dividend every three months, the investor has to pay special attention to these dates. Unlike German options, cash dividends are not deducted from the exercise price of the option. Many stock investors who, for safety reasons, had first bought the call option and want to acquire the underlying security at a later date through exercising the option, will exercise their options shortly before the ex-dividend date so as to receive the dividend payment together with the stock.

Depending on the preference of the call options buyer, the option is sometimes exercised both at the near and at the medium expiration date. In December 1976, for example, when the price of Chase Manhattan was quoted at $33, nearly all calls for the expiration months January and April 1977 were drawn shortly before ex-dividend. The greatest danger point the writer of a call encounters with the ex-dividend dates is when the option is exercised one day before ex-dividend, but the confirmation is only given on the day of ex-dividend. In that case, the investor has no chance to buy the stock on the market and to deliver before ex-dividend, which means that he has to pay the dividend in addition to the stock commissions. General Motors stocks, for example, carried a dividend of approximately $1.60. Since every options contract contains 100 shares, this can add up to a hefty, additional amount.

The buyer of a put can profit from the interim dividend on a high dividend payment. In 1977, General Motors puts were traded with a premium of $3½ at a stock price of $70. Since one could assume that owing to the good earnings in 1977 a surplus dividend would be declared in addition to the regular dividend of $1.70, and taking the interim dividend into account, the put actually traded with a premium of only about $½. Unlike the investor who short-sells the General Motors stocks, the buyer of a put does not have to deliver the dividend. The only exception would be if the buyer exercises his option and delivers the stocks to the writer of the put prior to the ex-dividend date. Since the dividend always belongs to the stock, and the ex-dividend day is also the clearing day of puts, every buyer of a put should make absolutely certain never to exercise his option one day before ex-dividend, because then he would have to deliver the dividend together with the security.

What About Commissions?

Exchange-traded United States options have become one of the main sources of income for brokerage houses because of an enormous boom in turnover on the CBOE and other exchanges. This fact alone seems sufficient for a great number of opponents of the options trade to roundly disqualify the options business itself. And yet, anyone who has ever dealt with, for example, a lawyer knows that he will get a juicy bill at the end regardless of whether the case was won or lost. But the lawyer has done his job and therefore has also earned his fee. Since the investor has asked the brokerage house to perform certain services for him, he will have to accept the fact that these services must be paid for. The cost for 1 option (100 shares) is in any case less than what he would have to pay to buy 100 shares of the stock. The lively and rapid turnover on the options exchanges proves that this new form of investment has filled a market gap. After all, no investor is forced to enter the options transactions. The commissions are legitimate remuneration for services rendered and should be respected as such.

The investor who buys 500 stocks at $50 has to pay $325.40 on an invested capital of $25,000 on the basis of the exchange's minimum commissions before May 1, 1975. (These commission rates were officially abolished on May 1, 1975, but they can still be used as a guideline.) The investment in options gives the investor better opportunities at a lower risk if he buys 5 options (equivalent to 500 shares) instead of the stocks themselves. At an options price of $5, the commission for a total capital investment of $2,500 (5 × 500) would be $82.95. This advantage, however, is only valid for the life time of the option, that is, a maximum of 9 months. If the investor only buys the option because he wants to be on the safe side during an uncertain market phase and only later exercises his option to receive the stocks, he will have to pay commission on both the stocks and the option. The commission on the options would in this case be the price for the safety margin the investor has acquired through the purchase of the right to exercise the option. However, the situation changes drastically if the investor buys 50 option contracts at $5 for $25,000. Instead of paying $325.40 commission, as necessary for the stocks, the investor will have to pay $520.80. But he can now exercise the option on 5000 shares instead of having 500 shares in his portfolio. If he tries to force high profits within the shortest time possible by means of constant buying and selling, the commissions will go up and can quickly reach several thousand dollars. It is one aspect of the options speculator's psychological makeup that he will ignore commissions as long as he makes a big profit. If he were to suffer losses due to taking positions with a high risk, however, he would frequently blame his broker.

The practice of giving options orders to the exchange with a set limit price has proved very useful because the investor does not have to pay extremely high prices if the market price of a stock fluctuates strongly. Such orders have the disadvantage, however, that at times either no executions are received at all or they come only in installments. The person who asks his broker to buy 10 options at the price of $5 on one day, will have to pay about $140.70 for this order. If he is unlucky and only 1 option can be executed at $5 each day, he may end up paying $250 for the same order because 1 option normally has a $25 commission. It is therefore up to the investor to lower the commission by adjusting the given limit so that the options can all be bought on the same day. Then he can take advantage of the fact that commissions are progressively reduced with a rising number of contracts. Even if the limit is changed several times during one day so that 10 different prices are obtained for 10 options, all options on the same stock with the same exercise price and expiration date are considered one order at the end of the day. Therefore the investor benefits from the lower commission on large orders.

With the chart for calculating options commissions, presented below, the investor can check up on the commissions for order of up to 50 options and up to an options price of $10. The chart for stock commissions, which is also included, enables one to compare the commissions for stocks and options. Both the calculation basis and the commission charts are only guidelines, which can change at any time, and are not used by every brokerage house.

The basis for calculating the purchase or sale of an option could be as follows (these were roughly the calculations before May 1, 1975):

Amount:

100–$2499	⅓% of the stock price plus $12
2500–$4777	0.9% of the stock price plus $22
4778–$29,999	$65

For the sale or purchase of *more than one* option:

100–$2499	1.3% of the stock price plus $12
2500–$19,999	0.9% of the stock price plus $22
20,000–$29,999	0.6% of the stock price plus $82

Both for the sale or purchase of one or more options, the following amounts have to be added:

1 − 10 options—another $6 per option

11 options and more—another $4 per option + 10% of the commission computed so far

Example: five options at $7 correspond to 500 shares at $7 = $3500 cost of the option portion

$3500 × 0.09	=	$31.50
		+ 22.00
		$53.50
5 options × $6		+ 30.00
		$83.50
10% of the total		+ 8.35
Total commission		$91.85

The following chart shows the commission rates of an American broker of 1 through 50 options contracts at an option price of $¹/₁₆ through $10 on December 31, 1977.

Commissions for stocks

The focal point for stocks in the list of exchange determined minimum commissions before Jan. 5, 75

SHARE PRICE	5	10	20	25	30	50	75	100	200	300	500	1000
S 1						7.60	8.79	9.98	19.96	29.94	49.90	99.80
2					7.60	8.08	8.79	12.36	24.72	37.08	61.80	116.42
3				7.60	8.79	9.98	10.57	14.73	29.46	44.19	73.06	129.49
4			7.60	8.08	8.79	9.98	12.36	17.11	34.22	51.33	80.78	140.18
5		7.60	8.55	9.03	9.50	11.17	14.14	19.48	38.96	58.44	88.51	150.88
6		8.08	8.55	9.39	9.50	12.36	15.92	21.86	43.72	63.44	93.85	168.91
7		8.55	9.03	9.98	10.22	13.54	17.70	24.24	48.48	68.07	99.20	180.09
8		9.03	9.98	10.57	10.93	14.73	19.48	26.61	53.22	72.71	104.54	191.27
9		9.50	10.93	11.17	11.64	15.92	21.27	28.16	56.32	76.39	109.89	202.45
10	7.60	9.98	11.40	11.76	12.36	17.11	23.05	29.70	59.40	79.60	115.24	213.62
11	7.84	10.45	12.83	11.76	13.07	18.30	24.62	31.24	62.48	82.80	126.00	224.80
12	8.08	10.93	13.31	12.36	13.78	19.48	25.78	32.79	65.58	86.01	131.65	235.98
13	8.32	11.40	13.78	12.95	14.49	20.67	26.95	34.33	68.19	89.22	137.25	247.16
14	8.55	11.88	14.26	13.54	15.21	21.86	28.10	35.88	70.33	92.43	142.83	258.34
15	8.79	12.36	14.73	14.14	15.92	23.05	29.26	37.42	72.47	95.63	148.24	269.51
16	9.03	12.83	14.73	14.73	16.63	24.24	30.41	38.97	74.61	98.84	154.01	280.69
17	9.27	13.31	15.33	15.33	17.34	25.01	31.58	40.51	76.74	106.69	159.60	291.87
18	9.50	13.78	15.92	15.92	18.06	25.78	32.73	42.06	78.88	104.00	165.19	303.05
19	9.74	14.26	16.51	16.51	18.77	26.56	33.89	43.60	81.02	113.40	170.78	314.23
20	9.98	14.73	17.11	17.11	19.48	27.32	35.05	45.14	83.16	116.75	176.36	325.40
21	7.72	11.40	17.58	19.96	20.20	28.10	36.21	46.69	85.30	120.11	181.96	332.86
22	7.84	11.64	18.06	20.43	20.91	28.87	37.37	48.23	87.44	123.45	187.54	340.31
23	7.96	11.88	18.53	20.91	21.62	29.65	38.52	49.78	89.58	126.81	193.14	347.76
24	8.08	12.12	19.01	21.38	22.33	30.41	39.68	51.32	91.71	130.16	198.72	355.21
25	8.20	12.36	19.48	21.86	23.05	31.19	40.85	52.87	93.85	133.52	204.31	362.66
26	8.32	11.64	20.67	23.64	23.76	31.96	42.00	53.94	100.35	136.87	209.90	370.12
27	8.43	18.06	24.39	24.24	24.39	32.73	43.16	55.00	102.59	140.23	215.49	377.57
28	8.55	18.53	24.85	24.62	24.85	33.50	44.31	56.07	104.82	143.58	221.08	385.02
29	8.67	19.01	24.43	25.16	25.42	34.28	45.48	57.14	107.06	146.93	226.67	392.47
30	8.79	12.36	19.48	21.86	25.78	35.05	46.63	58.21	109.30	150.28	232.25	399.92
31	8.91	19.96	23.64	27.71	26.24	35.82	47.79	59.28	111.53	153.64	237.85	404.89
32	9.03	20.43	24.24	28.10	26.71	36.59	48.95	60.35	113.77	156.99	243.43	409.86
33	9.15	20.91	24.62	28.57	27.17	37.37	50.11	61.42	116.00	160.35	249.03	414.83
34	9.27	21.38	27.64	28.87	27.64	38.13	51.03	62.49	118.24	163.70	254.61	419.80
35	9.39	21.86	25.40	29.26	28.10	38.91	51.83	63.56	120.47	167.05	260.20	424.76
36	9.50	22.33	25.78	27.71	28.56	39.68	52.63	64.63	122.71	170.40	265.79	429.73
37	9.62	22.81	26.17	28.10	29.03	40.46	53.44	65.70	124.95	173.76	271.38	434.70
38	9.74	23.28	26.56	28.87	29.48	41.22	54.24	66.77	127.18	177.11	276.97	439.67
39	9.86	23.76	26.95	29.26	29.95	42.00	55.04	67.83	129.42	180.47	282.56	444.64
40	9.98	24.24	27.32	29.65	30.41	42.77	55.84	68.90	131.65	183.82	288.14	449.60
41	10.10	24.55	27.71	30.88	30.88	43.55	56.65	69.97	133.89	187.16	291.87	454.57
42	10.22	24.85	28.10	31.34	31.34	44.31	57.45	71.04	136.12	190.52	295.60	459.54
43	10.34	25.16	28.87	31.81	31.81	45.09	58.24	72.11	138.36	193.59	299.32	464.51
44	10.45	25.47	28.87	32.27	32.27	45.86	59.04	73.18	140.59	197.23	303.05	469.48
45	10.57	25.78	29.26	32.73	32.73	46.63	59.85	74.25	142.83	200.59	306.77	474.44
46	10.69	26.09	29.65	33.65	33.20	47.40	60.65	75.32	145.07	203.94	310.50	479.41
47	10.81	26.40	30.03	33.65	33.65	48.18	61.45	76.38	147.30	207.30	314.23	484.38
48	10.93	26.71	30.41	33.81	34.11	48.95	62.26	77.22	149.54	210.64	317.95	489.35
49	11.05	26.87	30.80	34.58	34.58	49.72	63.06	77.22	151.77	214.00	321.68	494.32
50	11.17	27.32	31.19	35.05	35.05	50.49	63.86	77.22	154.01	214.50	325.40	499.28

SHARE PRICE	5	10	20	25	30	50	75	100	200	300	500	1000
S 51	11.29	17.34	27.64	31.58	35.51	51.03	64.66	80.73	156.24	220.70	329.13	504.25
52	11.40	17.58	27.94	31.96	35.97	51.56	65.46	80.73	158.47	224.06	332.86	509.22
53	11.52	17.82	28.25	32.35	36.44	52.10	66.27	80.73	161.05	227.40	336.58	514.19
54	11.64	18.06	28.56	32.73	36.90	52.63	67.07	80.73	161.46	230.76	340.31	519.16
55	11.76	18.30	28.96	33.12	37.37	53.17	67.87	80.73	161.46	234.12	344.03	524.12
56	11.88	18.53	29.18	33.50	37.82	53.70	68.67	80.73	161.46	237.47	347.76	529.09
57	12.00	18.77	29.48	33.89	38.29	54.24	69.48	80.73	161.46	240.83	351.49	534.06
58	12.12	19.01	29.80	34.28	38.75	54.77	70.28	80.73	161.46	242.19	355.21	539.03
59	12.24	19.25	30.10	34.67	39.21	55.31	71.07	80.73	161.46	242.19	358.94	544.00
60	12.36	19.48	30.41	35.05	39.68	55.84	72.06	80.73	161.46	242.19	362.66	548.96
61	12.47	19.72	30.73	35.43	40.14	56.38	72.68	80.73	161.46	242.19	365.15	553.93
62	12.59	19.96	31.03	35.82	40.61	56.91	73.48	80.73	161.46	242.19	367.63	558.90
63	12.71	20.20	31.34	36.21	41.07	57.45	74.28	80.73	161.46	242.19	370.12	563.87
64	12.83	20.43	31.54	36.61	41.54	57.97	75.08	80.73	161.46	242.19	372.60	568.84
65	12.95	20.67	31.96	36.98	42.00	58.51	75.89	80.73	161.46	242.19	375.08	573.80
66	13.07	20.91	32.27	37.37	42.45	59.04	76.69	80.73	161.46	242.19	377.57	578.77
67	13.18	21.15	32.57	37.76	42.92	59.58	80.73	80.73	161.46	242.19	380.05	583.74
68	13.31	21.38	32.89	38.13	43.38	60.11	80.73	80.73	161.46	242.19	382.54	588.71
69	13.42	21.62	33.19	38.52	43.85	60.65	80.73	80.73	161.46	242.19	385.02	593.68
70	13.54	21.86	33.50	38.91	44.31	61.18	80.73	80.73	161.46	242.19	387.50	598.64
71	13.66	22.10	33.81	39.30	44.78	61.72	80.73	80.73	161.46	242.19	389.99	603.61
72	13.78	22.33	34.13	39.68	45.24	62.25	80.73	80.73	161.46	242.19	392.47	608.58
73	13.90	22.57	34.43	40.07	45.71	62.79	80.73	80.73	161.46	242.19	394.96	613.55
74	14.02	22.81	34.74	40.46	46.17	63.32	80.73	80.73	161.46	242.19	397.44	618.52
75	14.14	23.05	35.05	40.85	46.63	63.86	80.73	80.73	161.46	242.19	399.92	623.48
76	14.26	23.28	35.36	41.22	47.09	64.39	80.73	80.73	161.46	242.19	402.41	628.45
77	14.37	23.52	35.66	41.61	47.55	64.93	80.73	80.73	161.46	242.19	403.65	633.42
78	14.49	23.76	35.97	42.00	48.02	65.46	80.73	80.73	161.46	242.19	403.65	638.39
79	14.61	24.00	36.28	42.38	48.48	66.00	80.73	80.73	161.46	242.19	403.65	643.36
80	14.73	24.24	36.59	42.77	48.95	66.53	80.73	80.73	161.46	242.19	403.65	648.32
81	14.85	24.39	36.90	43.16	49.41	67.07	80.73	80.73	161.46	242.19	403.65	653.29
82	14.97	24.55	37.21	43.55	49.87	67.60	80.73	80.73	161.46	242.19	403.65	658.26
83	15.09	24.70	37.52	43.93	50.34	68.14	80.73	80.73	161.46	242.19	403.65	663.23
84	15.21	24.85	37.82	44.32	50.71	68.67	80.73	80.73	161.46	242.19	403.65	668.20
85	15.33	25.01	38.13	44.70	51.03	69.21	80.73	80.73	161.46	242.19	403.65	673.16
86	15.44	25.16	38.45	45.09	51.34	69.74	80.73	80.73	161.46	242.19	403.65	678.13
87	15.56	25.32	38.75	45.48	51.67	70.28	80.73	80.73	161.46	242.19	403.65	683.10
88	15.68	25.47	39.06	45.86	51.99	70.80	80.73	80.73	161.46	242.19	403.65	688.07
89	15.80	25.63	39.36	46.25	52.30	71.34	80.73	80.73	161.46	242.19	403.65	693.04
90	15.92	25.78	39.68	46.63	52.63	71.87	80.73	80.73	161.46	242.19	403.65	698.00
91	16.04	25.93	39.99	47.02	52.95	72.41	80.73	80.73	161.46	242.19	403.65	702.97
92	16.16	26.09	40.29	47.40	53.27	72.94	80.73	80.73	161.46	242.19	403.65	707.94
93	16.27	26.24	40.61	47.78	53.59	73.48	80.73	80.73	161.46	242.19	403.65	712.91
94	16.39	26.37	40.41	48.18	53.91	74.01	80.73	80.73	161.46	242.19	403.65	717.88
95	16.51	26.56	41.22	48.57	54.24	74.55	80.73	80.73	161.46	242.19	403.65	722.84
96	16.63	26.71	41.54	48.95	54.50	75.08	80.73	80.73	161.46	242.19	403.65	727.81
97	16.75	26.86	41.84	49.33	54.87	75.62	80.73	80.73	161.46	242.19	403.65	732.78
98	16.87	27.01	42.15	49.72	55.20	76.15	80.73	80.73	161.46	242.19	403.65	737.75
99	16.99	27.17	42.45	50.11	55.51	76.68	80.73	80.73	161.46	242.19	403.65	742.72
100	17.11	27.32	42.77	50.49	55.84	77.22	80.73	80.73	161.46	242.19	403.65	747.68

145

Options Contract

Price in $		2	3	4	5	6	7	8	9	10	11	12	13	14	15
1/16	3.65	4.25	4.88	5.50	6.13	6.75	7.38	8.00	8.63	9.25	9.88	10.50	11.13	11.75	12.38
1/8	4.25	5.50	6.75	8.00	9.25	10.50	11.75	13.00	13.50	13.50	14.75	16.00	17.25	18.50	19.75
3/16	4.88	6.75	8.63	10.50	12.38	13.50	14.13	16.00	17.88	19.75	21.63	23.50	25.38	27.25	29.13
1/4	5.50	8.00	10.50	13.00	13.50	16.00	18.50	21.00	23.50	26.00	28.50	31.00	33.50	36.00	38.50
5/16	6.13	9.25	12.38	13.50	16.63	19.75	22.88	26.00	29.13	32.25	35.38	38.50	41.63	44.75	47.88
3/8	6.75	10.50	13.50	16.00	19.75	23.50	27.25	31.00	34.75	38.50	42.25	46.00	49.75	53.50	57.25
7/16	7.38	11.75	14.13	18.50	22.88	27.25	31.63	36.00	40.38	44.75	49.13	53.50	57.88	62.25	66.63
1/2	8.00	13.00	16.00	21.00	26.00	31.00	36.00	41.00	46.00	51.00	56.00	61.00	66.00	71.00	76.00
9/16	8.63	13.50	17.88	23.50	29.13	34.75	40.38	46.00	51.63	57.25	62.88	68.50	74.13	79.75	85.38
5/8	9.25	13.50	19.75	26.00	32.25	38.50	44.75	51.00	57.25	63.50	69.75	76.00	82.25	88.50	94.75
11/16	9.88	14.75	21.63	28.50	35.38	42.25	49.13	56.00	62.88	69.75	76.63	83.50	90.38	97.25	102.57
3/4	10.50	14.00	23.50	31.00	38.50	46.00	53.50	61.00	68.50	76.00	83.50	91.00	98.50	103.50	107.25
13/16	11.13	17.25	25.38	33.50	41.63	49.75	57.88	66.00	74.13	82.25	90.38	98.50	103.82	107.88	111.94
7/8	11.75	18.50	27.25	36.00	44.75	53.50	62.25	71.00	79.75	88.50	97.25	103.50	107.88	112.25	116.63
15/16	12.38	19.75	29.13	38.50	47.88	57.25	66.63	76.00	85.38	94.50	100.33	106.16	111.94	116.63	121.32
1	24.00	30.26	38.29	46.32	54.35	62.38	70.41	78.44	86.47	94.50	100.33	106.16	111.99	117.82	123.65
1-1/16	24.00	30.44	38.55	45.68	54.80	62.92	71.04	79.16	87.28	95.40	101.52	107.24	113.16	119.08	125.00
1-1/8	25.00	30.62	39.10	47.04	55.25	63.46	71.67	79.87	88.08	96.29	102.30	108.31	114.32	120.33	126.34
1-3/16	25.00	30.80	39.10	47.40	55.70	63.99	72.29	80.59	88.89	97.19	103.28	109.38	115.48	121.58	127.68
1-1/4	25.00	30.98	39.37	47.75	55.14	64.53	72.92	81.30	89.69	98.08	104.27	110.45	116.64	122.83	129.02
1-5/16	25.00	31.16	39.64	48.11	56.59	65.07	73.54	82.02	90.50	98.97	105.25	111.53	117.80	124.08	130.36
1-3/8	25.00	31.34	39.90	48.47	57.04	65.60	74.17	82.73	91.30	99.87	106.23	112.60	118.97	125.33	131.70
1-7/16	25.00	31.52	40.17	48.83	57.48	66.14	74.79	83.45	92.11	100.76	107.22	113.67	120.13	126.58	133.04
1-1/2	25.00	31.69	40.44	49.18	57.93	66.67	75.42	84.16	92.91	101.65	108.20	114.74	121.29	127.83	134.38
1-9/16	25.00	31.87	40.71	49.54	58.38	67.21	76.05	84.88	93.71	102.55	109.18	115.82	122.45	129.09	135.72
1-5/8	25.00	32.05	40.98	49.90	58.82	67.75	76.67	85.59	94.52	103.44	110.17	116.89	123.61	130.34	137.06
1-11/16	25.00	32.23	41.24	50.26	59.27	68.28	77.30	86.31	95.32	104.34	111.15	117.94	124.78	131.59	138.26
1-3/4	25.00	32.41	41.51	50.61	59.72	68.82	77.92	87.02	96.13	105.23	112.13	119.03	125.94	132.84	139.19
1-13/16	25.00	32.59	41.78	50.97	60.16	69.36	78.55	87.74	96.93	106.12	113.12	120.11	127.10	133.93	140.12
1-7/8	25.00	32.77	42.05	51.33	60.61	69.89	79.17	88.45	97.74	107.02	114.10	121.18	128.26	134.79	141.05
1-15/16	25.00	32.95	42.32	51.69	61.06	70.43	79.80	89.17	98.54	107.91	115.08	122.25	129.34	135.66	141.98
2	25.00	33.12	42.58	52.04	61.50	70.96	80.42	89.88	99.34	108.80	116.06	123.32	130.14	136.52	142.90
2-1/16	25.00	33.30	42.85	52.40	61.95	71.50	81.05	90.60	100.15	109.70	117.05	124.40	130.95	137.39	143.83
2-1/8	25.00	33.48	43.12	52.76	62.40	72.04	81.68	91.31	100.95	110.59	118.03	125.25	131.75	138.26	144.76
2-3/16	25.00	33.66	43.39	53.12	62.85	72.57	82.30	92.03	101.76	111.49	119.01	125.99	132.56	139.12	145.69
2-1/4	25.00	33.84	43.66	53.47	63.29	73.11	82.93	92.74	102.56	112.38	119.99	126.73	133.36	139.99	146.62
2-5/16	25.00	34.02	43.93	53.83	63.74	73.65	83.55	93.46	103.37	114.27	120.79	127.48	134.17	140.86	147.55
2-3/8	25.00	34.20	44.19	54.19	64.19	74.18	84.18	94.17	104.17	114.17	121.47	128.22	134.97	141.72	148.47
2-7/16	25.00	34.38	44.46	54.55	64.63	74.72	84.80	94.89	104.98	115.06	122.15	128.96	135.78	142.59	149.40
2-1/2	25.00	34.55	44.73	54.90	65.08	75.25	85.43	95.60	105.78	115.95	122.83	129.70	136.58	143.45	150.33
2-9/16	25.00	34.73	45.00	55.26	65.53	75.79	86.06	96.42	106.58	116.75	123.51	130.45	137.38	144.32	151.26
2-5/8	25.00	34.91	45.27	55.62	65.97	76.33	86.68	97.03	107.39	117.19	124.19	131.19	138.19	145.19	152.19
2-11/16	25.30	35.09	45.53	55.98	66.42	76.86	87.31	97.75	108.19	117.81	124.87	131.93	138.99	146.05	153.11
2-3/4	25.00	35.27	45.80	56.33	66.87	77.40	87.93	98.46	109.00	118.43	125.55	132.67	139.80	146.92	154.04
2-13/16	25.00	35.45	46.07	56.69	67.31	77.94	88.56	99.18	109.66	119.05	126.23	133.42	140.60	147.79	154.97
2-7/8	25.00	35.63	46.34	57.05	67.75	78.47	89.18	99.89	110.22	119.67	126.91	134.16	141.41	148.65	155.90
2-15/16	25.00	35.81	46.61	57.41	68.21	79.01	89.81	100.61	110.78	120.29	127.59	134.90	142.21	149.52	156.83
3	25.00	35.98	46.87	57.76	68.65	79.34	90.43	101.32	111.33	120.90	128.27	135.64	143.01	150.38	157.75
3-1/8	25.00	36.34	47.41	58.48	69.55	80.62	91.69	102.75	113.16	122.14	129.64	137.13	144.62	152.12	159.61
3-1/4	25.00	36.70	47.95	59.19	70.44	81.69	92.94	103.74	113.56	123.38	131.00	138.61	146.23	153.85	161.47
3-3/8	25.00	37.06	48.48	59.91	71.34	82.76	94.19	104.73	114.68	124.62	132.36	140.10	147.84	155.58	163.32
3-1/2	25.00	37.42	49.02	60.62	72.23	83.83	95.44	105.72	115.79	125.85	133.72	141.58	149.45	157.31	165.18
3-5/8	25.00	37.77	49.56	61.34	73.12	84.91	96.53	106.71	116.80	127.09	135.08	143.07	151.06	166.23	174.58
3-3/4	25.00	38.13	50.09	62.05	74.02	85.98	97.39	107.70	118.00	128.33	136.44	144.55	152.67	168.04	176.62
3-7/8	25.00	38.49	50.63	62.77	74.91	87.05	98.26	108.69	119.13	129.57	137.80	146.04	161.24	169.65	178.46
4	25.00	38.84	51.16	63.48	75.80	88.12	99.12	109.68	120.24	130.80	139.16	147.52	162.92	171.66	180.40
4-1/8	25.00	39.20	51.70	64.20	76.70	89.20	100.06	111.18	122.47	133.28	141.89	150.49	159.29	169.05	182.35
4-1/4	25.00	39.56	52.24	64.91	77.59	90.05	100.86	111.66	122.45	133.42	141.89	150.84	159.10	167.70	186.23
4-3/8	25.00	39.92	52.77	65.63	78.49	90.79	101.72	112.65	123.59	134.52	143.25	158.84	167.97	177.10	186.23
4-1/2	25.00	40.27	53.31	66.34	79.38	91.53	102.59	113.64	124.70	135.75	144.61	160.39	169.65	178.91	188.17
4-5/8	25.00	40.63	53.85	67.06	80.27	92.28	103.46	114.63	125.81	136.99	152.56	161.95	171.33	180.72	190.11
4-3/4	25.00	40.99	54.38	67.77	81.17	93.02	104.33	115.63	126.93	138.23	153.98	163.50	173.02	182.53	192.05
4-7/8	25.00	41.35	54.92	68.49	82.06	93.76	105.19	116.61	128.04	139.47	155.41	165.05	174.70	184.34	193.99
5	25.00	41.70	55.45	69.20	82.95	94.50	106.05	117.60	129.15	140.70	156.83	166.60	176.38	186.15	195.93
5-1/8	25.00	42.06	55.99	69.92	83.57	95.25	106.92	118.59	130.27	148.33	158.68	169.71	179.77	189.94	199.81
5-1/4	25.00	42.42	56.53	70.63	84.19	95.99	107.79	119.58	131.38	149.64	159.66	169.71	179.74	189.78	199.81
5-3/8	25.00	42.78	57.06	71.35	84.81	96.73	108.65	120.57	132.50	150.94	161.10	171.26	181.43	191.59	201.75
5-1/2	25.30	43.13	57.60	72.06	85.43	97.47	109.52	121.56	133.61	152.23	162.52	172.81	183.11	193.40	203.69
5-5/8	25.00	43.49	58.14	72.78	86.05	98.22	110.39	122.55	140.80	153.52	163.95	174.37	184.79	195.21	205.63
5-3/4	25.00	43.85	58.67	73.49	86.67	98.96	111.25	123.54	141.97	154.82	165.37	175.92	186.47	197.02	207.57
5-7/8	25.00	44.21	59.21	74.21	87.29	99.70	112.12	124.43	142.13	156.11	166.77	177.42	188.15	198.83	209.51
6	25.00	44.56	59.74	74.92	87.90	100.44	112.98	125.52	144.29	157.40	168.21	179.02	189.83	200.64	211.45
6-1/8	25.00	44.92	60.28	75.64	88.52	101.19	113.85	126.51	145.46	158.70	169.64	180.58	191.52	202.46	213.40
6-1/4	25.00	45.28	60.82	76.35	89.14	101.93	114.72	127.50	146.62	159.99	171.06	182.13	193.20	204.27	215.34
6-3/8	25.00	45.64	61.35	76.85	89.76	102.67	115.58	134.29	147.79	161.29	172.48	183.68	194.88	206.08	217.28
6-1/2	25.00	45.99	61.89	77.34	90.38	103.41	116.45	135.32	148.95	162.58	173.91	185.23	196.56	207.89	219.22
6-5/8	25.00	46.35	62.43	77.84	91.00	104.16	117.32	136.36	150.12	163.87	175.33	186.79	198.24	209.70	221.16
6-3/4	25.00	46.71	62.96	78.33	91.62	104.90	118.18	137.39	151.28	165.17	176.78	188.34	199.93	211.51	223.10
6-7/8	25.00	47.07	63.50	78.83	92.24	105.64	119.05	138.43	152.45	166.46	178.18	189.89	201.61	213.32	225.04
7	25.00	47.42	64.03	79.32	92.85	106.38	119.91	139.46	153.61	167.75	179.60	191.44	203.29	215.13	226.98
7-1/8	25.00	47.78	64.53	80.14	93.47	107.13	120.78	140.49	154.77	169.05	181.02	193.00	204.97	216.94	228.92
7-1/4	25.00	48.14	65.11	80.81	94.09	107.87	127.13	141.53	155.94	170.34	182.45	194.55	206.65	218.76	230.86
7-3/8	25.00	48.50	65.64	81.31	94.71	108.61	128.04	142.57	157.10	171.64	183.87	196.10	208.34	220.57	232.80
7-1/2	25.00	48.85	66.18	81.30	95.33	109.35	128.94	143.60	158.27	172.93	185.29	197.65	210.02	222.38	234.74
7-5/8	25.11	49.21	66.72	81.80	95.95	110.10	129.85	144.64	159.43	174.22	186.72	199.21	211.70	224.19	236.68
7-3/4	25.29	49.57	67.25	82.29	96.57	110.84	130.75	145.67	160.60	175.52	188.14	200.76	213.38	226.00	238.62
7-7/8	25.47	49.93	67.79	82.79	97.19	111.58	131.66	146.71	161.76	176.81	189.56	202.31	215.07	227.81	240.56
8	25.64	50.28	68.32	83.28	97.80	112.32	132.56	147.74	152.92	178.10	190.98	203.86	216.74	229.62	242.50
8-1/8	25.82	50.64	68.86	83.78	98.42	113.07	133.47	148.78	164.09	179.40	192.41	205.42	218.43	231.44	244.45
8-1/4	26.00	51.00	69.40	84.27	99.04	113.81	134.38	149.81	165.25	180.69	193.83	206.97	220.11	233.25	246.39
8-3/8	26.18	51.36	69.88	84.77	99.66	119.71	135.28	150.85	166.42	181.99	195.25	208.52	221.79	235.06	248.33
8-1/2	26.36	51.71	70.25	85.26	100.28	120.49	136.19	151.88	167.58	183.28	196.68	210.07	223.47	236.87	250.27
8-5/8	26.54	52.07	70.62	85.78	100.90	121.27	137.09	152.92	168.75	184.57	198.10	211.63	225.15	238.68	252.21
8-3/4	26.72	52.43	70.99	86.25	122.04	122.04	138.00	153.95	169.91	185.87	199.52	213.18	226.84	240.50	254.16
8-7/8	26.90	52.79	71.34	86.75	102.14	122.82	138.90	154.99	171.08	187.16	200.95	214.73	228.52	242.30	256.09
9	27.07	53.14	71.73	87.24	102.75	123.59	139.81	156.02	172.24	188.45	202.37	216.28	230.20	244.11	258.03
9-1/8	27.25	53.50	72.11	87.74	103.37	124.37	140.72	157.06	173.40	189.75	203.79	217.83	231.87	245.91	259.97
9-1/4	27.43	53.86	72.48	88.23	103.99	125.15	141.62	158.09	174.57	191.00	205.22	219.39	233.56	247.74	261.91
9-3/8	27.61	54.22	72.85	88.73	104.61	125.92	142.53	159.13	175.73	192.34	206.64	220.94	235.25	249.55	263.85
9-1/2	27.79	54.57	73.22	89.22	105.23	126.70	143.43	160.16	176.90	193.63	208.06	222.50	236.93	251.36	265.79
9-5/8	27.97	54.93	73.59	89.72	105.85	127.48	144.34	161.20	178.06	194.92	209.49	224.05	238.61	253.17	267.73
9-3/4	28.15	55.29	73.96	90.21	106.47	128.25	145.24	162.23	179.23	196.22	210.91	225.60	240.29	254.98	269.67
9-7/8	28.33	55.65	74.33	90.71	107.09	129.03	146.15	163.27	180.39	197.51	212.33	227.15	241.97	256.79	271.61
10	28.50	56.00	74.70	91.20	107.70	129.80	147.05	164.30	181.55	198.80	213.75	228.70	243.65	258.60	273.55

Options Contract

Price in $	16	17	18	19	20	21	22	23	24	25	30	35	40	45	50
1/16	13.00	13.50	13.50	13.50	13.50	14.13	14.75	15.38	16.00	16.63	19.75	22.88	26.00	29.13	32.25
1/8	21.00	22.25	23.50	24.75	26.00	27.25	28.50	29.75	31.00	32.25	38.50	44.75	51.00	57.25	63.50
3/16	31.00	32.88	34.75	36.63	38.50	40.38	42.25	44.13	46.00	47.88	57.25	66.63	76.00	85.38	94.75
1/4	41.00	43.50	46.00	48.50	51.00	53.50	56.00	58.50	61.00	63.50	76.00	88.50	101.00	107.25	113.50
5/16	51.00	54.13	57.25	60.38	63.50	66.63	69.75	72.88	76.00	79.13	94.75	105.69	113.50	121.32	129.13
3/8	61.00	64.75	68.50	72.25	76.00	79.75	83.50	87.25	91.00	94.75	107.25	116.63	126.00	135.38	144.75
7/16	71.00	75.38	79.75	84.13	88.50	92.88	97.25	101.32	103.50	105.69	116.63	127.57	138.50	149.44	160.38
1/2	81.00	86.00	91.00	96.00	101.00	103.50	106.00	108.50	111.00	113.50	126.00	138.50	151.00	163.50	176.00
9/16	91.00	96.63	101.63	104.44	107.25	110.07	112.88	115.69	118.50	121.32	135.38	149.44	163.50	177.57	191.63
5/8	101.00	104.13	107.25	110.38	113.50	116.63	119.75	122.88	126.00	129.13	144.75	160.38	176.00	191.63	207.25
11/16	106.00	109.44	112.88	116.32	119.75	123.19	126.63	130.07	133.50	136.94	154.13	171.32	188.50	205.69	222.88
3/4	111.00	114.75	118.50	122.25	126.00	129.75	133.50	137.25	141.00	144.75	163.50	182.25	201.00	219.75	238.50
13/16	116.00	120.07	124.13	128.19	132.25	136.32	140.38	144.44	148.50	152.57	172.88	193.19	213.50	233.82	254.13
7/8	121.00	125.38	129.75	134.13	138.50	142.88	147.25	151.63	156.00	160.38	182.25	204.13	226.00	247.88	269.75
15/16	126.00	130.69	135.38	140.07	144.75	149.44	154.13	158.82	163.50	168.19	191.63	215.07	238.50	261.94	285.38
1	129.48	135.31	141.14	146.97	152.80	158.63	164.46	170.29	176.12	181.95	208.90	235.85	262.80	289.75	316.70
1-1/16	130.91	136.83	142.75	148.67	154.59	160.51	166.43	172.35	178.05	183.50	210.76	238.02	265.28	292.54	334.29
1-1/8	132.34	138.35	144.36	150.37	156.38	162.39	168.40	174.02	179.53	185.05	212.62	240.19	267.75	308.70	337.52
1-3/16	133.77	139.87	145.97	152.07	158.17	164.27	169.87	175.44	181.02	186.60	214.47	242.35	270.23	311.61	340.76
1-1/4	135.20	141.39	147.58	153.77	159.95	165.59	171.23	176.87	182.50	188.14	216.33	244.52	272.70	314.52	343.99
1-5/16	136.63	142.91	149.19	155.47	161.19	166.89	172.59	178.29	183.99	189.69	218.19	246.68	287.64	317.43	347.23
1-3/8	138.06	144.43	150.80	156.67	162.43	168.19	173.95	179.71	185.47	191.24	220.04	248.85	290.23	320.34	350.46
1-7/16	139.49	145.95	152.02	157.84	163.67	169.49	175.31	181.14	186.96	192.78	221.90	262.38	292.82	323.26	353.69
1-1/2	140.92	147.25	153.13	159.02	164.90	170.79	176.67	182.56	188.44	194.33	223.75	264.64	295.40	326.17	356.93
1-9/16	142.35	148.30	154.25	160.20	166.14	172.09	178.04	183.98	189.93	195.88	225.61	266.91	297.99	329.08	360.16
1-5/8	143.34	149.35	155.36	161.37	167.38	173.39	179.40	185.41	191.42	197.42	227.47	269.17	300.58	331.99	363.40
1-11/16	144.33	150.41	156.48	162.55	168.62	174.69	180.76	186.83	192.90	198.97	239.70	271.43	303.17	334.90	366.63
1-3/4	145.32	151.46	157.59	163.72	169.85	175.99	182.12	188.25	194.38	200.52	241.64	273.70	305.75	337.81	369.87
1-13/16	146.31	152.51	158.70	164.90	171.09	177.29	183.48	189.68	195.87	220.06	243.58	275.96	308.34	340.72	373.10
1-7/8	147.30	153.56	159.82	164.07	172.33	178.59	184.84	191.10	197.35	203.61	245.52	278.23	310.93	343.63	376.34
1-15/16	148.29	154.61	160.93	167.25	173.57	179.89	186.20	192.52	198.84	205.16	247.46	280.49	313.52	346.54	379.57
2	149.28	155.66	162.04	168.42	174.80	181.18	187.56	193.94	200.32	206.70	249.40	282.75	316.10	349.45	382.80
2-1/16	150.27	156.72	163.16	169.60	176.04	182.48	188.93	195.37	201.81	217.67	251.35	285.02	318.69	352.36	386.04
2-1/8	151.26	157.77	164.27	170.78	177.28	183.78	190.29	196.79	212.49	219.29	253.29	287.28	321.28	355.28	389.27
2-3/16	152.25	158.82	165.39	171.95	178.52	185.08	191.65	207.18	214.04	220.91	255.23	289.55	323.87	358.19	392.51
2-1/4	153.24	159.87	166.50	173.13	179.75	186.38	193.01	208.67	215.59	222.52	257.17	291.81	326.45	361.10	395.74
2-5/16	154.23	160.92	167.61	174.30	180.99	187.68	203.16	210.15	217.15	224.14	259.11	294.07	329.04	364.01	398.98
2-3/8	155.22	161.98	168.73	175.48	182.23	188.98	204.58	211.64	218.70	225.76	261.05	296.34	331.63	366.92	402.21
2-7/16	156.21	163.03	169.84	176.65	183.47	198.88	206.01	213.13	220.25	227.38	262.99	298.60	334.22	369.83	405.44
2-1/2	157.20	164.08	170.95	177.83	184.70	200.24	207.43	214.62	221.80	228.99	264.93	300.87	336.80	372.74	408.68
2-9/16	158.19	165.13	172.07	179.01	194.35	201.60	208.85	216.11	223.36	230.61	266.87	303.13	339.39	375.65	411.91
2-5/8	159.18	166.18	173.18	180.18	195.64	202.96	210.28	217.59	224.91	232.23	268.81	305.39	341.98	378.56	415.15
2-11/16	160.17	167.24	174.30	189.59	196.94	204.32	211.70	219.08	226.46	233.84	270.75	307.66	344.57	381.47	418.38
2-3/4	161.16	168.29	175.41	190.78	198.23	205.68	213.12	220.57	228.01	235.46	272.69	309.92	347.16	384.39	421.62
2-13/16	162.15	169.34	184.50	192.01	199.52	207.03	214.55	222.06	229.57	237.08	274.63	312.19	349.74	387.30	424.85
2-7/8	163.13	180.29	185.67	193.24	200.82	208.39	215.97	223.54	231.12	238.70	276.57	314.45	352.33	390.21	428.09
2-15/16	164.13	171.44	186.83	194.47	202.11	209.75	217.39	225.03	232.67	240.31	278.51	316.72	354.92	393.12	431.32
3	165.12	180.29	187.99	195.70	203.40	211.11	218.81	226.52	234.22	241.92	280.45	318.98	357.50	396.03	434.55
3-1/16	167.10	182.49	190.32	198.16	205.99	213.83	221.66	229.50	237.33	245.16	284.34	323.51	362.68	401.85	441.02
3-1/4	176.12	184.69	192.65	200.62	208.58	216.54	224.51	232.47	240.43	248.40	288.22	328.04	367.85	407.67	447.49
3-3/8	178.79	186.89	194.98	203.07	211.17	219.26	227.35	235.45	243.54	251.63	292.10	332.56	373.03	413.49	453.96
3-1/2	180.86	189.09	197.31	205.53	213.75	221.98	230.20	238.42	246.64	254.87	295.98	336.09	378.20	419.30	460.43
3-5/8	182.93	191.29	199.64	207.99	216.34	224.69	233.05	241.40	249.75	258.10	299.86	341.62	383.38	425.14	466.90
3-3/4	185.00	193.49	201.97	210.45	218.93	227.41	235.89	244.37	252.85	261.34	303.74	346.15	388.55	430.96	473.37
3-7/8	187.07	195.69	204.30	212.91	221.53	230.13	238.74	247.35	255.96	264.57	310.68	350.68	393.73	436.78	479.84
4	189.14	197.88	206.62	215.36	224.10	232.84	241.58	250.32	259.06	267.80	311.50	355.20	398.90	442.60	486.30
4-1/8	191.21	200.08	208.95	217.82	226.69	235.56	244.43	253.30	262.17	271.04	315.39	359.73	404.08	448.43	492.62
4-1/4	193.28	202.28	211.28	220.28	229.28	238.28	247.28	256.28	265.27	274.27	319.27	364.26	409.25	454.25	499.24
4-3/8	195.35	204.48	213.61	222.74	231.87	241.00	250.12	259.25	268.38	277.51	323.15	368.79	414.43	460.07	499.24
4-1/2	197.42	206.68	215.94	225.20	234.45	243.71	252.97	262.23	271.48	280.74	327.03	373.32	419.60	465.03	503.55
4-5/8	199.49	208.88	218.27	227.66	237.04	246.43	255.82	265.20	274.59	283.98	330.91	377.84	424.78	468.91	507.87
4-3/4	201.56	211.08	220.60	230.11	239.63	249.15	258.66	268.18	277.69	287.21	334.79	382.37	429.95	472.79	512.18
4-7/8	203.63	213.28	222.93	232.57	242.22	251.86	261.51	271.15	280.80	290.45	338.67	386.90	435.13	476.67	516.49
5	205.70	215.48	225.25	235.03	244.80	254.58	264.35	274.13	283.90	293.68	342.55	391.43	440.30	480.55	520.80
5-1/8	207.77	217.68	227.58	237.49	247.39	257.30	267.20	277.10	287.01	296.91	346.44	395.96	445.75	484.44	525.12
5-1/4	209.84	219.88	229.91	239.95	249.98	260.01	270.05	280.08	290.12	300.15	350.32	400.49	450.67	488.32	529.43
5-3/8	211.91	222.08	232.24	242.40	252.57	262.73	272.89	283.06	293.22	303.38	354.20	405.01	450.65	492.20	533.74
5-1/2	213.98	224.28	234.57	244.86	255.15	265.45	275.74	286.03	296.32	306.62	358.08	409.54	454.10	496.08	538.05
5-5/8	216.05	226.48	236.90	247.32	257.74	268.16	278.59	289.01	299.43	309.85	361.96	414.07	457.55	499.96	542.37
5-3/4	218.12	228.68	239.23	249.78	260.33	270.88	281.43	291.98	302.53	313.09	365.84	418.17	461.00	503.84	546.68
5-7/8	220.19	230.88	241.56	252.24	262.92	273.60	284.28	294.96	305.64	316.32	369.72	421.19	464.45	507.72	550.99
6	222.26	233.07	243.88	254.69	265.50	276.31	287.12	297.93	308.74	319.55	373.60	424.80	467.90	511.60	555.30
6-1/8	224.33	235.27	246.21	257.15	268.09	279.03	289.97	300.91	311.85	322.79	377.49	427.22	471.35	515.49	558.18
6-1/4	226.40	237.47	248.54	259.61	270.68	281.75	292.82	303.89	314.95	326.02	381.37	430.24	474.80	519.37	561.05
6-3/8	228.47	239.67	250.87	262.07	273.27	284.47	295.66	306.86	318.06	329.26	385.25	433.26	478.25	523.25	563.93
6-1/2	230.54	241.87	253.20	264.53	275.85	287.18	298.51	309.84	321.16	332.49	389.13	436.28	481.70	527.13	566.80
6-5/8	232.61	244.07	255.53	266.99	278.44	289.90	301.36	312.81	324.27	335.73	393.01	439.30	485.15	531.01	569.68
6-3/4	234.68	246.27	257.86	269.44	281.03	292.62	304.20	315.79	327.37	338.96	396.03	442.32	488.60	534.03	572.55
6-7/8	236.75	248.47	260.19	271.90	283.62	295.33	307.05	318.77	330.49	342.20	398.92	445.34	492.05	536.62	575.43
7	238.82	250.67	262.51	274.36	286.20	298.05	309.89	321.74	333.58	345.43	401.20	448.35	495.50	539.20	578.30
7-1/8	240.89	252.87	264.74	276.67	288.79	300.77	312.74	324.71	336.69	348.66	405.17	451.37	498.95	541.70	581.18
7-1/4	242.96	255.07	267.17	279.28	291.38	303.48	315.59	327.69	339.79	351.90	406.38	454.39	502.40	544.38	584.05
7-3/8	245.03	257.27	269.50	281.73	293.97	306.20	318.43	330.67	342.90	355.13	408.97	457.41	505.85	546.97	586.93
7-1/2	247.10	259.47	271.83	284.19	296.55	308.92	321.28	333.64	346.00	358.37	411.55	460.43	509.30	549.55	589.80
7-5/8	249.17	261.67	274.16	286.65	299.14	311.63	324.13	336.62	349.11	361.60	414.14	463.45	511.60	552.14	592.68
7-3/4	251.24	263.87	276.49	289.11	301.73	314.35	326.97	339.59	352.21	364.83	416.73	466.47	513.70	554.73	595.55
7-7/8	253.31	266.06	278.82	291.57	304.32	317.37	329.82	342.57	355.32	368.07	419.32	469.49	516.20	557.32	598.43
8	255.38	268.26	281.14	294.02	306.90	319.78	332.66	345.54	358.42	371.30	421.90	472.50	518.50	559.90	601.30
8-1/8	257.45	270.46	283.47	296.48	309.49	322.50	335.51	348.52	361.53	374.53	426.67	477.03	523.10	565.08	607.05
8-1/4	259.52	272.66	285.80	298.94	312.08	325.22	338.36	351.50	364.63	377.63	427.62	478.54	523.10	566.67	609.93
8-3/8	261.59	274.86	288.13	301.40	314.67	327.93	341.20	354.47	367.74	381.01	430.39	481.56	525.40	567.67	609.93
8-1/2	263.66	277.06	290.46	303.86	317.25	330.65	344.05	357.45	369.46	379.93	432.25	484.58	527.70	570.25	612.80
8-5/8	265.73	279.26	292.79	306.31	319.84	333.37	346.90	360.42	371.53	382.09	434.84	487.17	530.00	572.84	615.68
8-3/4	267.80	281.46	295.12	308.77	322.43	336.09	349.76	362.97	373.60	384.24	437.43	489.18	532.30	575.43	618.55
8-7/8	269.87	283.66	297.45	311.23	325.02	338.81	352.61	364.90	375.67	386.40	440.02	491.19	534.60	578.02	621.43
9	271.94	285.86	299.77	313.69	327.60	341.52	355.43	366.93	377.74	388.55	442.60	493.20	536.90	580.60	624.30
9-1/8	274.01	288.06	302.10	316.15	330.19	344.24	358.02	369.17	379.81	390.71	445.19	495.22	539.20	583.19	627.18
9-1/4	276.08	290.26	304.43	318.61	332.78	346.95	359.42	370.80	381.88	392.87	447.78	497.23	541.50	585.78	630.05
9-3/8	278.15	292.46	306.76	321.06	335.37	349.67	361.82	372.89	383.95	395.02	450.37	499.24	543.80	588.37	632.93
9-1/2	280.22	294.66	309.09	323.52	337.95	352.39	363.71	374.87	386.02	397.18	452.95	501.25	546.10	590.95	635.80
9-5/8	282.29	296.86	311.42	325.98	340.54	354.37	365.61	376.85	388.09	399.34	455.54	503.27	548.40	593.54	638.68
9-3/4	284.36	299.06	313.75	328.44	343.13	356.18	367.51	378.84	390.16	401.49	458.13	505.28	550.70	596.13	641.55
9-7/8	286.43	301.25	316.08	330.90	345.72	357.99	369.41	380.82	392.23	403.65	460.72	507.29	553.00	598.72	644.43
10	288.50	303.45	318.35	333.35	348.30	359.80	371.30	382.80	394.30	405.80	463.30	509.30	555.30	601.30	647.30

DIFFERENCES OF EXCHANGE TRADE BETWEEN AMERICAN OPTIONS AND GERMAN OPTIONS

	United States	Germany
Kind of option	Calls Puts	Calls Puts
Exercise prices	Standardized exercise price ◇ Stock price between $10–$50, $5 apart. ◇ Stock price between $50–$200, $10 apart. ◇ Stock price above $200, $20 apart (exceptions are possible). Depending on the price development, new exercise prices can be introduced at any time.	Writer and purchaser negotiate exercise price. No standardization. The current stock price is usually the exercise price.
Expiration months and expiration days	Three cycles of expiration months ◇ January, April, July, October ◇ February, May, August, November ◇ March, June, September, December The expiration day is the third Saturday of an expiration month (exceptions are possible).	Three choices in expiration dates 2 months and 5 days 3 months and 5 days 6 months and 10 days Calculated as of the day of transaction
Size of contract	1 option = 100 shares (exceptions with stock dividends)	1 option = 50 shares or the same many times over
Trading	Calls and puts can be bought or sold at any time. The price is determined by supply and demand. The Option Clearing Corporation guarantees the rights of the buyer and the duties of the writer.	Options cannot be traded. A clearing institution (Lombard Kasse) guarantees the rights of the buyer and the duties of the writer.
Options buyer	The options buyer can either sell his right to exercise his option on	The right to exercise the option cannot be sold. The investor can at any

	United States	Germany
Kind of option	Calls Puts	Calls Puts
	the exchange or take delivery of the under-lying securities by exer-cising the option.	time exercise the option and thus receive the underlying securities with calls or offer delivery to the options writer in case of puts. If only the option is to be sold, he can do this by exercising the option and immediately selling the stocks at the market.
Options writer	The options writer can withdraw from the obli-gation of the options contract by buying back the option.	The writer of a put or call has no chance to with-draw from the obliga-tion to deliver or take delivery.
Cash dividends	No effect on exercise price.	Options investors receive credit. The amount of the dividend is de-ducted from the exer-cise prices.
Rights	An increase in capital is infrequently carried out in the form of 'rights.'	An increase in capital is often conducted through rights. If the trading term exceeds the exercise day of the option, the right has to be delivered to the buyer of a call or the writer of a put if he exercises the option. If the trading term of the right terminates on the exercise day of the option or before that day, the price of the right is deducted from the exercise price.
Stock splits and stock dividends	The number of securities is increased at the ratio of the stock split or stock dividend. The exercise price is correspondingly reduced.	The number of securities is increased at the ratio of stock split. The exer-cise price is corre-spondingly reduced.

149

The Options Exchange—An "Efficient Market"?

When the CBOE opened in 1973, questions arose of whether this exchange could overcome the disadvantages of the OTC option market and what influence it would have on the price movements of the underlying securities. To test the efficiency, studies were conducted that focused on the volatility and the marketability of the underlying securities. The results of these studies are as follows:

◇ The CBOE (and the other option exchanges) is an exchange where prices are determined by supply and demand. It has an almost perfect information system for all transactions and activities on the exchange. Every option is stored and filed with the exact date on which the transaction was executed. The investor can thus check all past transactions should there be a disagreement between him and his broker.

◇ During the market session (on an intraday basis) no influence of the options on the underlying securities could be discovered.

◇ During the opening period of the CBOE, the volatility of those stocks that were also traded in options on the CBOE was greater. After the CBOE had traded in options for several months, however, this "novelty effect" had worn off.

◇ It could not be established that the marketability of the stocks during "normal" times was influenced. (Normal times means the time from shortly after one expiration date until shortly before the next expiration date.)

A different picture was presented when the influence of the CBOE on stock prices shortly before and after the expiration date of the option was studied. In these cases, the underlying securities were influenced by the options. It is quite possible, however, that this merely indicated a change in investors' behavior. Whereas the turnover on the CBOE was extremely lively and active, the turnover on other exchanges remained the same or declined. The CBOE, however, can only be blamed for the negative effects on the stock market if the options premiums that are realized by covered writers are not reinvested.

If these premiums are reinvested in the equity market, the options exchange can, as a rule, have no negative influences. If, however, an options writer does not own the securities underlying the option (uncovered writer), the conditions governing supply and demand for the underlying securities can change. Such transactions can increase the volatility and reduce the marketability and volume, but the portion of uncovered options in relation to the entire options volume is very small.

The Securities Exchange Commission (SEC) watches the effect of the options exchanges on the stock market very closely. As of June 1977, five options exchanges received permission to trade put options. This indicates that the SEC, too—and despite the strict supervision it exercises over the options trade—welcomes and supports the options exchanges as a new form of investment that is in the interest of the investor. The extent of the supervision was called to mind again in October 1977, when the SEC announced a renewed and comprehensive investigation of the options business and at the same time put a stop to expansion plans or new establishments for the options trade. The SEC justified this step with the "serious fear" that the self-regulating mechanisms of the options exchanges concerned were obviously unable to sufficiently control the options trade and to prevent all offences against security laws after it had discovered some market manipulations. According to the SEC, these investigations could lead to the introduction of new and more stringent rules that would further safeguard the investor against possible manipulations in the options trade.

The individual investor is faced with the same question he came up against with the stock market: if and to what degree the options trade could be called an "efficient market." If the market were efficient, the investor would have no chance whatsoever to select by suitable analysis those stocks or options that in the long run would bring a return above the average market return. As far as the efficiency of the options market is concerned, the primary question is whether it is possible to find options that, measured by the trend of the stock price that can realistically be expected, are either over- or undervalued. But the matter of efficiency is so complex that the answer cannot be a straight yes or no. There are some indications that would support the assumption that the options market is not an efficient market. For one thing, it is much more complex and much less transparent than the stock market, since the options investor has to cope with the expiration date and the exercise price in addition to all the other problems that confront the stock investor. The requirement of complete market transparency is definitely not fulfilled. Moreover, unlike stocks, the life of options is limited to 9 months at the most. This automatically excludes the big, long-term investors.

The risks and opportunities of options investing are quite often not calculated carefully enough, and the necessity to make a decision before the expiration date (as well as the leverage effect) can easily lead to irrational and unduly speculative transactions. For these reasons, options are frequently overvalued. Many options would not survive the test of sober analysis; they exist only because a majority of investors is prepared to pay unjustifiable prices. The fact that a transaction in options requires a relatively small amount of capital, and thus favors speculative investments, increases the tendency toward overvaluation.

If the options market cannot be considered an "efficient market" because of these tendencies, it is, nevertheless, a market that offers an opportunity of above-average performance to the investor who is quick at figures and also possesses the necessary "cool." If, when analyzing the processes of pricing, it were possible to extricate those extreme fluctuations which are not caused by the irrational behavior of the options investor, the speculator could be "certain" of a profit. He would simply buy the options that are "undervalued" and sell those which are "overvalued." On the other hand, if the inefficiency of the market is caused by the irrational behavior of an army of speculators, the individual investor must guard himself against joining their ranks and adding to the inefficiency instead of profiting from it. Because of its possible inefficiency, the options market demands two character traits to a much greater degree than the stock market, *knowledge* and *discipline*.

THE NET PREMIUM

Meaning and Effects of the Net Premium

The net premium is that part of the price which reflects the investors' expectations about the future development of stock prices. The intrinsic value of the options price represents the difference between the current price and the lower exercise price (call) or the higher exercise price (put), but the net premium itself is pure bonus. This bonus is the result of emotions, intuition, and the speculative fever of the options buyer; it can be considered as the remuneration for the investor's ability to buy or sell stocks at a certain price and up to a certain expiration date by exercising the option. The net premium can quite often reach 15 to 20% of the stock price. When a stock price is subject to strong fluctuations, the gambler's instinct of the investor who is interested only in the option because he is chasing the fast buck, and not the underlying security itself, comes into full play. The size of the options volume makes this quite clear. For example, on certain days, IBM's option contracts had a trading volume of more than 8000 contracts at a specific exercise price in one expiration month, representing stock volume of more than 800,000 shares. In 1978, nearly 20,000 of IBM's options contracts for all exercise prices and expiration months, both calls and puts, were traded on one day for a total of 2 million shares! On that same day, IBM's volume was only about 200,000 shares on the New York Stock Exchange. IBM is the perfect example of how strongly the net premiums can fluctuate.

A short-term price increase of the stock from $270 to $274 in 1977 so excited the options buyer that at the exercise price of 280 in the near expiration date the net premium doubled and went from $2 to $4 in one day. When the price did not continue to go up as expected, the euphoric state was quickly forgotten and the net premium went down by half just as quickly as it had risen. Net premiums are incredibly sensitive to good or bad news. Speculation on changes in the net premium alone is extremely dangerous for every options buyer, especially in the near expiration month. The danger is increased by the effects of the remaining life of the options. As the expiration date approaches, the net premiums move faster and faster towards zero and become worthless on the expiration day. The effect of the remaining life and the decrease in net premiums can be profitably exploited by the options writer; this strategy is quite often successful and is a clearly recognizable mechanism in the writer's favor.

If an investor moves into the market and acquires a stock at the top price, he can still hope that it will recover at a later point if for a time the price refuses to budge or even declines. But if the stock price is not going up after the investor has bought a call, the loss is predetermined by the expiration date. For this reason, the careful investor will always choose a later expiration date and an exercise price that is close to or below the stock price. The net premiums increase with the option's lifetime. The buyer of a call or put pays a higher net premium because with the longer life of the option he is much more independent of short-term price fluctuations. The writer of a call or put demands higher net premiums for an extended life because, when writing an option, he is committed to

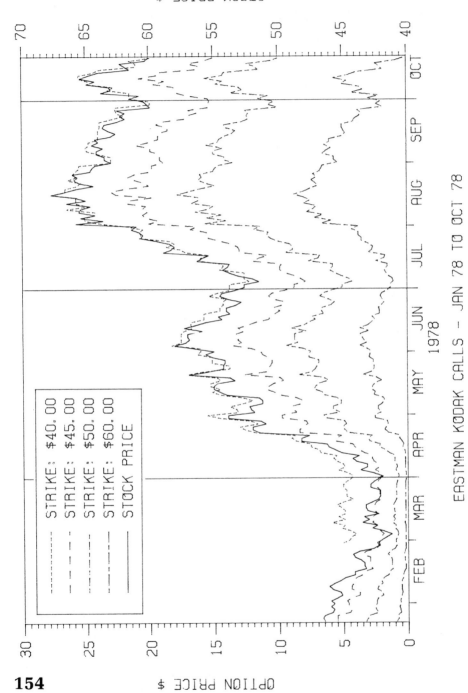

Figure 35 Parallel movement of option premiums—logarithmic scale
in dollars.

the obligations of the options contract and thus make no use of alternative investment forms. In addition, he has taken on the higher risk of having tomake (call) or take (put) delivery.

Many stocks have their own typical high or low net premiums. These normal net premiums are created through the dollar volatility of the stock and not through percentage changes in the stock price. Stocks such as IBM, Xerox, Eastman Kodak, or Polaroid tend toward a high net premium whereas stocks such as AT&T and Chase Manhattan rarely carry a high net premium. Both the volatility of the stock and the general state of the market determine the size of the net premium (Figure 35).

During a bullish market phase, the net premiums will be higher than in a period when the market is stagnating or declining. With calls, the net premiums are small in the exercise prices above the stock price, but compared to the stock price they tend to be overvalued. With exercise prices below the stock price, options are often traded without net premiums and are thus undervalued. The same situation exists for puts, but in the reverse; however, puts in general have a tendency to trade at lower net premium than calls. This might be caused by a psychological weakness in the investor that makes him hesitate to speculate on a bearish market, an assumption supported by the lower volume of the puts.

The net premium reflects the inefficiency of the options exchanges. The different information level, the diverse character of the investors, lack of discipline, varying financial resources, and wide divergencies in the individual risk preferences cause net premiums to fluctuate (see Figure 36). All those factors, which also influence the pricing of a stock, have an effect on the net premium of an option but in a much more concentrated form.

THE EVALUATION OF THE NET PREMIUM

Indicators for Predicting Net Premiums Movements

Stock analysis has a decisive impact on the success or failure of trading in options. Under certain circumstances, however, an exact analysis of the net premium can help make deductions about the short-term action of a stock price. Because of the leverage effect of options and because the risk with short expiration dates is so much

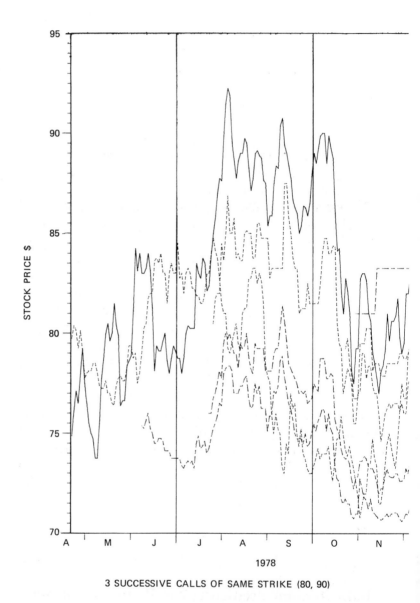

STOCK PRICE $

95

90

85

80

75

70

A   M   J   J   A   S   O   N

1978

3 SUCCESSIVE CALLS OF SAME STRIKE (80, 90)

Figure 36   Texas Instruments successive call option series from April 1978 through July 1979. Two Strikes: 80, 90.

156

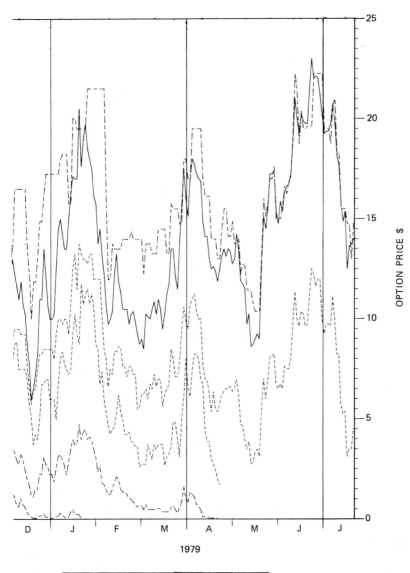

OPTION PRICE $

D   J   F   M   A   M   J   J

1979

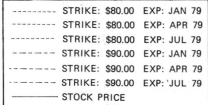

STRIKE: $80.00   EXP: JAN 79
STRIKE: $80.00   EXP: APR 79
STRIKE: $80.00   EXP: JUL 79
STRIKE: $90.00   EXP: JAN 79
STRIKE: $90.00   EXP: APR 79
STRIKE: $90.00   EXP: JUL 79
STOCK PRICE

157

greater than with stock investments, options investors react much more sensitively than stock investors. If a net premium increases within a short time, the options buyer will be certain that the stock price is going up. On the other hand, net premiums often decrease before stock prices turn weak.

A change in volume during the different expiration months and in the exercise prices of the options can—as with stock analysis—be used as an indicator for an options analysis. This kind of analysis is made difficult because there are so many different exercise prices and expiration dates the investor cannot possibly cope with all of them at the same time; this would run counter to every cost-return-analysis. Options whose exercise price is closest to the stock price and that trade in an expiration month that is at least two months away from the current price (which would be either the near expiration month, if it were 2 to 3 months away from the current stock price, or the medium expiration month) are most suitable for that purpose. Options with an exercise price far below the stock price are not representative, since they usually trade with a smaller net premium (i.e., they almost have only an intrinsic value) and therefore simply track the security, dollar for dollar. An exercise price that is far above the stock price is not representative either, because of the daily price fluctuations of the stock the net premium trend is not very pronounced. The net premium in an expiration month close to the current stock price is, on the other hand, too strongly influenced by the negative effects of the remaining life of the option, while the last expiration months up to nine months away trades on such limited volume that there is little if any interpretative value. An additional and important indicator can be the change in the "open interest." The "open interest" is an extremely complicated subject and is therefore discussed in detail.

Open Interest

Total volume consists of the total of all purchases and sales. Because every buyer of an option must be matched by a writer, the number of all purchases is the same as the number of sales each day. The "open interest" is the number of options contracts that are still open at the close of each market day—that is, they have not been terminated because the investor has neither liquidated the options contract nor exercised the option.

At the beginning of the life span of a new expiration date, there are no options contracts and therefore there is no open interest. During the trading hours of the first day of a new expiration month, the open interest develops as follows: if buyer *A* acquires from writer *B* an XRX October 60 call, the options contract is agreed upon. If buyer *C* purchases an option from *D*, the open interest has gone up to 2. And if, finally, Mr. *E* sells an option to Mr. *F*, the open interest has increased to 3 options contracts.

What happens now if existing options contracts are terminated? If, for example, Mr. *A* decides to terminate his options contract by selling his right to exercise the option to Mr. *G*—a new buyer—the sum of the open interest does not change. In this case, Mr. *G* has simply replaced Mr. *A* as the buyer of the options contract and therefore the number of open interests remains unchanged at 3 units. If, however, Mr. *A* 's offer to sell is accepted by Mr. *F*, who has sold an option that day, Mr. *A* 's sale is compensated by Mr. *F*, who buys back the contract. In that case, only 2 options contracts are left open, that is, the open interest is now reduced to 2 units.

This process could be summarized as follows:

◇ The open interest increases if a new purchase and a new sale is executed.

◇ The open interest remains the same if a new purchase is compensated for by the sale of an existing options contract.

◇ The open interest decreases if the sale of an existing options contract is compensated for by the repurchase of an option.

◇ The open interest decreases if the writer of an option delivers the underlying securities to the buyer of that option.

Since volume and open interest are closely connected, it is very important that the investor follows not only the volume but also the changes in the open interest. All these figures are useful only if they are seen in combination with the movement of a stock. Ideally, all these data should be collected on a chart because it is only then that they will attain their full explanatory value (see Figure 37*a* and *b*). To make the connections between the open interest and the volume more apparent, the four possible market situations with calls are explained briefly in the following.

Open Interest has Increased, the Stock Price Has Risen. As stated above, an increase in the open interest indicates the activities of both buyers and writers. If the stock price has increased as well, the buyers have influenced the premium on that day more aggressively.

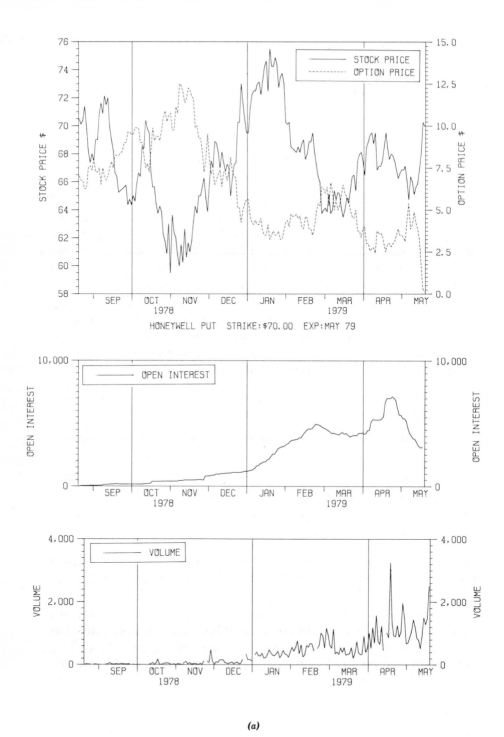

HONEYWELL PUT   STRIKE:$70.00   EXP:MAY 79

(a)

160   *Figure 37a   Honeywell option open interest and volume versus stock price.*

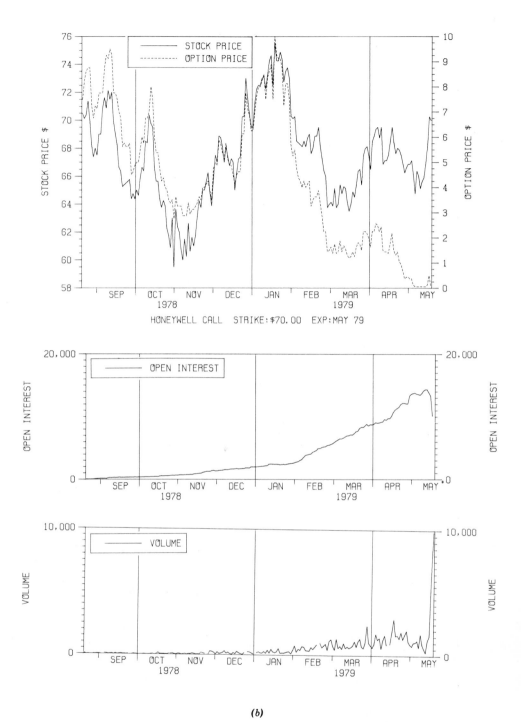

STOCK PRICE

OPTION PRICE

STOCK PRICE
OPTION PRICE

HONEYWELL CALL   STRIKE:$70.00   EXP:MAY 79

OPEN INTEREST

OPEN INTEREST

OPEN INTEREST

VOLUME

VOLUME

VOLUME

(b)

Figure 37b   Honeywell option open interest and volume versus stock price.

161

As a rule, this signifies the good technical state of a stock. The investor must be sure, however, that the option has not been maneuvered into a strongly overbought position; such a situation occurs if the open interest increases largely because of speculative purchases in combination with speculative rebuying of options.

Open Interest Increases, Stock Price Goes Down. The open interest increases if new buyers and sellers appear. This indicates that the speculative writers are in the majority and the investor should conclude that the stock is in a poor technical state.

Open Interest Decreases, Stock Price Declines. When the open interest decreases, the number of investors who liquidate is greater than the number of new buyers and writers. Because the prices are going down as well, it is probable that there are more buyers who are selling out (profit-taking) than writers covering their positions. This indicates an oversold options market.

Open Interest Goes Down, Stock Price Goes Up. In this case, the number of writers and buyers who liquidate their open positions is bigger than the number of buyers and writers entering the market. Since prices are going up, such investors who had previously sold their options and are now rebuying them are in the majority. This signifies a good technical state of the stock. The open interest can rarely be analyzed by an individual investor unless he is in constant contact with a brokerage house. The figures on volume, highest and lowest prices, and the open interest are published daily.

The difficulty with the evaluation of options prices is that it is simply not sufficient to identify, with the aid of analysis, the directional price movement of the underlying stock. In addition, one has to know the magnitude and the duration of the price move; otherwise, neither the exercise price nor the expiration month of the call can be chosen rationally. Options investment thus demands a much higher ability to predict developments than stock investment. The correct prognosis of an increase in stock prices means a sure profit for the stock investor. The options investor can only realize his profit if the price movement comes about before the expiration date; his time, therefore, is limited.

The options premium is a subject of great interest to theoreticians. If it were at all possible to recognize definitely an over- or undervaluation in time to benefit by it, arbitrage operations would lead to certain profit. The model of Black and Scholes, which is probably the best known in this area, is described briefly in the following.

The Mathematical Assessment of Options

The Black and Scholes Model. The investor attributes intuitively to all stocks he buys a certain probability that they will either rise or fall. In the final analysis, the sum of all these estimated probabilities about future price developments determines the total demand. The stock price is the result of supply and demand and the same holds true for options. Black and Scholes proceeded from the assumption that, to a certain degree, the stock market and the options market are independent of each other. This could mean that investors put a different valuation on stock prices and on net premiums. Black and Scholes developed their model in an attempt to catch these differing valuations and to make it possible to apply them in practice.

The probability of a stock price's movement can be calculated on the basis of the market data of the stock and by applying a probability calculation (*lemma by Ito*) which attributes a certain price to the option (Dan Galai, "Pricing of Options and the Efficiency of the Chicago Board Options Exchange," unpublished Ph.D. dissertation, the University of Chicago, 1975). This probability distribution is the basis for calculating a statistical options value, the so-called "fair value." A comparison can be made between the value the individual options buyer has put on the options—that is, the current options price on the one side—and the value that the option should have according to the calculations—the "fair value." These two values need not agree. Black and Scholes's formula (The Valuation of Options Contracts and a Test of Market Efficiency, *Journal of Finance*, Vol. 27, 1972, pp. 399–417) for calculating the fair value of options is:

$$w\,(x, t) = xN(d_1) - ce^{f(t-t^*)}N(d_2)$$

$$d_1 = \frac{\ln\dfrac{x}{c} + \left(r + \dfrac{1}{2}v^2\right)(t^* - t)}{v\sqrt{t^* - t}}$$

$$d_2 = \frac{\ln\dfrac{x}{c} + \left(r - \dfrac{1}{2}v^2\right)(t^* - t)}{v\sqrt{t^* - t}}$$

where:

x = Stock price
c = Exercise price
t = Expiration date of option

r = Interest rates of treasuries
v^2 = Variance of price development of stocks (volatility)
L_a = *logarithmus naturalis*
$N(d)$ = Functional value of the cumulative normal distribution at point d
$w(x,t)$ = Value of option during life at stock price x

Rather than discussing the formula in detail, we merely point out briefly the premises for the formula according to which valid interpretations about the "correct" fair value of options can be made:

◇ Stock prices follow a random walk.

◇ The variance of the options price is dependent on the stock price; if the stock price goes up, the variance of the options price increases as the square of the stock price increases, that is, the risk (standard deviation) increases disproportionately with the price increase.

◇ The rate of interest remains unchanged.

◇ All market participants are permitted to engage in short sales and to buy on margin.

It follows that with the given parameters, the options price is a function of the stock price and of that time period until the expiration date. The numerical determination of the functional range of cumulative normal distribution is so complicated and involved that this task can only be mastered by a computer. With the help of a computer, tables are established that can give information about the fair value that should be attributed to which option under certain prescribed conditions. (Incidentally, these tables can be purchased.) The fair value that is culled from the chart is compared with the current price of the option. The investor can then decide whether to buy the option (if it is undervalued) or whether he should sell it (if it is overvalued). Figure 38 is a reproduction of a page from such a table.

How is the table read?

Annual Std Dev = 0.20 Exercise Price = 40.

Price	Interest Rate = 0.05			Interest Rate = 0.10			Interest Rate = 0.15		
	3 Months	6 Months	9 Months	3 Months	6 Months	9 Months	3 Months	6 Months	9 Months
28.	0.00 (0.00)	0.01 (0.01)	0.07 (0.04)	0.00 (0.00)	0.02 (0.02)	0.12 (0.06)	0.00 (0.00)	0.04 •(0.03)	0.20 (0.09)
32.	0.02 (0.02)	0.18 (0.09)	0.44 (0.16)	0.03 (0.03)	0.26 (0.12)	0.65 (0.22)	0.04 (0.04)	0.37 (0.16)	0.93 (0.29)
36.	0.36 (0.19)	0.94 (0.31)	1.50 (0.38)	0.45 (0.23)	1.22 (0.37)	2.01 (0.46)	0.55 (0.26)	1.55 (0.44)	2.61 (0.55)
40.	1.85 (0.57)	2.76 (0.60)	3.51 (0.62)	2.12 (0.62)	3.31 (0.66)	4.35 (0.70)	2.41 (0.66)	3.92 (0.73)	5.27 (0.77)
44.	4.80 (0.87)	5.63 (0.82)	6.38 (0.80)	5.22 (0.89)	6.41 (0.86)	7.49 (0.86)	5.65 (0.92)	7.21 (0.90)	8.64 (0.90)
48.	8.54 (0.98)	9.18 (0.94)	9.83 (0.91)	9.02 (0.98)	10.08 (0.96)	11.11 (0.94)	9.49 (0.99)	10.97 (0.97)	12.39 (0.95)
52.	12.50 (1.00)	13.04 (0.98)	13.60 (0.97)	12.99 (1.00)	13.98 (0.99)	14.96 (0.98)	13.47 (1.00)	14.91 (0.99)	16.30 (0.99)

Annual Std Dev = 0.30 Exercise Price = 40.

Price	Interest Rate = 0.05			Interest Rate = 0.10			Interest Rate = 0.15		
	3 Months	6 Months	9 Months	3 Months	6 Months	9 Months	3 Months	6 Months	9 Months
28.	0.02 (0.01)	0.18 (0.07)	0.45 (0.14)	0.02 (0.02)	0.23 (0.09)	0.59 (0.17)	0.03 (0.02)	0.29 (0.11)	0.76 (0.21)
32.	0.19 (0.09)	0.70 (0.20)	1.27 (0.28)	0.23 (0.11)	0.86 (0.24)	1.58 (0.33)	0.27 (0.12)	1.04 (0.28)	1.9. (0.38)
36.	0.92 (0.29)	1.89 (0.39)	2.72 (0.45)	1.05 (0.32)	2.21 (0.44)	3.25 (0.51)	1.19 (0.35)	2.56 (49)	3.84 (0.56)
40.	2.63 (0.56)	3.85 (0.59)	4.84 (0.61)	2.89 (0.60)	4.36 (0.63)	5.59 (0.66)	3.16 (0.63)	4.?0 (0.68)	6.40 (0.71)
44.	5.36 (0.79)	6.55 (0.75)	7.54 (0.74)	5.73 (0.81)	7.22 (0.79)	8.?0 (0.78)	6.11 (0.83)	7.91 (0.82)	9.49 (0.82)
48.	8.79 (0.92)	9.78 (0.86)	10.70 (0.84)	9.23 (0.93)	10.58 (0.89)	11.82 (0.87)	9.68 (0.94)	11.38 (0.91)	12.94 (0.90)
52.	12.59 (0.97)	13.37 (0.93)	14.18 (0.90)	13.06 (0.98)	14.24 (0.94)	15.41 (0.92)	1?.53 (0.98)	15.11 (0.96)	16.63 (0.94)

Annual Std Dev = 0.40 Exercise Price = 40.

Price	Interest Rate = 0.05			Interest Rate = 0.10			Interest Rate = 0.15		
	3 Months	6 Months	9 Months	3 Months	6 Months	9 Months	3 Months	6 Months	9 Months
28.	0.12 (0.05)	0.55 (0.15)	1.09 (0.23)	0.13 (0.06)	0.65 (0.17)	1.30 (0.26)	0.15 (0.07)	0.76 (0.20)	1.54 (0.30)
32.	0.53 (0.17)	1.42 (0.29)	2.26 (0.36)	0.60 (0.19)	1.62 (0.32)	2.62 (0.40)	0.67 (0.20)	1.85 (0.35)	3.02 (0.44)
36.	1.57 (0.36)	2.88 (0.44)	3.96 (0.49)	1.72 (0.38)	3.22 (0.48)	4.49 (0.53)	1.87 (0.41)	3.58 (0.51)	5.06 (0.56)
40.	3.42 (0.56)	4.95 (0.59)	6.17 (0.61)	3.67 (0.59)	5.43 (0.62)	6.87 (0.65)	3.92 (0.61)	5.93 (0.66)	7.60 (0.69)
44.	6.04 (0.74)	7.57 (0.71)	8.82 (0.71)	6.38 (0.76)	8.18 (0.74)	9.67 (0.75)	6.72 (0.78)	8.80 (0.77)	10.56 (0.78)
48.	9.26 (0.86)	10.63 (0.81)	11.83 (0.79)	9.66 (0.87)	11.34 (0.83)	12.82 (0.82)	10.06 (0.88)	12.06 (0.85)	13.82 (0.85)
52.	12.85 (0.93)	14.01 (0.88)	15.11 (0.85)	1?.29 (0.94)	14.80 (0.89)	16.21 (0.87)	13.73 (0.95)	15.59 (0.91)	17.31 (0.90)

Annual Std Dev = 0.50 Exercise Price = 40.

Price	Interest Rate = 0.05			Interest Rate = 0.10			Interest Rate = 0.15		
	3 Months	6 Months	9 Months	3 Months	6 Months	9 Months	3 Months	6 Months	9 Months
28.	0.32 (0.11)	1.08 (0.22)	1.88 (0.30)	0.35 (0.11)	1.22 (0.24)	2.14 (0.33)	0.39 (0.12)	1.37 (0.27)	2.42 (0.36)
32.	0.99 (0.24)	2.23 (0.35)	3.32 (0.42)	1.07 (0.25)	2.46 (0.38)	3.71 (0.45)	1.16 (0.27)	2.71 (0.40)	4.12 (0.48)
36.	2.26 (0.40)	3.89 (0.48)	5.20 (0.52)	2.41 (0.42)	4.23 (0.51)	5.73 (0.56)	2.58 (0.44)	4.59 (0.54)	6.28 (0.59)
40.	4.21 (0.57)	6.05 (0.60)	7.49 (0.62)	4.44 (0.59)	6.51 (0.62)	8.15 (0.65)	4.69 (0.61)	6.97 (0.65)	8.83 (0.68)
44.	6.78 (0.71)	8.65 (0.70)	10.13 (0.70)	7.69 (0.73)	9.21 (0.72)	10.92 (0.73)	7.40 (0.74)	9.77 (0.74)	11.72 (0.76)
48.	9.85 (0.82)	11.60 (0.78)	13.07 (0.77)	10.22 (0.83)	12.25 (0.80)	13.9. (0.79)	10.59 (0.84)	12.91 (0.82)	14.87 (0.85)
52.	13.27 (0.89)	14.84 (0.84)	16.24 (0.82)	13.68 (0.90)	15.56 (0.86)	17.23 (0.84)	14.10 (0.91)	16.29 (0.87)	18.22 (0.86)

Figure 38 Option values and hedge-ratios for different stock prices and maturities, by standard deviation and interest rate. (Financial Analysts Journal, *July–August 1975.*)

Example: The table arrives at a fair value of $2.63 with the following data:
- ◇ Current stock price, $40.
- ◇ Exercise price of the option, 40.
- ◇ Interest rate for treasuries, 5%.
- ◇ Volatility of the stock, 0.30.
- ◇ Life of the option, 3 months.

This means that if the current options price with a stock price of $40 is below $2.63, the option is undervalued; if it is above $2.63, it is overvalued. The unknown quantity in this formula is the volatility of the stock. *Gastineau-Madansky, Kassouf* and others have developed models similar to the one by Black and Scholes. Even though the premises of these models are not perfect, they still offer some help to those investors who realize the limitations of these models and who know how to make use of the results within these limitations.

The Practical Utilization of Over- and Undervalued Options

Owing to the great number of negotiable options with their different exercise prices and expiration dates, the individual investor scarcely has a chance to use those formulas to calculate the over- or undervaluation of the options premiums. This market gap has been filled by several information services. The *Holt Trading Advisory*, for example, publishes a mathematically calculated fair value for all. expiration dates and exercise prices for those stocks with the highest options trading volume, and compares those values with the current value of the options. Figure 39 is a graphic representation of a combination of stock prices and options prices.

The first chart shows the trend of IBM during 1976 to 1978 on the basis of week-end closing prices. The weekly volume, the 200-day moving average, and the relative strength of IBM compared to other stocks gives information about the medium-term trend of the stock.

The second chart shows the trend of IBM on the basis of daily closing prices in the 4-week trend. The daily volume and the 50- and 200-day moving averages indicate the short-term trend of the stock.

The third chart shows those lines that give the mathematically computed price of IBM options in the expiration months of April, July, and October at exercise prices 240, 260, and 280.

The black squares mark the current price of the option. Point 1 is below line 1 (exercise price 280); this means that the current options price is undervalued by the theoretically computed options

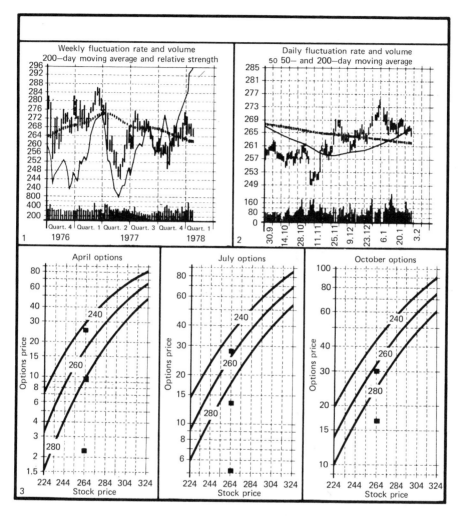

Figure 39   International Business Machines, stock price: 264¼, interest rate 4.3%, P/E 14. (The Holt Trading Advisory, T. S. Holt & Company, Inc., New York.)

value. If point 1 is above line 1, then this indicates that the option is overvalued. If the investor were to concentrate solely on this evaluation of the option, all of the IBM options would be worth buying at this price. If the theoretical value is computed correctly, the undervalued current options price should move closer to the theoretical value and thus offer an opportunity for profit. Before buying an option, however, the investor should look at the stock price. The investor can only buy the option if he receives a buying signal through stock price analysis (see the discussion of stock price analysis in Chapter 2). The assessment of the option is therefore only an auxiliary aid for reinforcing a decision after it has been made as regards buying, selling, or short-selling a stock.

GUIDE FOR BUYING AND SELLING PUTS AND CALLS

A brief survey of options strategies will give some idea of what alternatives are suitable for which type of investor before these strategies are discussed in detail. This classification is extremely important because each options strategy should be used only under quite specific conditions and should not be applied aimlessly by every investor. The major advantage of options—and one that is still widely unknown—lies in the fact that there is an optimum options strategy for all kinds of investors. The following classifications and valuations can, of course, only give a rough picture because investors' mentalities, risk preferences, investment horizons, and know-how really cannot be assembled under one uniform heading. Still, no investor can include options as an integral part of his portfolio without a definite object in view. We can make rough subdivisions of investors.

Types of Investors

Speculator: aggressive investment strategy. Desires big leverage effect in capital investment. Investment horizon is extremely short. Minimal diversification. Concentration instead of diversification. High risk preferences. Main object in view: "all or nothing."

Conservative investor: Prudent investment strategy. Diversification of the portfolio through stocks, treasuries, and options. Low risk preference. Main object in view: maintenance of capital and realistic capital growth.

Each of these investors will have different ideas about how to invest his capital. It is vital to know the answer to the following questions: how much time can the investor spare for his capital investment? Does he have any experience with the market, and how extensive is that experience? Does he have a good advisor? How intensively does he keep watch over individual transactions? Does he calculate changes in the portfolio with regard to timing? These and other considerations allow further subdivisions:

Professional investor: extensive know-how and experience in the market.

◇ Sufficient time to work out portfolio strategies.

◇ Constant supervision of the individual transactions, control of accounts, and monthly evaluation of the state of the portfolio.

◇ Close contact with brokers and banks.

Nonprofessional investor: little or no know-how and experience in the market.

◇ Makes his investment decisions on the basis of advertisements, pamphlets, and the like.

◇ Depends on an advisor to a great extent and is unable to recognize the risks of capital investments or to supervise them.

◇ Has no control over individual transactions or monthly changes in the portfolio.

◇ Tends to hesitate when decisions have to be made (profit taking, limitation of losses).

Depending on which of these groups the investor feels he belongs to—that is, whether he thinks he is conservative or speculative and whether he administers and supervises his capital investment professionally—he has to decide what percentage of his capital he wants to invest in options. Here again two categories can be distinguished:

◇ A very high percentage of the capital at his disposal (in extreme cases, 100%).

◇ A small portion of the capital at his disposal (approximately 10 to 20%).

With these criteria, a corresponding classification and valuation for each options strategy can be set up. This has been attempted in Figure 40, which gives three ratings: recommended, conditionally recommended, and useless. The investor who cannot be bothered with the intensive study of all the options strategies described can pick from this table the strategy suitable for himself and limit himself to that.

At this point it must be made very clear that none of the categorizations and appraisals can be complete; they reflect, above all, the author's own experience. But without such a classification, the presentation of the various possibilities in options would in all probability only create more confusion and be of no help at all. The classification certainly is not meant as a moral valuation; it is a

Strategy	Type of Investor	Speculator		Conservative Investor	
		Pro-fessional	Nonpro-fessional	Pro-fessional	Nonpro-fessional
1 Buyer call	Total capital (up to 100%)	+	–	–	–
	Partial amount (10–20%)	0	+	+	0
2 Writer uncovered call	Total capital (up to 100%)	–	–	–	–
	Partial amount (10–20%)	0	–	+	–
3 Covered writer	Total capital (up to 100%)	N/A	N/A	N/A	N/A
	Partial amount (10–20%)	–	–	+	+
4 Buyer put	Total capital (up to 100%)	+	–	–	–
	Partial amount (10–20%)	0	+	+	0
5 Writer uncovered put	Total capital (up to 100%)	N/A	N/A	N/A	N/A
	Partial amount (10–20%)	0	–	+	–

Legend: + = recommended; – = useless; 0 = conditionally recommended; N/A = not applicable.

Figure 40

simple, objective statement. A person with a full-time job cannot be expected to show as much and as intensive concern about his investments as the investor who can concentrate totally on his portfolio. The table shows the chances everyone can have, no matter what his limitations.

RISKS AND OPPORTUNITIES WITH CALLS AND PUTS

Strategy I: The Purchase of Calls

To give an idea of the possibilities open to the options buyer due to price fluctuations of stocks in the various exercise prices and expiration months, we can study the behavior of Xerox and its options during a period of 4 days with the actual prices (commissions excluded):

Example:

Date	Oct. 2	Oct. 13		Oct. 18		Nov. 11	
Stock price	55	60		58½		54	
Expiration month	Options price	Options price	Change in %	Options price	Change in %	Options price	Change in %
October							
Exer- 50	5⅛	13⅝	+164	9¼	−32	expired	−100
cise 60	⅝	3⅛	+490	1⅞	−54	expired	−100
price 70	⅛	⅛	—	⅛	—	expired	−100
January							
Exer- 50	7⅜	14½	+ 96	11¼	−22	7½	− 33
cise 60	2¾	7	+154	5⅜	−23	2½	− 58
price 70	1	3⅛	+212	2⅛	−32	¼	− 76
April							
Exer- 50	10¼	15⅜	+ 49	12⅞	−16	9½	− 26
cise 60	4¾	8⅛	+ 71	7⅜	− 9	4¾	− 36
price 70	2⅛	3⅞	+ 82	3⅞	—	2⅛	− 45

With this example, the influence of price movements of Xerox on the options in various expiration months and exercise prices can be studied.

The Speculative Buyer of Calls

Most calls are bought by investors who want to make a quick profit. The opportunity to achieve a profit of several hundred percent within a few weeks is not all that rare; this, of course, incites the avid speculator to take positions in calls time and again. The opportunities are at the optimum if the price trend of the underlying securities can be determined accurately. But the investor who overestimates his own capability of prognosis and therefore takes too many positions can suffer a total loss, from which he may not recover, within a very short period if he miscalculates the price trend. The investor who speculates in the near expiration months according to the motto "all or nothing" has several choices in the different exercise prices. Xerox again serves as an example for studying the movements of options prices in the near expiration months.

Example:

Date Stock price in dollars	Octo-ber 2 55	Octo-ber 13 60	Profit + loss in%	Octo-ber 18 58½	Profit + loss in%	Octo-ber 24 56
Exercise price October						
50	5⅛	13⅝	+164	9¼	−32	expired
60	⅝	3⅛	+490	1⅞	−54	expired
70	⅛	⅛	—	⅛	—	expired

The movement of the options prices is graphically represented in Figures 41 and 42.

Before the options speculator takes a position, he has to decide which one of the following two possibilities comes closer to his risk preference:

◇ The exercise price above the stock price (out of the money) with the higher percentage of opportunities but greater risk,

or

◇ The exercise price below the stock price (in the money) where options are more expensive but all in all much safer.

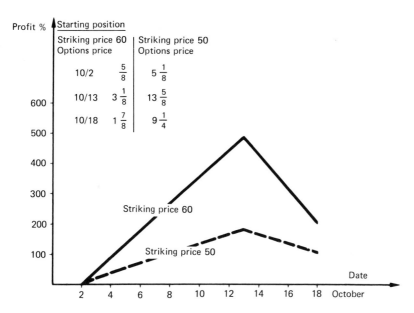

Figure 41 *Percentage value of the increase/decrease of the option prices.*

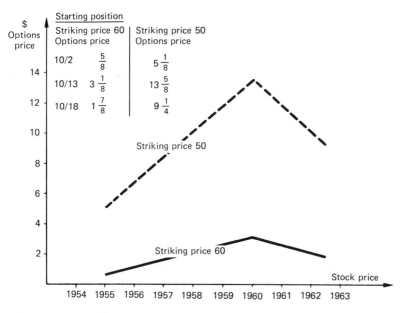

Figure 42 *Dollar value of the increase/decrease of option prices.*

173

October 50 Call

If the investor wants to achieve the biggest increase in profit in dollars, he will have to take positions in the low exercise price 50. The option at this point has the lowest net premium ($⅛ on October 2) and an intrinsic value of $5.

The investor can be certain that the option will go up by nearly the same dollar amount if the stock price goes up, since the intrinsic value (difference between the stock price and the lower exercise price) always remains intact. With the price increase of the stock from $55 on October 2 to $60 on October 13, the options price increased from $5⅛ to $13⅝. Within this period, the speculative investor not only achieved a profit through the increase of the intrinsic value of the option by $5, but in addition the net premium increased from $⅛ on October 2 to $3⅝ on October 13. Within 10 market days, the investor earned $8½ on his investment. His expectations were completely realized.

Between October 13 and October 18, the stock price fell from $60 to $58½—that is, the investor has lost very little through the price fluctuation of the stock, but nearly the entire net premium. The net premium fell disproportionately fast because the effect of the very short remaining life until the expiration date of October 24, together with the declining price, was so strong that no investor had any interest in paying a surplus price in the shape of the net premium for this option. The options buyer who acquired the option on October 13 and speculated that it would continue to rise lost $4⅜ on his investment within 5 days. The only way the investor can succeed with this strategy is to employ extremely good timing.

October 60 Call

Investors who want to achieve a higher percentage of profits with a bigger leverage effect than the exercise price 50 offers buy calls at an exercise price above the stock price. Here the options price consists solely of the net premium. Compared to the purchase price of $5⅛ in the exercise price 50, the options price on October 2 of $⅝ with the exercise price 60 is really quite low. With the same investment, the investor can purchase approximately 20 times as many options contracts. Within 10 days, the stock price increased by $5 to $60 and the option went up to $3⅛, or by 490%. Since the remaining life has a particularly strong effect on the net premium shortly before the expiration date, the option fell back to $1⅞ within the week before October 18, which meant a loss of 54% for the investor who had bought his options on October 13. If the investor did not sell his option at its residual value before October 24, he would suffer a total loss of his investment because the option expires on that day. The danger of purchasing an option with a net premium not only lies in the fact that the future stock price development is difficult to predict, but there is also the danger that the net premium will deteriorate before the expiration date on October 23. But despite the high risk, many investors take positions in these options—an action that is clearly supported by the high volume. Emotions, intuitions, or greed cause the investor to forget all rational investment strategies, Such a capital "investment" becomes, in fact, a lottery with a 100% risk of total loss.

October 70 Call

How small the interest is in the more distant exercise prices shortly before the expiration date is shown by the influence of Xerox price movements on the options price October 70 call, which remained practically unchanged.

The Prudent Purchaser of Calls

The investor who does not want to emphatically force a profit buys options in a more distant expiration date and invests in calls no more than is necessary for exercising the option for the number of shares he wants to own. If, for example, 500 Xerox at $50 cost $25,000, the purchase of 5 options for Xerox is sufficient (5 options is equivalent to 500 shares). He can choose from among the various exercise prices and expiration dates, with which he can regulate the size of the options price and thus the risk of the investment as well. In our example, he could have bought the option Xerox at the January exercise price 60 at $2½ instead of in the near expiration October 60 call at $⅝. The figures up to the expiration date in January are as follows:

Example:

Stock price	Profits + losses of Xerox share	Cost of call	Total profit + loss	Profit + loss in %
70	10	−2,5	+7,5	+300
68	8	−2,5	+5,5	+220
66	6	−2,5	+3,5	+140
64	4	−2,5	+1,5	+ 60
62	2	−2,5	+0,5	− 20
60	0	−2,5	−2,5	−100
58	0	−2,5	−2,5	−100
56	0	−2,5	−2,5	−100
54	0	−2,5	−2,5	−100
52	0	−2,5	−2,5	−100

In the example shown in Figure 43, the options buyer would have had neither a profit nor a loss in January if Xerox had traded at approximately $63 (commissions excluded). If the price were at $66, the option could be sold with a considerable profit of $3½. If the price were to fall below $60, the loss would never be more than

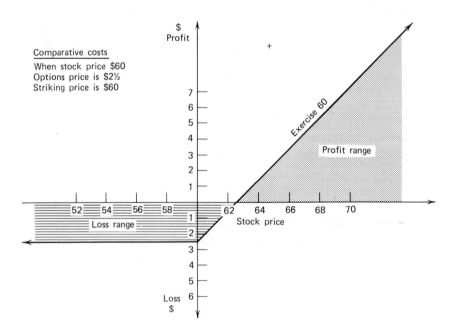

Figure 43   Purchase of a call.

$2½, or 100%. Until the expiration date in January, the investor has plenty of time to watch the price trend and to decide whether he wants to sell or hold the option. With the more distant expiration date, the investor has purchased a much greater range for his decision making, but he must pay the higher options price.

Unlike the speculator who has no interest in the purchase of underlying securities, the conservative investor can try to compensate for lack of timing with options. He can first buy the call and decide later to exercise the option and thus acquire the shares. It is definitely safer and cheaper to buy the option instead of buying stocks on margin. If the stock price goes up, the options price will follow suit dollar by dollar if the exercise price is below the stock price, since the intrinsic value of the option is very high (the difference between the exercise price and the stock price) and the net premium is very small. The options investor is by no means at a disadvantage compared to the stock investor. If the stock price goes down, the option will lose dollar by dollar parallel to the stock until the exercise price is reached. With the option, however, the loss is limited to the amount of the options price; a stock can drop considerably below the exercise price of the option and the loss in dollars compared to that of options can be considerably higher. The only disadvantage the options buyer has is that he cannot benefit from dividend payments on the stocks.

There is a further argument in support of the purchase of options; an investor is convinced that the price of a stock will go up and wants to secure the stock for a certain date. If he does not have the necessary funds at the time to purchase the stock, the option can help bridge this period because it requires a smaller capital input. The purchase of a call not only offers a wide investment spectrum to the options buyer, but it is also a useful supplement for safeguarding short-sale positions in stocks. This can be done either immediately, in order to limit the risk with the short-sold stock right from the beginning, or the investor can buy the call at a later date to secure the return that has been achieved without having to buy the stocks again at that time.

Example: In September 1977, Eastman Kodak shares were traded at $60. The investor who sold short at that time was able to protect the securities against a price increase with a call for $2 at exercise price 60 January. If the price increased, the loss in the stock could never exceed $2 before the

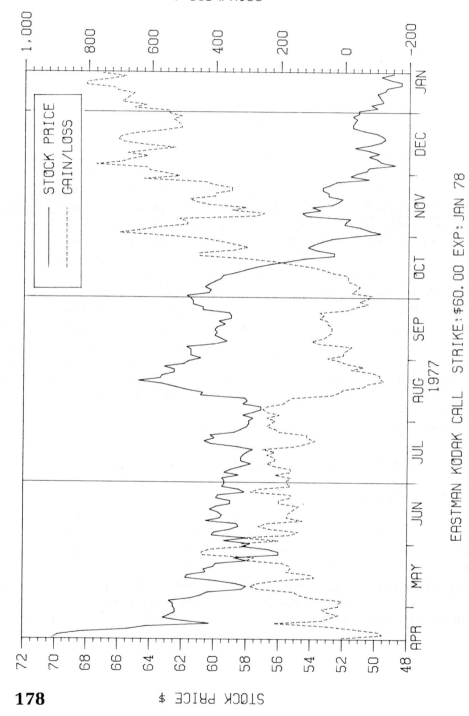

GAIN/LOSS $

STOCK PRICE $

EASTMAN KODAK CALL   STRIKE:$60.00 EXP:JAN 78
1977

STOCK PRICE
GAIN/LOSS

178

Figure 44   Eastman Kodak results of sell 100 shares of stock; buy one call as protection.

expiration date in January. To supplement this strategy, the protection of the short sale could be deferred. When Eastman Kodak was traded in October at $50, the investor had to decide whether he should buy the shares again with a profit or whether he should protect the profit he had achieved by purchasing a call option January 50 at $2 and watch the price trend. In any case, the profit of $8 was protected through the purchase of the option, no matter how much the price of Eastman Kodak would increase until the expiration date in January.

Summary

Most people automatically conjure up the picture of the speculative buyer of calls when they hear the word "options"—either from ignorance or because of the pushy advertisements they see. The huge and rapid turnover on the American options exchanges proves, however, that investors welcome this new form of investment, which allows them to take either more conservative or more speculative positions than the stock market offers. With a 10% price increase in the stock the investor can make a 100% profit or more with the option; this is such a great temptation that he tends to forget or disregard all rational considerations. Options are often bought because this form of investment is popular; the most fundamental rules are consequently pushed aside, viz: that with opportunities for large profits the risk increases disproportionately. It never pays to make risky speculations that put a strain on the investor's financial resources or to put all one's eggs in one basket. Options investing is an extremely complicated field, and the highest degree of skill and expertise is required if the investor wants to make proper use of the many investment choices offered and select the right exercise prices and expiration dates. Even though the table in Figure 40 definitely facilitates the choice of the "right" strategy, it can never hurt to study the options trade in all its aspects and ramifications.

The following conditions generally prevail for the buyer of calls:

◇ The greatest possible loss is the total options price. This loss occurs if the stock price is below the exercise price on the expiration date.
◇ There are "unlimited" opportunities for profit if the stock price is above the exercise price of the option up to the expiration date.

The following can be said about the call prices in the various exercise prices and expiration dates:

◇ The more the stock price exceeds the exercise price of the option, the higher the options price.

◇ The more the exercise price exceeds the stock price, the lower the options price.

◇ The further away the expiration date, the higher the options price in all exercise prices.

Valid Strategies

● 1. **The Professional Speculator**

His strategy

◇ Not closer than about 6 weeks before the near.

◇ Expiration date or medium expiration month.

◇ Purchase of calls at exercise price close to the current price of the stock.

Why Recommended for Full Capital Investment?

◇ The big leverage effect of options is the aim of an aggressive investment policy.

◇ The risk can be limited with extensive know-how, market experience, discipline, and good timing.

◇ A wide diversification in different stocks, expiration months, and exercise prices is possible and decreases the risk even further.

Danger

◇ Total loss is possible if always fully invested and not well enough diversified, and if the timing goes wrong.

Why Conditionally Recommended for 10−20% of Total Capital Investment?

◇ The leverage effect is not big enough with the smaller capital investment.

◇ Compared to other opportunities involving a small capital investment this strategy requires too much time and energy for planning and execution.

Advantages

◇ The psychological pressure is not so great with the smaller capital input. Therefore suitable for professional speculators who want to familiarize themselves with the conditions and requirements of options.

● 2. **The Nonprofessional Speculator**

His strategy

◇ Purchase of calls during medium or most distant expiration month.

◇ Purchase of calls with exercise price at or below the stock price.

Why Not Recommended for Full Capital Investment?

◇ An aggressive investment policy is often destructive if possibilities for supervision of positions and strategies are lacking.

◇ Poor timing or no timing of decisions at all plus very little discipline, know-how, and market experience lead to misjudgment of opportunities and risks in options.

◇ The risk of a total loss cannot be avoided by furnishing a third person with full powers.

Why Recommended for 10−20% of Total Capital Investment?

◇ The leverage effect of options can lead to disproportionally large profits compared with other forms of investment, even with a small capital input and thus considerably improve the total return of a portfolio.

◇ The risk remains managable.

◇ Mistakes do not entail the total loss of the capital.

◇ Distant expiration dates and low exercise prices can to a certain degree be a compensation for lack of timing.

◇ A good advisor can make up for the investor's lack of time and other weak points as well, so that the investor does not have to forego all opportunities of options.

◇ By investing small amounts the investor can test whether he is qualified for options with a greater capital commitment.

● 3. The Professional Conservative Investor

His strategy

◇ Purchase of calls in medium or distant expiration month.

◇ Purchase of calls with exercise price near or below the stock price.

◇ Number of options contracts: only as many that the available capital is sufficient to buy the underlying securities.

Why Not Recommended for Full Capital Investment?

◇ Investment form too agressive to allow the realization of the aim of capital growth and maintenance.

◇ Conservative strategies are better equipped to realize expected returns at less risk.

◇ No dividends or other return from options.

Why Recommended for 10–20% of Total Capital Investment?

◇ A well-diversified portfolio with treasuries and stocks can be enriched by partial investment in options.

◇ The risk can be limited to a calculated amount with know-how, experience, and good timing.

◇ Total loss in options has little effect on the total investment.

◇ Calls can be used at a maximum not only to achieve an additional yield but also to protect short-positions in stocks.

● **4. The Conservative Nonprofessional Investor**

His strategy

◇ The purchase of calls.

Why Not Recommended for Full Capital Investment?

◇ Strategy is wrong for investor's mentality and investment aims.
◇ No qualification.
◇ Leverage effect of options is too great.

Why Conditionally Recommended for 10–20% of Total Capital Investment?

◇ A good advisor can to a certain degree make up for some of the investor's lack of qualification and thus the opportunities of options can be applied at a maximum in the investors interest. The risk remains within the scope of the avowed goal.

HOW TO GET 25 TO 1 LEVERAGE, AND MORE, WITH "CHART SEGMENTS"

In 1970 the *Key-Volume Strategies* stock advisory service introduced a new market timing tool, *Chart Segments*, for catching 40 point and larger moves of the DJI (Dow Jones Industrial Average) in both directions.

Before you proceed to the Option Trading discussion below, refer to Figure 45 to learn:

1. *How a new "chart segment" is signaled.*

2. *How 40 and 71 point profit targets are set. The 71-point strategy, called* optimization, *was added to the original trading system in 1975.*

3. *How option trades can be timed to coincide with chart segments.*

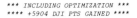

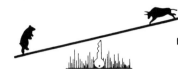

KEY-VOLUME STRATEGIES, INC.

P.O. BOX 407

WHITE PLAINS, N.Y. 10602

BULLETIN # _7811_
DATE: _3/11/78_

| CHART SEGMENTS |

SIGNAL: _BUY_
DJI: _746_

Quick short term market moves can be caught, and usually profitably traded, using the trading tool: "CHART SEGMENTS". Since February 1970, a total of _+5287_ DJI equivalent points have been gained. Today's bulletin announces a NEW SIGNAL and describes the basic trading rules.

HOW THE NEW CHART SEGMENT HAS BEEN SIGNALLED

To catch such signals, you need only a daily DJI (Dow Jones Industrials) chart. Our source is the Wall Street Journal. Draw in the steepest possible short term trendline (*1) connecting at least two of the latest intraday lows or highs. Now all you need to do is make three easy observations:

● 1. HAS THE TRENDLINE JUST BEEN BROKEN? If yes .....
● 2. WAS THE CLOSING ACROSS THE BROKEN TRENDLINE, ON THE DAY OF THE BREAK? If the answer is yes again .....
● 3. DID THE CLOSING EXCEED THE LAST 4 OR MORE CLOSINGS JUST PRIOR TO IT (OR 5 OUT OF THE LAST 6) ?

If the answer is YES to all three questions, we have a SIGNAL. CHART SEGMENT # _215_, the NEW SIGNAL, is illustrated in the box. Note the BREAKING of the TRENDLINE. The CLOSING on the day of the break (_3/8_) is circled, and an ELBOW SHAPED ARROW points to it. You can count the immediately preceding closings which have been EXCEEDED, _BELOW_ the ELBOW. It is evident that the signal day's closing is _ABOVE_ the _7_ closings just prior to the signal. We express this as: "CE" = _7_ . "CE" means Closings Exceeded.

If a signal is given by the UPSIDE CROSSING of a DOWNTREND LINE, it is a BUY signal. Conversely, if a signal is given by the DOWNSIDE CROSSING of an UPTREND LINE, it's a SELL signal. Clearly, the NEW signal is: _BUY_ . This is indicated by the arrowhead △ in the box.

MINIMUM AND OPTIMAL TARGETS FOR THE SIGNALLED MOVE. On the TWO trading days immediately following the signal, namely _3/9_ and _3/10_ , the _LOWEST_ DJI level has been, or is expected to be _746_ . Based on several years of experience, a MINIMUM gain of 40 and an OPTIMAL gain (*1) of 71 DJI pts can be projected from this level. Accordingly, our projections are: MINIMUM TARGET = DJI _786_ ; OPTIMAL TARGET = DJI _817_ . One possible exception:

If on either of the two trading days mentioned above a SELL signal should occur (meaning: a CHART SEGMENT signal in the OPPOSITE direction), this would NEGATE segment # _215_, for a ZERO result. For this segment, such negation is: still possible ___ / no longer possible _✓_.

OPTION TRADES. Coincident with the new signal, subscribers who regularly follow CHART SEGMENTS and our STOCK/OPTION recommendations as well, were able to take positions in these selections: _N SEMI MAY20_ *@* _1/4_ *and* _CTL DATA AUG30_ *@* _1/2_ *. Among the selections on the latest TRADER'S ACTION REPORT, these two appeared BEST priced when it was time to act on this new CHART SEGMENT.* --- If you are satisfied with the profit(s) you have by the time the CHART SEGMENT reaches its 40 pt or 71 pt target (or the segment is closed on "STOP", see below), TAKE PROFITS. Optionally you may hold any position until the next ...

CONSENSUS TARGET is reached (assuming this gives the DJI further to go). CONSENSUS TARGETS, based on SIX original Key-Volume tools including CHART SEGMENTS, appear at the bottom of the SHORT TERM OUTLOOK page. What if the DJI does not "deliver"? How long to hold positions before settling for a small profit or even a loss? For a specific TIME LIMIT date for EVERY selection, simply refer to the current TRADER'S ACTION REPORT

IS THERE A "STOP" FOR THIS CHART SEGMENT? Yes, the segment may be CANCELLED, or the TIME LIMIT rule may cause its liquidation, short of the target. ● 1. CANCELLATION. If segment # _215_ has been active for only "CE" (= _7_) trading days or less, and an opposing SELL signal should occur, then liquidation would be required at the action point of the opposing signal. Watch for possible cancellation in this range of dates: _3/10_ thru _3/20_ .

● 2. TIME LIMIT. If the target is not reached, nor has the segment been cancelled by the time it is TWICE "CE" = _14_ trading days old, liquidate on this "time limit" day, or no later than the next day. The TIME LIMIT day for the segment just announced is _3/30_ .

COMPLETION OF THE PREVIOUS CHART SEGMENT. The final IN & OUT levels for segment # _214_ were _774_ and _739_ , respectively, for a result of _+35_ DJI pts. Reason for liquidating this segment is checked: TARGET REACHED ___ ; CANCELLATION ___ ; TIME LIMIT _✓_.

(*1) See the TRADER'S GUIDE to CHART SEGMENTS for exceptions & added detail. The information in the TRADER'S GUIDE and BULLETINS obsoletes the earlier TRADING BROCHURE series.

TRADER'S ACTION REPORT featuring individual stock & option selection & summaries, based on "PPS", a PRO'S PERSONAL TRADING SYSTEM, appears on p. 1 of each Key-Volume RELEASE.

184   *Figure 45*

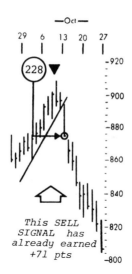

—Oct—

| 29 | 6 | 13 | 20 | 27 |

228 ▼

This SELL
SIGNAL has
already earned
+71 pts

Figure 46

	EAS KD	GM	WESTGH	IBM	MESA P	MEDIAN
SEG #210	APR50p	APR60p	APR20p	APR260p	APR35p	
1/ 3/78	B 2.25	B 2.13	B 2.25	B 4.25	B .75	
SELL	S 3.88	S 3.88	S 3.00	S 6.00	S 1.50	
RESULTS ▶	+ 72%	+ 82%	+ 33%	+ 41%	+ 100%	+ 72%
	------	------	------	-------	------	------
SEG #217	JUL45	JUL60	JUL15	JUL260	JUL35	
3/29/78	B 1.13	B 2.38	B 1.81	B 1.38	B 1.13	
BUY	S 2.81	S 4.88	S 4.38	S 2.88	S 2.75	
RESULTS ▶	+ 150%	+ 105%	+ 141%	+ 109%	+ 144%	+ 141%
	------	------	------	-------	------	------
SEG #221	JUL60	JUL60	JUL20	JUL280	JUL35	
5/31/78	B 1.19	B 2.56	B 1.88	B 1.75	B 1.56	
BUY	S 2.00	S 4.25	S 3.88	S 6.00	S 2.63	
RESULTS ▶	+ 68%	+ 66%	+ 107%	+ 243%	+ 68%	+ 68%
	------	------	------	-------	------	------
SEG #223	OCT60	OCT60	OCT25	OCT280	OCT35	
7/10/78	B 1.31	B 1.81	B .63	B 2.75	B 1.56	
BUY	S 4.25	S 4.00	S 1.38	S 9.38	S 2.31	
RESULTS ▶	+ 224%	+ 121%	+ 120%	+ 241%	+ 48%	+ 121%
	------	------	------	-------	------	------
SEG #228	JAN60p	JAN60p	JAN20p	JAN260p	JAN35p	
10/16/78	B 3.00	B 2.06	B .75	B 5.00	B .56	
SELL	S 6.00	S 5.88	S 3.75	S 8.50	S 4.13	
RESULTS ▶	+ 100%	+ 185%	+ 400%	+ 70%	+ 633%	+ 185%
	------	------	------	-------	------	------

● AVERAGE OF ALL MEDIAN GAINS, 5 BEST SIGNALS .... + 117%

To assess the profit potential of trades in *listed put and call options* in conjunction with chart segments, KVS compiled statistics for the full year 1978 using the options of the same five widely traded stocks: *Eastman Kodak, General Motors, Westinghouse, IBM and Mesa Petroleum*. From the 24 chart segment signals of 1978, KVS chose the five most successful and the five least successful signals for this analysis. The five best signals, identified in the left column of the trade summary table, resulted in these gains, in DJI points: *71 points each for segments 210, 221, and 228; and 100 points each for segments 217 and 223*. So that readers may see an example for a sell signal to supplement the buy illustration in the bulletin, *segment 228 is reproduced in Figure 46*, as it appeared in the KVS market release which reported its completion with a 71 point gain.

Basic rules for trading listed options in conjunction with chart segments:

◇ *Buy calls if the signal was buy; buy puts if the signal was sell.*

◇ *Favor slightly out-of-money options expiring no sooner than the second month following signal.*

◇ *Take positions within two trading days of the chart segment signal, at the best prices you can.*

◇ *During the first few days try for a gross gain of at least 75%, but lower your sights to a gross gain of 30½ or better thereafter.*

◇ *By the end of the second calendar week following the week of the chart segment signal, close all positions taken on that signal.*

Examine the table and note that the *median gain* of the five best signals ranged from +68% to +185%. The average of the five median gains was +117%. The average holding time was seven trading days. The total DJI gain of the five chart segments was +413 points, or an average of +83 points. This translates to an average DJI gain of +10.12%, the average DJI level having been 820 for starting the chart segments (the two sells occurred @823 and 872, and the three buys @753, 835 and 815). On first look, the *leverage* appears to be only about 11 to 1 (117% divided by 10.12%). However, the average holding time for realizing the full chart segment gains was 35 trading days, exactly five times as long as the seven day average holding time for the options. To calculate *true leverage*, therefore, the result of the division must be multiplied by 5. The math works out like this: $117:10.12 = 11.56 \times 5 = 57.8$. The true leverage thus approximated 58 to 1 on the *best* trades. Commissions not considered.

The five *worst* trades gained only a total of +29 DJI points, in an average time of only five trading days, because each of these chart segments was *cancelled*: #211, BUY @773 (1/18/78); #213, BUY @767 (2/1/78); #216, SELL @761 (3/22/78); #218, SELL @837 (5/3/78); and #229, BUY @810 (11/1/78). The average DJI level for acting on these unsuccessful segments was 790. The average point gain of six (rounded) amounted to .76%. Since the average holding time was only five trading days, and there are approximately 250 trading days a year, the annualized result was $.76\% \times (250:5) = +38\%$. The corresponding option trades, for which no table is provided due to space limitation, achieved these *median gains* for the five signals: even (0%), +32%, +16%, +62% and +23%, in chronological order. The average of the five median gains was +27%, considerably below the +117% achieved by the best signals.

Yet even on these "worst" results, an average *gain* was possible, offering fairly high leverage compared to the result in DJI points. The average holding time for the options was again 7 trading days, therefore the math for computing the annualized result works like this: $27\% \times (250:7) = +964\%$. The leverage was in excess of 25 to 1 (964% : 38%).*

---

* Each individual option trader's own typical result, using CHART SEGMENT signals, is likely to differ with experience.

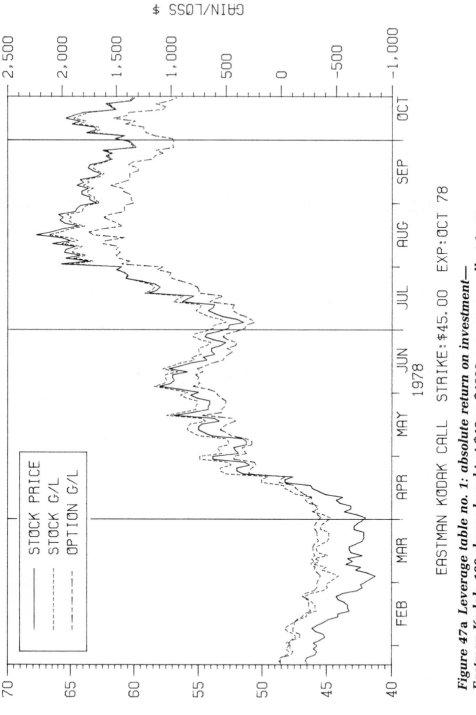

Figure 47a Leverage table no. 1: absolute return on investment—
Eastman Kodak, 100 shares bought at $46 or $4600 versus one call at $4.60
or $460 (excluding commissions and margin effects).

188

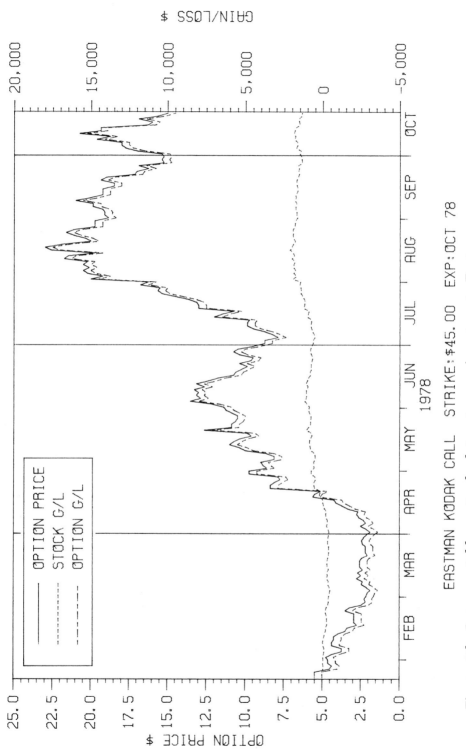

Figure 47b Leverage table no. 2: absolute return on investment—Eastman Kodak, 100 shares bought at $46 or $4600 versus 10 calls at $4.60 or $4600 (excluding commissions and margin effects).

189

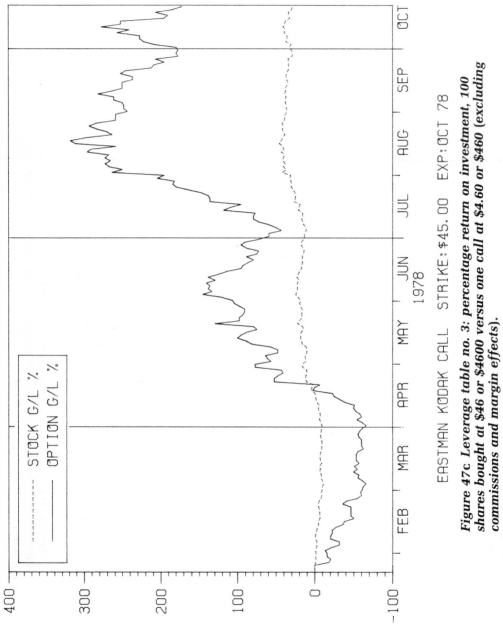

EASTMAN KODAK CALL STRIKE:$45.00 EXP:OCT 78

Figure 47c Leverage table no. 3: percentage return on investment, 100 shares bought at $46 or $4600 versus one call at $4.60 or $460 (excluding commissions and margin effects).

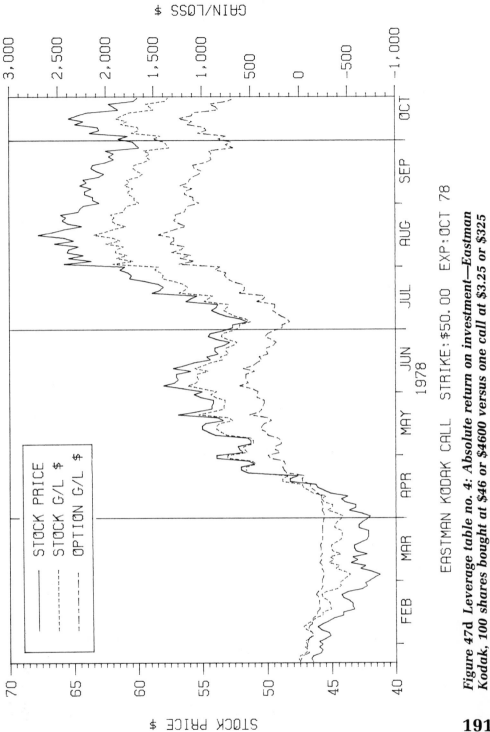

Figure 47d *Leverage table no. 4: Absolute return on investment—Eastman Kodak, 100 shares bought at $46 or $4600 versus one call at $3.25 or $325 (excluding commissions and margin effects).*

191

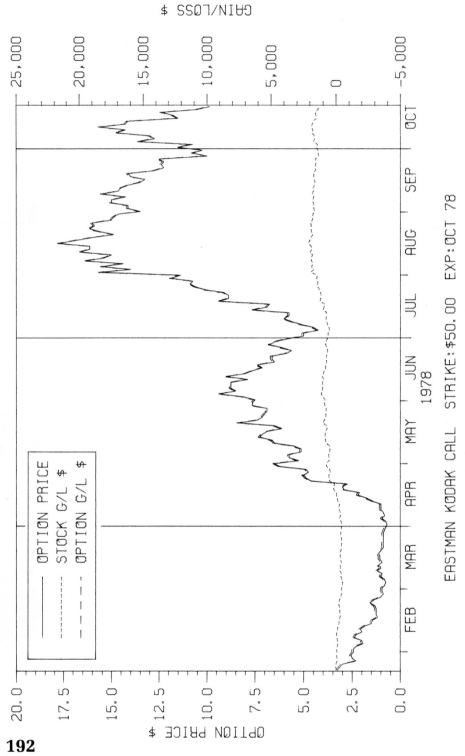

Figure 47e Leverage table no. 5: Return on 100 shares at $46 versus 15 calls at $3.25; total investment: $4600 (excluding commissions and margin effects).

192

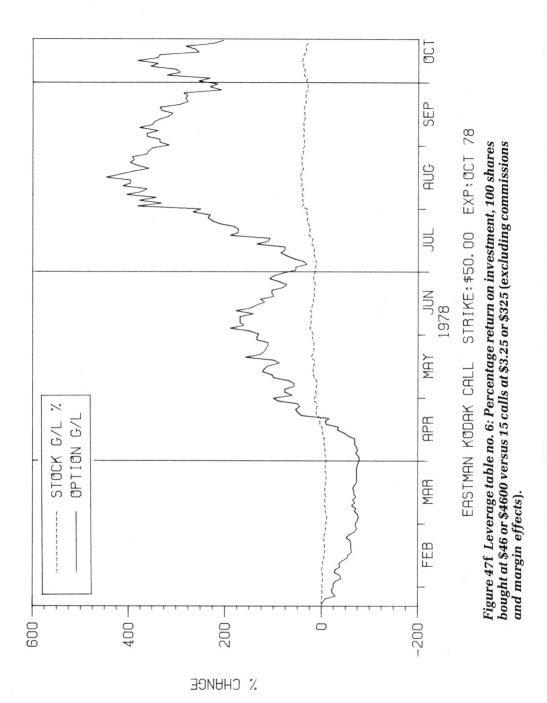

EASTMAN KODAK CALL STRIKE: $50.00 EXP: OCT 78

Figure 47f Leverage table no. 6: Percentage return on investment, 100 shares bought at $46 or $4600 versus 15 calls at $3.25 or $325 (excluding commissions and margin effects).

193

Strategy II: The Writer of Uncovered Calls

The small investor rarely acts as an options writer. The majority of options sales are covered writing transactions and are almost exclusively conducted by big investors. We discuss later the various motivations investors have for writing calls, but their prevailing intention is to increase the return on the portfolio with a regular income from net premiums. The net premium is paid immediately when the call is written.

It is not true that the purchase of a call option is more dangerous than writing a call. Both options forms require an in-depth knowledge of the subject and each can prove the best investment strategy for any one individual investor. But even if an investor turns to options writing, it does not free him from the necessity of good timing judgment and the constant supervision of his positions. If he wants to be successful in writing options, the sound selection of exercise prices and expiration dates is just as important as with the purchase of an option.

The big investors prefer the writing of calls, and particularly covered writing transactions, to other strategies, since on principle they act more prudently. If they are institutional investors, they follow the requirements of their statutes, or they may just have an aversion against speculations with a high risk. These investors consider options a supplementary operation and not primarily a means to double an investment within a very short time. Like all long-term investors in stocks, they have plenty of time, enough capital, stamina, and a great fund of experience to formulate strategies that further their interests. Their investment strategies are designed with the long-term maintenance of capital in mind, and an expected return of 10 to 20% per year. Any salesman who tries to talk a speculator into buying options and has the audacity to mention these figures will not be very successful in his canvassing. But the options writer often benefits from the stupidity of the options buyer who does not hesitate to pay net premiums of up to 15 or 20% of the stock value. The effects of the remaining life of an option also work to the advantage of the options writer because they cause the net premiums to deteriorate as the expiration date approaches and thus clearly support the profit-making process. In the following, we examine the wide spectrum of possibilities available to the writer of a call and the risks and opportunities connected with this operation.

The American investor, unlike his German counterpart, is allowed to write uncovered calls for exchange traded options, that is, he can write the option without owning the underlying securities. Instead of buying the stocks, he deposits a sum of at least 30% (exchange minimum) of the stock value as a margin with his brokerage house. (Brokerage houses have somewhat different house rules.) The writer of a call pledges to deliver the underlying securities until the expiration date of the option at exercise price, whenever the purchaser exercises the option. For this commitment he receives the options price. If he does not own the underlying security when the option is exercised, he has to buy it at the current market price and make delivery at the exercise price. The writer of a naked call therefore speculates on a declining or stagnating stock price. If he is right, and has correctly interpreted the market situation he can make a substantial profit with a small capital investment (if the stocks go down). If he was wrong, however, his loss is—theoretically—unlimited, depending on the price increase of the stock.

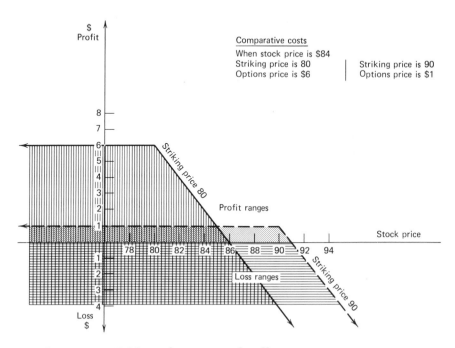

Figure 48   Writing of uncovered calls.

The writer of an uncovered call should take a position in the near expiration month. He should try to exploit the inevitable depreciation of the net premium to his advantage. But if he not only wants to profit by the depreciation of the net premium but also to participate in the depreciation of the intrinsic value of the option owing to the price decline of the stock, he will select an exercise price that is below the stock price. If he only wants to speculate on the net premium, he chooses an exercise price above the stock price. To show the extent of risks and opportunities with this form of investment, the various possibilities are demonstrated with Texas Instruments (TXN).

Example:

	Stock price of TXN					$84
	October 80 call					6
	October 90 call					1

	Option exercise price 80			Option exercise price 90		
Stock price	Profit + loss share	Return options	Total profit + loss	Profit + loss share	Return from options	Total profit + loss
94	−14	+6	−8	−4	+1	−3
92	−12	+6	−6	−2	+1	−1
90	−10	+6	−4	0	+1	+1
88	− 8	+6	−2	0	+1	+1
86	− 6	+6	±0	0	+1	+1
84	− 4	+6	+2	0	+1	+1
82	− 2	+6	+4	+0	+1	+1
80	0	+6	+6	+0	+1	+1
78	0	+6	+6	+0	+1	+1
76	0	+6	+6	+0	+1	+1

The investor was able to write an uncovered call exercise price 80 for $6 with the stock price at $84. If the stock remains at $84 until the expiration date, the net premium of $2 is the profit. If the price declines, the investor can make an additional profit through the depreciation of the intrinsic value of the call. The profit can never be more than the options price of $6, however, no matter how far below $80 the stock is traded on the expiration day. If the stock price goes up, the investor will lose dollar by dollar as soon as it starts rising above $86.

It is obvious how dangerous such a position can be. Short-term price increases can come about at any time. The investor is unprotected unless he rebuys his position at a loss. The options premium will depreciate very quickly as the expiration date approaches. If the option trades without net premium and there is an upward trend, the investor is faced daily with the possibility that he will be called upon to deliver. Such risky speculations therefore are only for the investor who is able to make a relatively accurate forecast about the probability of a price decline with the help of suitable analytical tools.

The business failure of several specialists on the exchange floor is ample proof of the dangers inherent in writing uncovered calls at low exercise prices. These traders are the only group of investors in the market who steadily make good returns, since they can tap the incoming orders for insider knowledge. Nevertheless, they too make wrong decisions in options again and again. The amount of margin calls can in some cases prove too much for the financial resources of the trader.

The investor who, in the TXN example, had written an option for $1 at high exercise price 90 in the near expiration month with the stock price at $84 can feel much more secure. He has purposely refused to participate in the profit possible with declining stock prices and instead acquired a large safety margin with the high exercise price—he falls in to the red only if the stock price rises above $91. Since the effects of the remaining life of the option are such that the net premium will hardly increase, even if there were a short-term rally to $88 or $89, the investor can carry out these transactions without precise analytical tools. Even if the stock should rise above $90, he can still repurchase the option on the exchange with a minimal loss; possibly he would break even.

This form of investment appeals strongly to all conservative option investors who want to realize a supplementary return on their treasury bills. Before nearly every expiration date, such stocks as Texas Instruments, IBM, and Eastman Kodak, offer the possibility to write uncovered options at a high exercise price (see Figure 49). Even with a net premium of only $5/16, the investor can realize a net amount of $250 by selling 10 calls naked. This relatively safe form of achieving a supplementary return is certainly not used enough, either for the stock portfolio or the treasuries investment. Because hardly a month passes without an expiration date that offers such

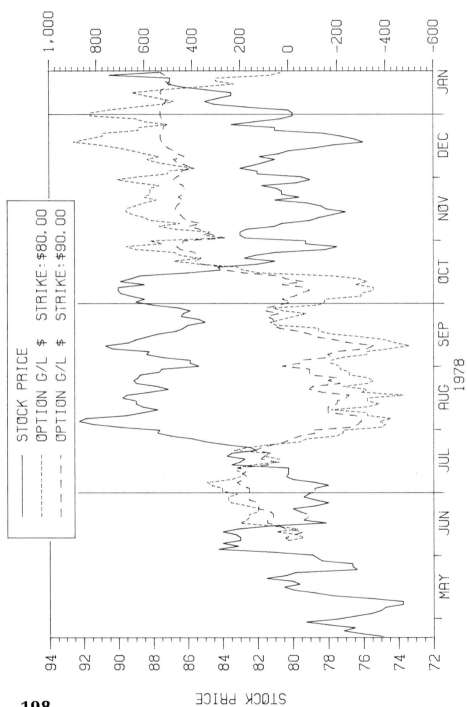

Figure 49   Stock price versus naked call Texas Instruments option: Jan. 80, 90.

advantageous premiums, a profitable and safe investment strategy could be to search for those opportunities and the continuous income from net premiums derived from them. The investor has to keep in mind that at least 30% of the value of 100 shares has to be deposited with the brokerage account for each uncovered call written. Therefore no more calls should be sold naked or the investor is able to buy the shares if he is exercised.

Summary

The writing of uncovered calls is often represented as the most risky form of speculation and therefore most options investors prefer to stay away from it. This interpretation is wrong. It is only theoretically possible that the investor will suffer an unlimited loss if he writes an uncovered call at an exercise price below the stock price. The investor can at any time liquidate his position on the exchange and thus limit the possible loss. The time that leads to the depreciation of net premiums works for the options writer. The net premium is a safety margin that no options buyer can command.

The investor has not only the safety margin of the expiring net premium in his favor during the near expiration month when he writes uncovered calls at an exercise price above the stock price; he also has the safety margin between the current stock price, and the higher exercise price protects him even further. Even though high exercise prices in the near expiration month bring only small net premiums, these amounts can improve the total return because they are a steady supplement to the stock portfolio return. The margin of 30 to 40% of the portfolio presents a barrier that stops the investor from taking too many positions in options. The investor who is careful by nature and refuses to invest too much money in options will not be deterred by this margin. The failure of most investment strategies with this type of options trading is mainly owing to the fact that many investors cannot bring themselves to follow through with an investment speculating on a bearish market. They jump back and forth in their evaluation of the possible price fluctuation. Furthermore, this form of options trading is still not widely known.

Valid Strategies

● 1. The Professional Speculator

His strategy

◇ Writes uncovered calls in the near or medium expiration month.

◇ Writes uncovered calls at exercise price below the stock price.

Why Not Recommended for Total Capital Investment?

◇ Because of the safety margin, at the most 70% of the total capital can be used for options.

◇ Leverage effect with uncovered calls written is smaller than that with calls purchased.

◇ Profit is limited to the amount of the options price received, whereas theoretically there is no limit to the loss if the stock price increases.

◇ Additional insecurity, since the investor has to be prepared at all times to deliver the underlying securities.

Why Conditionally Recommended for 10−20% of Total Capital Investment?

Advantage:

◇ Risk can be calculated with know-how, market experience, and discipline as well as good timing.

◇ Since the net premium becomes worthless on the expiration date, the remaining lifetime of an option always has an advantageous effect.

◇ The danger that the option may be exercised can be avoided by the timely repurchase of the options contract.

◇ The psychological pressure is less with small capital investment.

Disadvantages

◇ The leverage effect is too small compared to that of the total capital commitment.

◇ The investor has to spend too much time on this strategy for the resulting opportunities.

● **2. The Nonprofessional Speculator**

His strategy

◇ Writing of uncovered calls.

Why Not Recommended for Both Full Capital Investment and Investment of 10–20% of Total Capital Investment?

◇ Aggressive investment policy as a rule becomes disastrous when active supervision is lacking.

◇ Unlimited risk if market is judged wrongly.

◇ Additional risk in case the option is exercised.

● **3. The Conservative Professional Investor**

His strategy

◇ Writes uncovered calls in near or medium expiration month.

◇ Writes uncovered calls with exercise price above the stock price.

Why Not Recommended for Full Capital Investment?

◇ Because of safety margin, 70% at the most of the total capital can be used for options.

◇ Form of investment is too aggressive to ensure maintenance of capital and capital growth aimed for by the investor.

◇ Expected returns can be realized better with conservative strategies with less risk.

Why Recommended for 10–20% of Total Capital Investment?

◇ Return of a well-diversified portfolio with stocks and treasuries can be improved at low risk by writing uncovered calls.

◇ Application of know-how, experience, and good timing can virtually eliminate risk.

◇ Writing uncovered calls in the near or medium expiration month with high exercise prices promises small (50¢–$1) but safe returns.

◇ The risk that the option may be exercised is relatively small because of the high exercise price.

◇ The necessary safety margin is supplied by stocks and treasuries held in the portfolio.

● **4. The Conservative Non-Professional Investor**

His strategy

◇ Writes uncovered calls.

Why Not Recommended for Both Total and 10–20% of Total Capital Investment?

◇ Selection of suitable options is too difficult.

◇ The risk cannot be controlled and does not suit the investor's mentality.

Strategy III: The Sale of Covered Calls

There are several choices for selling a stock. The conservative stock investor prefers the strategy of the covered writer. The investor first buys a stock and writes calls against it, either immediately or later on. If the option has expired or has not been exercised, a new call can be written either at once or at a later time. The purpose of the whole process is that the investor increases his return and receives in addition to the regular income from dividends the net premiums from writing options. Because experience has shown that less than half the options are exercised, the written calls yield a good supplementary income to those investors who have too little time to watch the stock price fluctuations closely.

Basically, the writing of calls against securities in the portfolio can be considered a strategy with a "limited risk." The limitation of risk, however, always entails a limitation of earnings as well. One cannot claim therefore that covered calls have only advantages. The strategy works best if the entire stock market moves up and down in short fluctuations, as occurred in 1976 to 1977. During this period IBM 280 calls could have been written four times with a total net premium income of approximately $60 without the security having once been called. As Figure 50 shows, IBM fluctuated between $245 and $286 during this time.

Because an option can be repurchased at any time, an adjustment to the market fluctuations of IBM and many other stocks could be

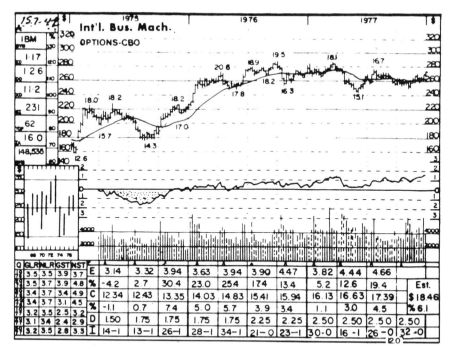

Figure 50   IBM.

made by writing the option as a covered writer's position when the calculation with technical tools indicated that the stock price was going to rise greatly. With a price decline, the drop in the stock price could be compensated to a great degree by the depreciation of the net premium. If the net premium still traded with a residual value and the expiration date was still far enough away, the repurchase of the option made sense. The stock was allowed to pass the next price increase without an option having been written, but at the next higher level, the option was written again. This example is based on factual market data of IBM, but it should nevertheless only be seen as a stimulus and suggestion for a profitable investment strategy because this strategy, usually very effective, also contains some dangers and cannot always be applied successfully. Good timing is an absolute necessity for the covered writers strategy although it is only needed when the stock price has decreased by the amount of the net premium—that is, the very last point when a timing decision has to made about whether:

◇ The stock should be sold.

◇ A new call should be written against the security at a lower exercise price.

◇ The stock has enough strength to go up again.

The investor who purchases a stock hopes to make a profit with the price increase. When he simultaneously writes a call, he hopes to receive an additional return in the net premium. Since by writing the call he has also undertaken the obligation to deliver the underlying securities at the exercise price (if exercised), he in reality sells the stock at the exercise price plus the net premium. If the price declines, the investor uses the options price to protect himself at least in part against a loss in the stock price.

A Practical Example to Emphasize the Above

Xerox (XRX) could be bought for $60 in October. At the same time, the investor could write the option XRX April 60 call for $9. Although this net premium may seem high, it corresponds to the current market price. It is rare that net premiums of about 15% of the stock value are paid, but it does happen occasionally. Expressed in figures, this example would appear as follows on the expiration date of the option (without commissions):

Example:

Stock price XRX $60 in October
XRX April 60 call at $9

Stock price	Profit + loss stock	Profit + loss stock	Return from option written	Total profit + loss
70	+10	−10	+9	+9
68	+ 8	− 8	+9	+9
66	+ 6	− 6	+9	+9
64	+ 4	− 4	+9	+9
62	+ 2	− 2	+9	+9
60	0	0	+9	+9
58	− 2	0	+9	+7
56	− 4	0	+9	+5
54	− 6	0	+9	+3
52	− 8	0	+9	+1
50	−10	0	+9	−1
48	−12	0	+9	−3

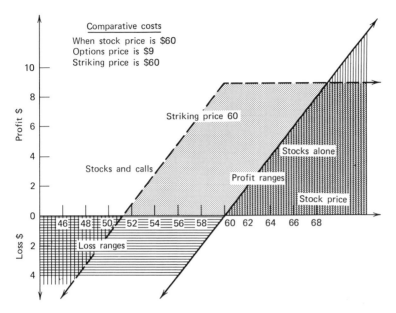

Comparative costs
When stock price is $60
Options price is $9
Striking price is $60

Profit $

Loss $

Striking price 60

Stocks and calls

Stocks alone

Profit ranges

Stock price

Loss ranges

Figure 51   Writing of covered calls.

The graphic representation of this situation appears in Figure 51. With the purchase of the Xerox at $60 and the simultaneous writing of the April 60 call at $9, the investor was in the following position: as the covered writer he had reduced the basic delivery price of the securities, 60 − 9 = $51, by receiving the $9 net premium (without commissions). If the stock price went below $51 before the expiration day, the investor would incur losses with his stock if he had no other way of protecting himself against a further decline in the market. As long as the stock price fluctuates between $51 and $60 up to the expiration day, it depends on the options buyer's calculations as to whether he suffers a loss or can gloat over a profit—commissions included—if he exercises the option. If on the expiration day the price is above the exercise price of $60, the buyer will certainly exercise his option and demand delivery of the underlying securities. Even if the stock price is above the exercise price 60 when the buyer exercises the option, the writer has to deliver at exercise price 60. But since he has already received the net premium of $9 from the options sold, his total sales price of the stock will be $69 in any case (without commission). However, the writer cannot achieve a larger return, no matter how much higher the price of the stock will rise. Because in this example the investor has purchased the stock at $60, he will realize a return of 15% on his capital in six months when the purchaser exercises his option.

How To Combine Various Exercise Prices and Expiration Dates

In the example just discussed, the underlying assumption was that the investor had written the April 60 call at exercise price $9 at the same time he had acquired the stock for $60. Since there are several exercise prices and expiration dates, however, the investor in this case can have the choice between the following possibilities:

October	Premium in $	January	Premium in $	April	Premium in $
Exercise price 50	13	Exercise price 50	15	Exercise price 50	17
Exercise price 60	4	Exercise price 60	7	Exercise price 60	9
Exercise price 70	$5/16$	Exercise price 70	3	Exercise price 70	$4\frac{1}{2}$

On the one hand, the basic strategy of the investor is aimed toward the highest possible supplementary return from his investment (he wants the highest premium). On the other, he wants to have the best possible protection against a price decline (he wants the highest exercise price). The investor will achieve the highest net premium and thus the highest return on the option, if the exercise price and stock price are very close to each other (in this case, an exercise price of 60) and the expiration month is as far away as possible (April).

The April 50 call seems to be the best choice because it has the highest premium of $17. However, since the options price is a combination of the $10 intrinsic value (stock price of $60/minus exercise price $50 = $10) the net premium is only $7; the exercise price of an April 60 call has in fact the highest net premium of $9 and therefore the highest returns. Returns on options can only be based on the net premium, never the intrinsic value. Quite often the investor is not satisfied with the highest possible return but wants to have the optimum protection for his stock against a possible price decline. The investor can manage this if he chooses a lower exercise price. The following alternatives are possible:

October 50 call at $13
January 50 call at $15
April 50   call at $17

Mathematically, the investor has reduced the stock price to $60 - 17 = \$43$ (without commission) when he wrote the April 50 call for $17. But since with the options contract he has undertaken the obligation to deliver the underlying security at the exercise price at any time, he immediately takes the loss of $10 (the difference between the stock price 60 and the exercise price 50) into account with this strategy. With the options price of $17, which is the combination of the $10 intrinsic value with the $7 net premium, only $7 remain as a profit from his investment—that is, 13% with fully paid stocks. Given the maximum profit of $7, the stock can decrease to $43 before the investor starts to lose.

If the investor is more speculatively inclined and convinced that the price will undergo at least a medium-term favorable development, he can also use exercise price 70 for his investment strategy. Using the same example of Xerox, the investor can choose between January, with exercise price 70 and a net premium of $3, or April, with exercise price 70 and a net premium of $4½. If he takes the exercise price of 70 in April he has essentially sold his stocks at the price of $74½ = (70 + 4½). Compared to the opportunities obtainable with exercise price 50 or 60, the investor gets the best return with the April 70, provided the stock price is at $70 or more on the expiration day. In that case, he can make a profit of $10 on the stock [exercise price $70 - \$60$ (purchase price stock) = $10] and $4½ net premium—that is, he can realize $14½ on the expiration date. With the higher return, however, the investor has a smaller safety margin against a price decline; in this case, the stock should not fall below $55½.

The changes in the separate exercise prices up to the expiration date are graphically represented in Figure 52.

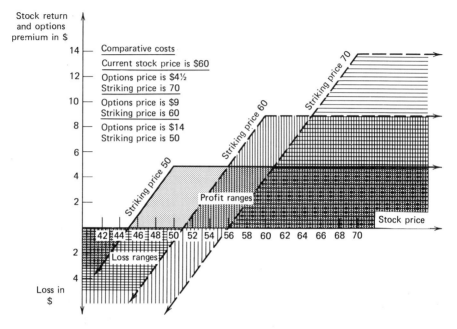

Figure 52   Writing of covered calls.

How To Protect Stocks With Calls Against A Price Decline

If the investor cannot handle the timing aspect but wants to protect his stocks against falling prices, the exchange traded options offer him an alternative: he can protect against the price decline by writing calls at the lower exercise price several times over.

For example on May 5, Xerox was bought at $76. The market was in good shape at the time, and there was no reason to suspect that the price would materially deteriorate. At the same time the stock was purchased, an October call exercise price 80 was written with a premium of $10⅛. The investor had decreased the delivery price per share to about $66 (76 − 10⅛ = 65⅞) by writing the net premium exercise price 80. When in July the stock price fell below $70, and the capital investment approached the loss range, the October 80 call written previously could now be repurchased for $1⅛. The investor had at that point realized a return of $9. At the same time, a new option could be written at exercise price 70 with a net premium of $6⅝. With this net pre-

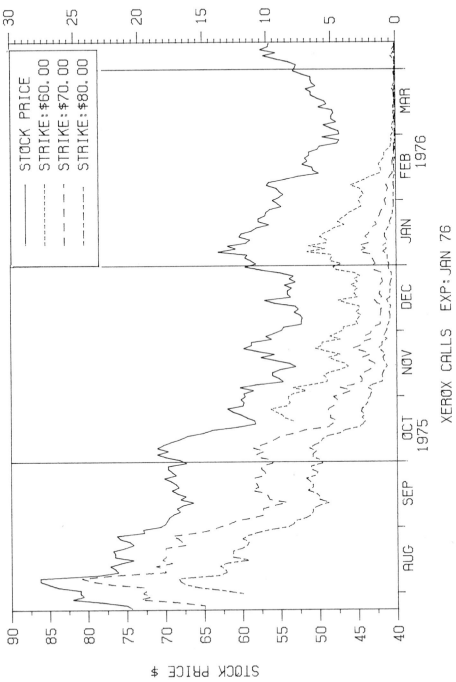

Figure 53   Xerox, covered writing data, three calls and stock movement.

mium, the investor was protected with $6⅝ against a further price decline. Although all indications were against a further price decline of Xerox, the price again deteriorated when it became known that the company was going to sell its computer division and would suffer such losses that dividend payments would be made for the third quarter, 1975. The price fell below $60 (see Figure 53). Now the investor could repurchase his option October exercise price 70 at $1¼ and write a new October 60 call for $6½.

The process once again in figures:

Date		Expenses (in $)	Return (in $)
5/22	Purchase of 1000 Xerox at $76	76,000.00	
	Commissions	628.00	
5/22	10 XRX October 80 calls with a net premium of $10⅛		10,125.00
	Commissions for writing 10 options	192.31	
6/16	Price of Xerox at $68		
	Repurchase of 10 XRX October 80's at $1⅛	1,125.00	
	Commissions for repurchase of options	95.29	
6/16	10 XRX October 70 calls written for $6⅝		6,625.00
	Commission for writing 10 options	161.75	
7/24	Price of Xerox at $58		
	Repurchase of 10 XRX October 70's at $1¼	1,250.00	
	Commission for repurchase of options	93.20	
7/24	10 XRX October 60 calls written at $6½		6,500.00
10/24		Options expire. Option has not been exercised since the price is below $60	
		79,545.55	23,250.00
	Net premiums received	23,250.00	
	Purchase price of the stocks with options prices taken into account	56,295.55	

Although the investor who had bought the stock at the price of $76 had suffered a loss of $17,000 or 23.5% when Xerox was quoted with $59 on October 26, the investor who had protected himself with writing calls against a price deterioration could still show a return of $2276.45 or approximately 3.8% (59,000 − 56,295.55 − 428 commission = $2276.45).

Whenever an investor writes a new call at a lower exercise price, he has to estimate whether the stock price will continue to fall or go up again. Covered writing transactions can be considered an insurance against price deterioration, but good timing strategy is still the foremost requirement.

Criteria for Covered Writers' Transactions

Criterion 1: The Options Price. If a stock is to be kept in the portfolio, a protection against a price decline only makes sense if, in addition to that protection, the investor can also expect a good return when he writes the option. With a stronger upward price movement, the profit from the stock is limited to the amount of the net premium if the exercise price of the option is below the stock price. Therefore, the investor should only write a call with a net premium of 10 to 15% of the stock price when the exercise price is below the stock price. If he chooses an exercise price above the stock price, the expected return is greater when the stock price goes up, but the protection against a price decline is smaller.

Criterion 2: The Exercise Prices. Good protection can only be granted if a sufficiently large safety margin exists against a possible price deterioration right from the beginning. This safety margin can be achieved by the selection (or existence) of the proper exercise price. For a safety strategy, the call should trade not only one but at least two exercise prices below the stock price. For the exercise price closest to the stock price, a net premium of 12 to 15% should be realized for the option. New exercise prices are introduced only after a stock price has gone up or down, and therefore the two exercise prices below the actual stock price are of paramount importance when the stock is bought. How valuable these two existing low exercise prices can be is illustrated with the case of Houston Oil & Minerals. On February 2, 1978, the security was still traded at $29. When the company announced that the oil and gas reserves had been overestimated, the stock price went down to about $20 within two days. Since a call of 20 was not available for trading, a protection of the stock by means of writing such a call was not possible. After it had been introduced, the options price had declined so sharply that it made no sense to write a call at 20 because of the small net premium.

Criterion 3: The Expiration Month. An optimum safety strategy is only practicable with a correspondingly high premium. Only the medium and distant expiration months are suitable for the investor on the lookout for a good return.

Criterion 4: The Termination of the Options Contract at No Loss. To ensure an optimum protection against a price decline the investor may be forced to switch to a lower exercise price. This, however, only makes sense if the options price had declined in dollars as much as the stock, because only then is the price loss from the stock compensated by the profit from the written call. This is shown with the aid of the Xerox example. It depends on the remaining lifetime and leverage of the option whether the options price will decrease as quickly as the stock price.

Criterion 5: The Price Level of the Stock. Given two stocks, one at $20, and the other $100, the lower-priced stock will always fall more quickly (by 10%) from $20 to $18 than the more expensive stock (by 10%) from $100 to $90, as previous experience has shown. The less expensive the security is in dollars, therefore, the more the degree of uncertainty in the safety strategy is magnified. The degree of uncertainty is further increased by the difference of the exercise prices among each other. With a stock price below $50, the graduation of the exercise price is always $5. Although the difference between 50 and 45 is only 10%, the percentage difference between exercise price 25 and 20 comes to 20%. The safety margin with inexpensive securities is therefore greatly restricted by the difference in the exercise prices. The investor should try to protect those stocks with options whose net premium is greater than the difference of two exercise prices, that is, with a stock price of $50, the options price should at least be $5 (the difference of exercise price 45 to exercise price 50 = 5).

Criterion 6: The Influence of Commissions. The question of commissions plays a very important role in a successful safety strategy when stocks are purchased and combined with written options. Since the cost reduction is very big with an increasing number of stocks and options, the investor should not buy fewer than 500 shares of one stock and write five calls against them.

The preceding criteria are only valid if the investor wants to take as little risk as possible. For those investors who want to retain the stocks in any case, it is best to choose an exercise price above the stock price because in addition to the net premium, he can realize a profit from the stocks if they go up. The investor who is only interested in the additional return should write the options at a high exercise price in the near expiration month several times a year because

◇ Although the return is very small because of the high exercise price, it is extremely safe.

◇ There is hardly any danger that the underlying securities will have to be delivered.

It is not true that a covered writer who has written an option with a medium expiration month always has to wait for the option to expire. A strong short-term price increase of a stock such as that of Pittston PCO, which rose in 1976 within three weeks from $35 to $45, (as shown in Figure 54) causes the total deterioration of the net premium. Many option buyers discover a strong yearning to exercise the option in order to get possession of the stocks. In the case of Pittston, the covered writer had to deliver after three weeks, but he could take the net premium income of 15% as a profit.

Summary

The purchase of stocks combined with the writing of calls is the strategy preferred by conservative investors who engage in call transactions. They consider the option an auxiliary means to achieve safe returns. The investor is primarily interested in the stock that he wants to hold in his portfolio on a long-term basis. Through the variation of exercise prices and expiration dates, it is possible to use these covered writer combinations either more aggressively or more conservatively. With a more aggressive strategic aim, good timing becomes ever more important.

Covered writing combinations are certainly no magic formula for hitting the jackpot every time. If a stock such as Eastman Kodak or Burroughs, to mention only two, decreases within a few months by more than 50% of its value, the loss can be kept smaller by writing the calls, but not totally eliminated. The well-considered purchase

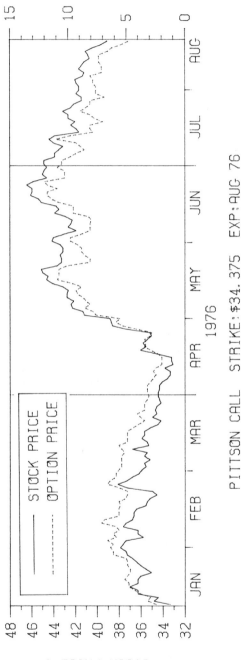

PITTSON CALL   STRIKE:$34.375   EXP:AUG 76

214

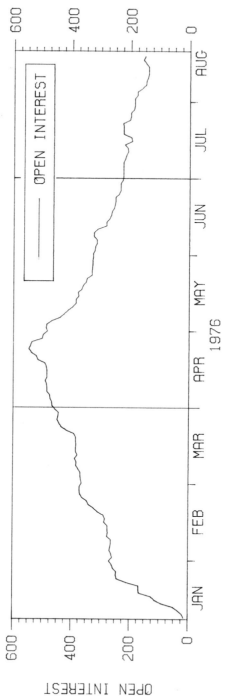

Figure 54 Pittston covered writing data, stock and option movement.

215

of options, therefore, can often be a much better strategy than the covered writing combination if one only has the return in mind. If the investor wants to put his capital in stocks, the covered writing combinations are often preferable to the exclusive investment in stocks. Good covered writers positions—that is, those with high net premiums—are not always available. It is therefore recommended that the investor who wants to take such a position await the "proper" time. Daily papers, market letters, and brokerage houses give out information about the various options prices and thus offer help in making decisions about when would be the best time to enter these transactions.

Valid Strategies

- **1.The Professional Speculator**

    His strategy

    ◇ Writing of covered calls

    Why Not Recommended for Both Full and Limited Capital Investment:

    ◇ Since capital is tied to stocks in the portfolio, only a small part of the entire capital is available for calls.

    ◇ The leverage effect of the option can only be used in a limited way.

    ◇ Expected returns are small, measured by an aggressive investment policy.

    ◇ Compared to the opportunities the small capital investment offers the investor has to spend too much time on this strategy.

    ◇ Once the covered call is written, active participation is no longer possible.

- **2. The Nonprofessional Speculator**

    His strategy

    ◇ Writing of covered calls

Why Not Recommended for Both Full and Limited Capital Investment:

◇ The same arguments apply as for the professional speculator.

● **3. The Conservative Professional Investor**

His strategy

◇ Purchases stocks.

◇ Writes calls in near, medium, or distant expiration month.

◇ Writes calls at exercise prices below, at, or above the current stock price.

Why Not Recommended for Full Capital Investment:

◇ The strategy is not applicable because most of the capital is tied to the stocks in the portfolio and only a small portion of the entire capital is available for calls.

Why Recommended for 10 to 20% of Total Capital Investment:

◇ Know-how, experience, and timing strategies have been predominantly gained from working with stocks.

◇ The writing of the call requires no additional safety margin because it is covered by stocks in the portfolio.

◇ The writing of calls is an auxiliary means for protection against price losses with stocks and a means to achieve a safe additional return.

◇ Dividend payments on stocks and other return from stocks are not affected.

◇ The selection of expiration months and exercise prices enables the investor to follow a more conservative or a more speculative strategy without negating the aims of capital preservation and capital growth.

◇ Stocks can be liquidated at any time since the investor can repurchase the option on the exchange.

◇ The investor does not have to wait for the expiration date of the option but can make use of good timing indicators. Short-term adaptation to market fluctuations is possible.

Danger:

◇ The investor must be prepared for the necessity of delivering the underlying securities when the stock price is above the exercise price of the option.

● **4. The Conservative Nonprofessional Investor**

His strategy

◇ Purchases stocks.

◇ Writes calls in the most distant expiration month.

◇ Writes calls at exercise prices below or near the stock price.

◇ Net premium of approximately 10 to 15%.

Why Not Recommended for Full Capital Investment:

◇ Capital is tied to stocks in the portfolio and only a small portion of the entire capital is available for options.

Why Recommended for 10 to 20% of the Total Capital Investment:

◇ The desired aim of capital preservation and capital growth is guaranteed.

◇ A high net premium ensures good return if the stock price increases, and offers good protection if the price goes down.

◇ The strategy can be carried out without an advisor, market experience, and timing. The study of the market page in the papers is sufficient.

◇ With the contract agreed upon, the investor need concern himself with the option again only when the stock price has decreased by 10 to 15%.

◇ Dividends and other returns from stocks are not affected.

Strategy IV: The Purchase of Put Options

Listed put options were introduced in June 1977, and the investor then had the opportunity to profit either speculatively or conservatively from a price decline in stocks. Puts offer the same wide investment spectrum as calls, but for a poor market. We find the same naive and unsophisticated speculator in this arena, too: with the battle cry "all or nothing" he jumps head over heels into the market—in the near expiration month, without a sense for timing, without an investment strategy, but with tremendous (and erroneous) self-confidence. He will be flabbergasted and righteously incensed, nonetheless, if he loses his entire capital within a very short time, since he has no sense of his own shortcomings. Of course, once in a while he will hit the jackpot, make a profit of several hundred percent in a single transaction, and promptly and proudly ascribe this success to his immense qualifications as a speculator. Measured by the degree of speculation in calls, the speculation in put options is really quite modest. Most investors encounter psychological difficulties with speculating on a price decline, and therefore the volume of puts tends to be essentially smaller than the volume of comparable calls. The lower volume is also reflected in the comparatively smaller premiums of puts.

The conservative investor who considers puts practically a down payment on the short sale of a stock or does not fool himself that his timing is perfect finds a wide spectrum of investment strategies in the various exercise prices and expiration months. The purchase of a put is often preferable to short-selling the stock. The investor has nearly the same opportunities for making a profit as with the short sale of stocks, but the risk is limited to the loss of the capital investment. The big problem here, as with the call, is the tendency of the investor to underestimate the leverage effect of the options. Many investors cannot restrain themselves so as to buy only one put instead of short selling 100 shares. Although this one put would suffice to obtain opportunities similar to those the short sale of 100 shares provides, the investor somehow feels compelled to buy 5 or 10 put options. Many investors seem to think it simply ridiculous to invest only $100 in an option instead of $10,000 in stocks, and to leave the remaining capital in the account in fixed-interest bearing securities.

Some Examples of the Effect of Different Expiration Dates and Exercise Prices

In September 1977 IBM was quoted at $260 and had the following put prices:

Example: Puts

Month	Exercise price	Option price	Month	Exercise price	Option price	Month	Exercise price	Option price
October	280	21	January	280	23	April	280	25
October	260	5	January	260	7	April	260	9
October	240	1	January	240	2½	April	240	4

The Speculative Buyer of Puts

As with calls, the greatest interest concentrates on puts in the near expiration date. This is plainly indicated by the relatively high volume. Since the price of IBM (in dollars) can fluctuate greatly at any time, the speculative interest focuses on the exercise price near the stock price $260 (exercise price 260) or below it (exercise price 240), although at this point the options trade with a net premium, which will be zero on the expiration day. That the danger of a total loss is at its peak with these near exercise prices is consciously or subconsciously suppressed—and understandably so, since nobody likes to think about losses. The more prudent speculator should therefore take a position in the high exercise price of 280, because at that level the option trades practically without net premium and it will move parallel to the stock price, dollar by dollar. As with calls, the speculator in the near expiration date has to struggle with two troublesome factors:

◇ The proper judgment of the stock price movement and
◇ The mandatory expiration of the net premium.

The Conservative Buyer of Put Options

The conservative speculator in puts buys his options in a more distant expiration date. The net premiums are a little bit higher, but the safety margin until the expiration date of the option is decidedly greater. Furthermore, the negative influences of the remaining lifetimes of the options make themselves very much less felt in the more distant expiration months. The investor can decide to exercise his options at any time up to the expiration date, depending on how he judges the price development of the stock. It seems to make much more sense and is safer, too, to take a position with the IBM January 260 put at $7 than to purchase the same option in the expiration month October at $5. In figures, the possibilities of profit and loss on the expiration date January are as follows:

Example:

Stock prices	Profit + loss (stock IBM)	Cost of option	Profit + loss total	Profit + loss (in %)
266	0	−7	−7	−100
264	0	−7	−7	−100
262	0	−7	−7	−100
260	0	−7	−7	−100
258	2	−7	−5	− 70
256	4	−7	−3	− 43
254	6	−7	−1	− 14
252	8	−7	+1	+ 14
250	10	−7	+3	+ 43
248	12	−7	+5	+ 70

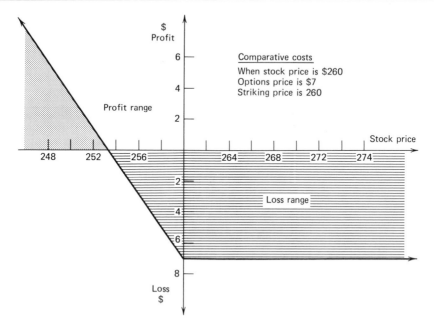

Figure 55 Purchase of a put.

The graphic representation of the changes is shown in Figure 55.

The net premium of the 260 put in this example amounts to $7. In the graphic representation, the profit-loss line crosses the zero line at 253 and turns favorable with continuing declining prices. The investor loses his entire net premium if the option trades above the exercise price of $260 on the expiration date. With a price of $250, the investor makes $3 profit. If the stock trades between $253 and $260 on the expiration date, the investor retains the intrinsic value of the option if he sells it or exercises it—that is, he purchases the stock for $258 at the market and sells it to the options writer at the exercise price $260, as stipulated in the options contract. The speculator, however, expects the stock to trade below $253 *before* the expiration date. In that case, the options price will definitely be traded well above $7, and the investor can close out his position with a profit. No matter how high the stock price rises above $260, the loss can never become greater than the $7 options price.

Unlike the pure speculation in options, the purchase of puts offers itself as a conservative alternative to the short sale of a stock. A short sale burdens the investor with the risk of a unlimited loss if the stock price increases. The buyer of a put, however, can never lose more than his capital investment, even if the price of the stock increases, because he profits from the price decline dollar by dollar as soon as the price moves below 253. These advantages can be clearly demonstrated with IBM.

Example: When IBM was trading at $260 in September 1977, the IBM January 260 put was at $7. If the investor wanted to sell short 100 IBM, he had to deposit 50% of the share value or $13,000 as a security with his broker. Depending on whether IBM increased or declined, he could gain or lose dollar by dollar, parallel with the price movement of the stock. If the investor had alternatively chosen to acquire an IBM January 260 put, it would have cost him only $700. No matter how much IBM went up, his loss could never surpass $700. If the difference between the $13,000 minus $700 = $12,300 had been invested in fixed-interest-bearing securities, the possible loss on the put would again have been considerably reduced through the interest income.

As owner of the put, the investor could sit back quietly and watch the constant up and down movement of the stock price without any great concern. If IBM had declined until January, a profit could be realized through selling the put. If IBM goes up and the favorable trend is stabilized, the put can be sold at its residual value on the exchange at any time, and a total loss of $700 can thus be avoided. The buyer of a put is much better off with his strategy than the investor who sells short the stock—both in a rising and a declining market. Another advantage is that unlike the investor who holds short positions in his portfolio beyond ex-dividend day, he does not have to deliver the dividend. However, as attractive as the possibility to invest only $700 in the put instead of the $13,000 necessary for the short sale would seem to the unbiased observer, this kind of investment strategy nonetheless goes against the grain of many investors. As a rule, the person who wants to take a position wants to do it wholeheartedly and immediately invest every cent set aside for that purpose. And if he cannot do it with stocks, he will turn to options. It is a rare achievement in investors' circles to do nothing but sit back quietly and watch market developments without taking a position. The individual options strategies have no built-in weaknesses; rather, the inability of those investors who cannot sustain a strategy even though they have recognized its validity makes them seem unreliable.

Conclusion

All those aspects of the options trading described before, which the buyer of calls has to weigh carefully, also must be considered by the purchaser of a put option. There is one difference: the buyer of calls counts on rising stock prices, whereas the buyer of puts bets on falling prices.

Basically, the following is true for the purchaser of puts:

◇ The maximum loss is the entire options price if the stock price is above the exercise price on the expiration date.

◇ "Unlimited" opportunities for profit if the stock price is below the exercise price of the option until the expiration date (stock cannot go under zero).

For the individual put prices in the various exercise prices and expiration months the following applies:

◇ The option is more expensive the higher the chosen exercise price is above the current stock price.

◇ The options price is smaller the lower the exercise price is below the current stock price.

◇ The options price in all exercise prices is greater the further the expiration day is away from the current stock price.

The purchase of a put not only offers the investor a wide range of investment strategies but is also a sensible supplement to protect stocks purchased. This protective action can be set in motion immediately after the purchase so as to limit the risk for the stocks right from the beginning. Alternatively, the investor can buy the put at a later date and thus ensure the profit he has achieved without having to sell the stocks.

Example: At the beginning of 1977, Inexco Oil was quoted at $14 and had increased to $28 by the middle of the year. The investor who had bought this stock at the right time was faced after this sharp price rise with the question whether he should take his profit from the stock by selling it or whether the stock should be held because it could be expected to go even higher.

The purchase of a put at exercise price 30 for $2½ was the sensible strategy which saved the investor from his quandary. With the purchase of this put option, the investor locked in the profit from the stock, no matter how much more the price would decline afterward. Also, he could still participate in a further price increase, with the exception of the $2½ he had paid for the put. The price movement of Inexco, which in November 1977 was back at $18½, shows that the purchase of the put really would have been quite the best strategy in this case (see Figure 56).

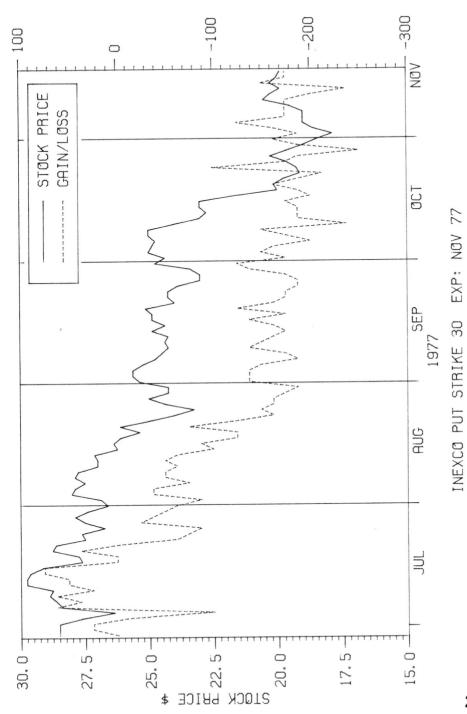

GAIN/LOSS $

STOCK PRICE $

INEXCO PUT STRIKE 30   EXP: NOV 77

STOCK PRICE
GAIN/LOSS

1977

Figure 56 Inexco, buying one put as protection of stock gains—100 shares.

225

Valid Strategies

● **1. The Professional Speculator**

His strategy

◇ Purchase of puts no nearer than approximately 6 weeks to the near expiration date or in the medium expiration month.

◇ Purchase of puts at exercise price close to the current stock price.

Why Recommended for Full Capital Investment:

◇ Big leverage effect of the option corresponds to the goal of an aggressive investment policy.

◇ Risk can be limited through expertise, market experience, discipline, and good timing.

Furthermore:

◇ Wide diversification in stocks, expiration months, and exercise prices can reduce the risk even more.

Danger:

◇ Total loss, if always fully invested and timing decisions fail completely.

Why Conditionally Recommended for 10 to 20% of Total Capital Investment:

Disadvantages:

◇ Leverage effect compared to that of the entire capital is too small.

◇ Compared to the opportunities that exist with the small capital investment, the investor has to spend too much time with this strategy.

Advantages:

◇ Psychological pressure is smaller than when fully invested. Therefore it is suitable for professional speculators who want to familiarize themselves with options.

● **2. The Nonprofessional Speculator**

His strategy

◇ Purchase of puts in the medium or most distant expiration month.

◇ Purchase of puts at an exercise price above the stock price.

Why Not Recommended for Full Capital Investment:

◇ Aggressive investment policy can prove disastrous if supervision of positions and strategies are lacking.

◇ Poor timing combined with little discipline, know-how, and market experience leads to misinterpretation of opportunities and risks in options.

◇ The risk of a total loss cannot be eliminated by giving power of attorney to a third party.

Why Recommended for 10 to 20% of the Total Capital Investment:

◇ The leverage effect of options can, even with a small investment, lead to disproportionally high profits compared with other forms of investment and thus improve the total return of a portfolio considerably.

◇ Risk can be estimated.

◇ Mistakes do not lead to total loss of capital.

◇ A distant expiration date and high exercise price can compensate for lack of timing to a certain degree.

◇ A good advisor can compensate for lack of time and other weak points on the part of the investor so that he does not have to forego the opportunities of the options.

◇ The use of small investments is a good test of whether options are suitable for bigger investments later on.

● **3. The Conservative Professional Investor**

His strategy

◇ Purchases puts in the medium or distant expiration month.

◇ Purchases puts at an exercise price near or below the stock price.

◇ Keeps the number of stocks sold through puts below the number of short sales (100 shares = 1 option).

Why Not Recommended for Total Investment Capital:

◇ Investment form is too aggressive to support the goal of capital preservation and growth.

◇ Better returns can be achieved with conservative strategies at less risk.

◇ No dividends or other returns are had from options.

Why Recommended for 10 to 20% of the Total Capital Investment:

◇ A well-diversified portfolio with treasuries and stocks can be attractively enriched by partial investment in options.

◇ Risk can be determined by know how, experience, and good timing and kept within reason.

◇ Total loss in options has little effect on the total capital.

◇ Puts can be used to achieve additional returns and also to protect stocks in the portfolio.

● **4. The Conservative Nonprofessional Investor**

His strategy

◇ Purchase of puts

Why Not Recommended for Full Capital Investment:

◇ The strategy is wrong for the mentality and goals of the investor.
◇ There is a lack of qualification.
◇ Leverage of options is too great.

Why Conditionally Recommended for 10 to 20% of Total Capital Investment:

◇ A qualified advisor can compensate for the lack of qualification in the investor to a certain extent. Thus the possibilities of options can be applied to a maximum degree in the investor's interest. In that case, the risk would be within the permissible range.

Strategy V: The Writing of Uncovered Puts

The writer of an uncovered call has earned the full net premium if the stock price is below the exercise price on the expiration date. The writer of an uncovered put, on the other hand, has fully realized his profit if the stock price is above the exercise price of the option on the expiration date. Only at that point can he be certain that the purchaser of the put will not exercise his option and deliver the stock at the exercise price. At first glance, the strategy of the uncovered put may seem absolutely paradoxical, but the conservative professional investor will follow this strategy if he considers the stock to be overpriced but would buy if only the stock price were lower, or if he expects a continuing price increase that would bring him an additional income from net premiums by writing the put. While the covered writing of calls is just another variety of stock sales, writing puts is a real alternative to the buying of stock, which could be elected instead. The writer of an uncovered put reduces the delivery price of a stock by means of the net premium received. Until the time when he might be tendered the underlying security, he invests the amount of purchase price of the stock in treasuries. He can also avoid taking delivery of the stock at any time if he repurchases the uncovered put on the exchange. Now, how big is the risk for the writer of an uncovered put? Another example will illustrate.

Example: In September 1977, Eastman Kodak was quoted at $60. With the exercise price April 60, the put commanded a net premium of $4. The price trend in figures was as follows:

Stock price	Return + loss stock	Premium option	Return + loss total
64	0	+4	+4
62	0	+4	+4
60	0	+4	+4
58	− 2	+4	+2
56	− 4	+4	+0
54	− 6	+4	−2
52	− 8	+4	−4
50	−10	+4	−6

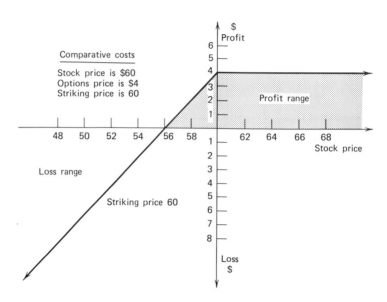

Figure 57   Writing of an uncovered put.

The graphic representation is shown in Figure 57. If the stock is at $56 on the expiration date, the investor has realized neither a profit nor suffered a loss. The buyer of the option will exercise his option, acquire the stock at the market for $56 and deliver to the writer at the exercise price of 60. Since, however, the writer has collected a net premium of $4 in advance, he does not lose anything on this trade. If the stock price rises above $56, the writer of the option begins to make a profit. With a stock price of more than $60, the buyer of the put will no longer exercise his option, since in that case he would have to buy the stock at the current price, possibly $65, and then make delivery at $60. The writer of the put has devised for himself a safety margin with the net premium that will cover him up to $56. The risk of incurring an unlimited loss with falling prices can be modified by repurchasing the puts written, so that the investor does not have to buy the stock at exercise price of 60. He can also switch to a lower exercise price; that is, he rebuys the option with an exercise price of 60 and immediately writes a new put with an exercise price of 50. Less speculatively inclined writers of puts will choose an exercise price below the stock price, in any case. Although the net premium is decidedly smaller with that exercise price, the safety margin is much greater and it is less likely that the option will be exercised.

Another judicious strategy for writing puts might be to write several options at different exercise prices. If the investor wants to buy 200 shares of Avon Products which are quoted at $47, he might write one put exercise price 45 for $1, and at the same time a second put exercise price 50 for $4. The average net premium per option, which is immediately paid over to the investor, would be $2.5. If the stock rises above $50, the investor receives the net premiums of both options, that is, a total of $5. If the stock price remains unchanged at $47 up to the expiration date, the option at 50 will be exercised, and the writer will leave to take delivery of the stock at $50. However, since he has already received $5 net premium, the actual delivery price for the 100 shares is $45. If the stock price falls below $45, both options will be exercised. The investor now has 200 shares which he acquired for an average price of $47.50. Since he has also received the net premium, the delivery price of the stock is reduced by another $2.50 to $45.

Valid Strategies

● 1. **The Professional Speculator**

   His strategy

   ◇ Write an uncovered put in the near or medium expiration date.

   ◇ Write uncovered puts with exercise price above the stock price.

   Why Not Recommended for Full Capital Investment?

   ◇ At most, only 70% of the capital is available for options, since the investor has to deposit margin.

   ◇ Leverage effect with the written put is not as large as with the purchase of puts.

   ◇ Profit is limited to the amount of the options price received, and losses can be painfully large if prices go down.

   ◇ An additional danger is that the investor has to be prepared to take delivery of the underlying securities at exercise price at any time.

Why Conditionally Recommended for 10–20% of Total Capital Investment?

Advantages:

◇ Risk can be calculated with good know-how, experience, discipline, and a good timing strategy.

◇ Since the net premium becomes worthless on the expiration day, the remaining lifetime of the option always has an advantageous effect.

◇ The danger that the option will be exercised can be eliminated by repurchasing the options contract.

◇ The psychological pressure is not so great with a smaller capital investment.

Disadvantages:

◇ The leverage effect is not big enough compared to the one the entire capital investment would generate.

◇ Compared with the opportunities the investor has with this strategy, he has to spend too much time on it; it is too time-consuming for anticipated return.

● 2. **The Nonprofessional Speculator**

His strategy

◇ Writes uncovered puts.

Why Not Recommended for Both Full and Limited Capital Investment?

◇ As a rule, aggressive investment policy is disastrous because supervision is lacking.

◇ The possibility of incurring high losses is very great if the investor misinterprets the market situation.

◇ There is additional risk if the option is exercised.

● **3. The Conservative Professional Investor**

His strategy

◇ Write uncovered puts in the near or medium expiration month.

◇ Write uncovered puts at exercise price above or below the stock price.

◇ Limits the number of options contracts: only so many that he still has enough liquid assets to buy the shares tendered when the option is exercised.

Why Not Recommended for Full Capital Investment?

◇ At the most, 70% of capital is available for options because margin must be deposited.

◇ Investment form is too aggressive to guarantee goal of capital preservation and growth.

◇ Better returns can be realized with more conservative strategies at a lower risk.

◇ There are no dividends or other returns with options.

◇ There is the danger that option will be exercised.

Why Recommended for 10–20% of the Capital Investment?

◇ The return of a well-diversified portfolio containing stocks and other securities can be increased with minimal risk by writing uncovered puts.

◇ Risk can be nearly eliminated with know-how, experience, and good timing.

◇ Uncovered puts written in the near or medium expiration month at low exercise price yield small (50¢–$1) but safe additional returns.

◇ At the low exercise price it is relatively unlikely that the writer will have to take delivery.

◇ Stocks and securities in the portfolio provide the necessary margin.

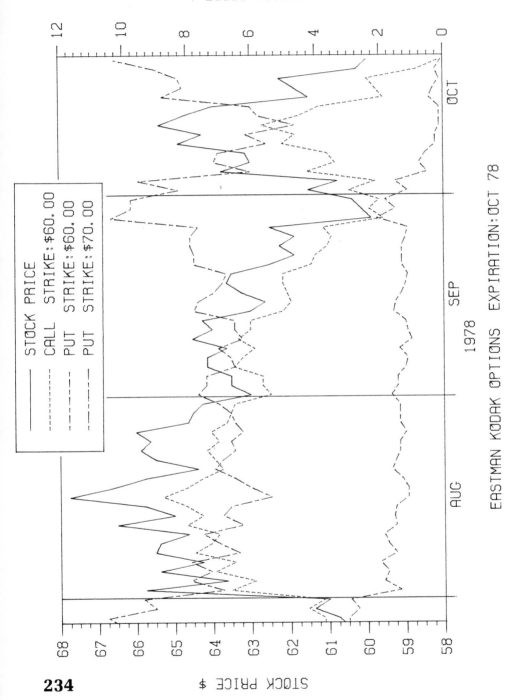

OPTION PRICE $

STOCK PRICE $

234

STOCK PRICE
CALL STRIKE:$60.00
PUT STRIKE:$60.00
PUT STRIKE:$70.00

EASTMAN KODAK OPTIONS   EXPIRATION:OCT 78

1978

AUG   SEP   OCT

Figure 58   Eastman Kodak, movement of call and put versus stock price.

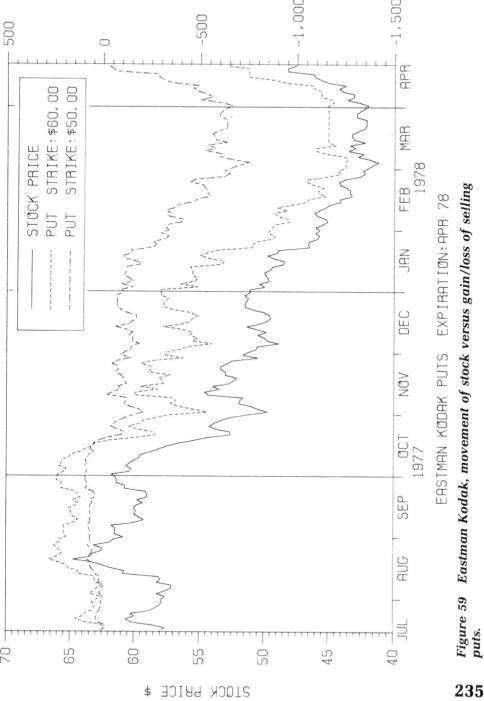

Figure 59 *Eastman Kodak, movement of stock versus gain/loss of selling puts.*

235

High Exercise Price:

◇ This exercise price should only be selected if the investor intends to keep the shares that are tendered to him.

● **4. The Conservative Nonprofessional Investor**

His strategy

◇ Writes uncovered puts.

Why Not Recommended for Full or Limited Capital Investment?

◇ Neither qualifications nor mentality of the investor are adequate for this strategy.

◇ The leverage effect of the option is too large.

Strategy VI: The Writing of Puts Combined with Stocks

As we have seen before, the purchase of a stock combined with the simultaneous writing of a call offers the conservative investor excellent possibilities of achieving a good return with both falling and rising stock prices.

This is possible because a loss can be considerably diminished when prices are going down by means of the premium received, even though the writing of the call limits the potential profit on the stock to the amount of the premium. A further safeguard against a price decline is offered by the possible switch to a lower exercise price. The effects of purchasing a stock combined with writing a put at the same time are illustrated by means of an example. In 1977 Eastman Kodak was traded at $60, and a put with our exercise price of 60 could be written for $4. With regard to the expiration date, the following picture presented itself:

Example: The development in figures:

Stock price	Profit/loss stock	Net put premium	Total profit + loss
66	6	+4	10
64	4	+4	8
62	2	+4	6
60	0	+4	4
58	− 2	+4	+ 2
56	− 4	+4	0
54	− 6	+4	− 4
52	− 8	+4	− 8
50	−10	+4	−12
48	−12	+4	−16

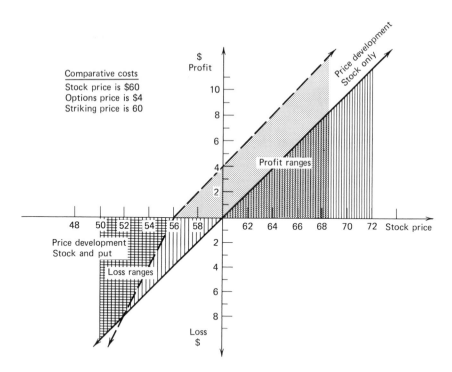

Figure 60   Purchase of a stock combined with the writing of a put.

The graphic representation of the price development is shown in Figure 60. The investor who buys this stock at $60 and at the same time writes a put against it increases his potential return by the $4 net premium, should the stock price rise. Compared to the pure stock purchase, the loss threshold is lowered from $60 to $56. Once it falls below $56, however, the investor loses twice as much (dollar for dollar, with the stock and the put) as he would have if he had bought the stock alone. With a stock price of $52, the investor would have lost only $8 on the stock; with the combination stock and written put, the loss would have amounted to $12. The combination of stock and written put therefore cannot be recommended to investors who are not absolutely certain of the price trend in the stocks concerned. Compared with the opportunity of making a $4 profit when prices go up, the possible losses from a price decline are simply exorbitant. This strategy can prove really treacherous, especially if the investor lacks the funds and finds himself unable to purchase the securities underlying the written put. He can, of course, at any time terminate the agreement by repurchasing the put, but as a rule this transaction means a certain loss.

Summary

The writing of puts is very attractive for two reasons. First, the acquisition cost of the stock can be reduced by the net premium received. This would make sense only, however, if the investor really intended to purchase the stock. Second, the investor can try to realize an additional income from net premiums. As with the writing of an uncovered call, the investor has the choice of either a more speculative or a more conservative strategy. If he writes a put with a high exercise price, the intrinsic value plus the net premium can be earned. For that, however, he needs a good timing system that enables him to make a correct short-term prognosis as to whether the stock price is going to rise. The full options price is completely realized only when the stock price on the expiration date is above the exercise price of the option written. If the investor fails to make a correct forecast of the price trend, he has to be prepared for the possibility that the option will be exercised, which means that he will have to take delivery of the stock. Therefore, it is decidedly safer to write an uncovered put in the near expiration month at an exercise price below the stock price. Even though the

net premiums are smaller, there is still a very good chance of realizing a sizeable income from net premiums if the investor rewrites
the option several times during one year. And if the stock price is
5–10% above the exercise price shortly before the expiration date, a
net premium of 50¢–$1 can still be realized with the lower exercise
price; thus the investor can nearly always count on a profit. Also, if,
contrary to all expectations, the stock price should decline strongly,
there will still be enough time to repurchase the option without
incurring too great a loss. The remaining lifetime of the option
always works in the interests of the investor. We do not intend to go
more fully into this combination of stocks purchased and puts written, since the opportunity to realize the options premium in addition to taking the profit from the stock if the price goes up compares
unfavorably with the risk of a double loss with both stock and
option if the price declines.

Strategy VII: The Purchase of Straddles

With a straddle, the investor combines the purchase of calls and
puts. This combination offers a possibility to make a profit when the
market is either going up or down, and the investor can leave aside
all timing strategies. IBM January options will show how this
works.

Example:

Stock price IBM 260 $ in September
Purchase January 260 call at $7
Purchase January 260 put at $6

   With the purchase of a call, the investor acquires the right to buy
the shares at 260 any time up to the expiration date. The purchase
of the put gives the investor the right to sell the shares at 260 at any
time up to the expiration date. What are the advantages of such a
combination? Like all options buyers, the buyer of a straddle can
lose no more than the capital invested in options. In this case, the
investment consists of the price for buying the call = $7 plus the
purchase of the put = $6; at the worst, the loss would be $13. The
$13, however, is only lost if the stock price on the expiration date of
the option is exactly $260. Since this is extremely unlikely, the

Profit + loss January	Call exercise price 260 $7		Put exercise price 260 $6		Total profit + loss
280	+20	−7	0	−6	+ 7
276	+16	−7	0	−6	+ 3
272	+12	−7	0	−6	− 1
268	+ 8	−7	0	−6	− 5
264	+ 4	−7	0	−6	− 9
260	+ 0	−7	0	−6	−13
256	0	−7	+ 4	−6	− 9
252	0	−7	+ 8	−6	− 5
248	0	−7	+12	−6	− 1
244	0	−7	+16	−6	+ 3
240	0	−7	+20	−6	+ 7

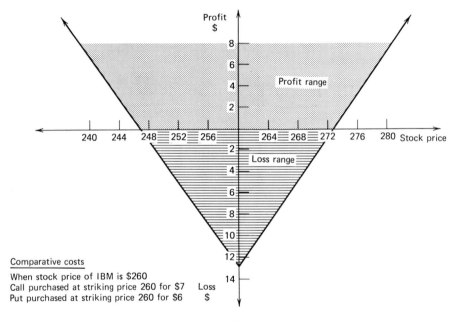

Figure 61   Purchase of a straddle.

danger of a loss the investor faces when buying a straddle is much less severe, no matter whether the stock is quoted above or below $260. The real potential of this combination lies in the fact that the investor will always profit from big price fluctuations in the underlying securities, regardless of whether the movement is up or down. The investor in our example begins to make a profit when the price either falls below $247 or when it rises above $273. From that point

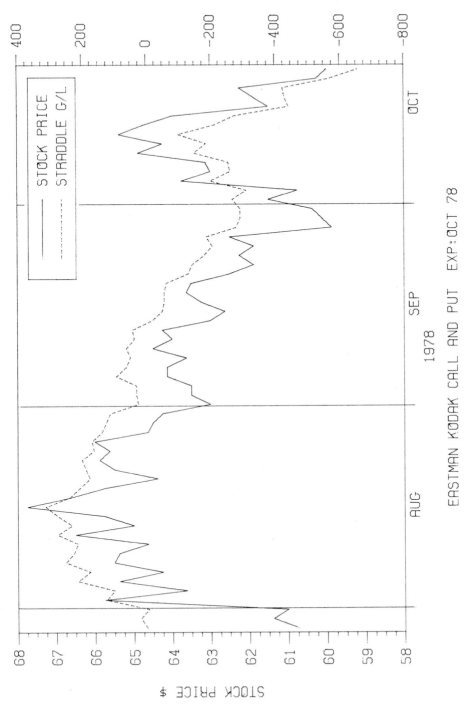

Figure 62a   Eastman Kodak, straddle purchase; price: $675.00 (call—
$375.00; put—$300.00).

241

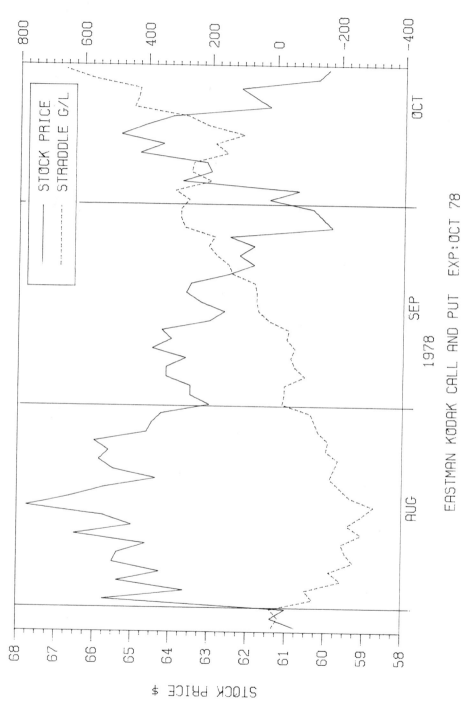

Figure 62b Eastman Kodak, straddle sale; price: $675.00 (call—$375.00; put—$300.00).

on, he profits dollar for dollar from continuing falling or rising stock prices.

The calculations in this example are based on the price at expiration date. However, since stocks such as IBM can be subject to stronger price fluctuations in dollars, a price of $247 or $273 only a few weeks after buying the straddle is quite within the realm of possibility. Since IBM usually trades with high net premiums until shortly before the expiration date, the investor may assume that he can terminate the straddle profitably even at a considerably lower trading range than $13. An additional example can be seen in Figure 62 which shows an Eastman Kodak straddle purchase and sale.

The straddles have a lot in common with the double options sold in Germany. The great advantages of the United States stock options: they are cheaper and traded on an exchange, and thus the investor can check the prices himself in the daily newspapers. In addition, the investor can compare the transactions executed on his behalf with the actual exchange prices and can also expect a perfect clearing system. Those investors who allow themselves to be impressed by the eternal loquaciousness of the high-pressure salesman, extolling the huge opportunities to be had with commodity double options, should first ask a United States broker about the conditions, opportunities, and risks involved in straddles. Here, he would be offered amenable alternatives.

DIVERSIFICATION AND HEDGING

In the chapter on risk analysis, three premises had already crystallized:

◇ A sensible definition of risk.

◇ A method for estimating the risk.

◇ Knowledge of the individual investor's attitude toward risk (i.e., his risk preference).

Risk is defined as the possibility of suffering losses while using an investment strategy. The risk increases when the probability of a loss and the amount of capital that might be lost increase. The counterpart of the risk is the opportunity of a capital investment, which is defined as the opportunity to make a profit. Risk and opportunity are closely connected; that is, if the opportunity increases, the risk will increase as well. These rules for the stock market can be equally applied to options. Because of the leverage effect, however, rational decisions require a much greater knowledge of one's own risk preference, a more extensive know-how with respect to opportunities and risk in options, and, above all, far more discipline.

If, to begin with, one considers the purchase of calls as a counterpart to buying stocks, the investor can choose between diversification and concentration. Since one can buy options on about 220 stocks, a risk variability in several industries is always possible. For the followers of the concentration idea (all eggs in one basket, but watch the basket!), the opening of the options exchanges was a godsend. The go-go funds had hurt most of their customers during the second half of the 1960s, but here was another chance, simply in a different guise to exploit the speculative inclinations of many investors and to offer even more risky forms of speculation than widely diversified stock investment. Still, it took the go-go funds several years to accomplish what speculative options investors, following the decrees of concentration, sometimes manage to achieve within a few months. The investor who does not know his own risk preference, and consequently commits himself too heavily, selects a near expiration date, with an exercise price far above the stock price to boot (that is the one with the biggest leverage). He will not have to wait too long before he discovers that he is absolutely broke, if his timing is off. Diversification, of course, may cut down on the disproportionally large opportunities for profit, but would seem to be the only strategy for those options investors "without timing" that would make sense.

The risk of a capital investment in the stock market can be divided into systematic and the nonsystematic risks, which is only conditionally possible with options. Because of the choice of different exercise prices and expiration dates, the risk structure of an options portfolio can only approximately be equated to that of a stock portfolio. For example, if the investor purchases options in the distant expiration month at an exercise price below the stock price, the options price will practically parallel the stock price, either up or down, because of the high intrinsic value and the low net premium. If he chooses a near expiration month or an exercise price above the stock price, the degree of risk will mount considerably and no longer allows equal comparison with stocks.

If one applies to options Markowitz's theory that all portfolios with an optimum diversification are placed on an efficient frontier line, the difficulties a maximum diversification in options presents become obvious. As a rule, the options investor is not only badly diversified (and for that reason alone is not on the efficient frontier), but with the near expiration date and an exercise price above the stock price he selects a degree of risk that is no longer honored by the market with a correspondingly high expected return.

The beta factors, which are of importance as a unit for measuring risk under a static view of a stock portfolio, can also have significance for that type of options portfolio, which includes options with a distant expiration month and an exercise price below the stock price. Since the studies about the efficiency of beta factors have shown that this measurement of risk remains stable for an entire portfolio during the expiration time, this is a welcome auxiliary aid for an options portfolio, such as described above. For example, if the arithmetic medium of the beta factors of all stocks with options held in the portfolio were 2, the stock portfolio would increase by 20% if the market increased by 10%, and vice versa. If it is possible to state as a fact that the degree of risk of an options portfolio is equal to that of the stock portfolio, the options portfolio gains very much in significance. With the same risk, the options portfolio with a high beta factor would increase more strongly because of the leverage effect if the entire market rises, while it would decline less than a comparable stock portfolio with a high beta factor. This question is investigated more thoroughly, because the result may prove to be of greatest importance to the conservative investor when he has to decide whether he wants to try options in order to achieve better results than with the stock market—and if so, to what extent.

A further possibility to decrease the risk with stocks is the hedge fund, which consists of long and short positions in stocks of various companies. Once an investor has overcome the psychological barrier and decided to speculate on a bearish market, hedge funds are an investment strategy for conservative investors who seek a stable return at low risk. A hedge fund with stocks promises the best results when the number of long and short positions is constantly changed. To determine the ratio of how many stocks should be bought or sold during any market phase, a multitude of technical analytic tools, such as described in the chapter about stock market forecasting, can be utilized. The hedge fund can carry a slightly higher degree of risk if the investor takes options instead of stocks into his portfolio. The stocks bought could be replaced by calls and the short positions by puts. The option hedge fund can be made more conservative or more aggressive than the hedge fund with stocks, depending for one thing on the choice of exercise prices and expiration dates and also on the percentage of options in the entire portfolio volume. How significant the percentage of options in a portfolio is for risk analysis is explained in the next chapter.

COMBINING CALLS WITH TREASURIES: IS THIS PREFERABLE TO STOCK INVESTMENT?

Case Study

In Chapter 3 it was shown by means of the capital asset pricing theory that the conservative investor would be safer if he were to choose a combination of stocks and treasuries instead of concentrating solely on stock investment. Compared to the pure stock investment, this combination of stocks and treasuries enables the investor to realize a higher expected return with the same risk or the same expected return with less risk. What are the factors that influence the relationship of expected return and risk, if calls instead of stocks are used in the portfolio? To answer that question, it is presumed that stocks and treasuries are apportioned in a certain way and that the ratio of expected return to risk that corresponds to this combination is taken as a unit to measure for judging a portfolio containing calls. In view of the 20% decline of the Dow Jones Industrial Average in 1977, these considerations are especially important.

In general, the net effect of replacing stocks with call options, which offer the same opportunities as the stocks, is that the investor requires much less capital. The remaining liquid assets can then be invested in treasuries and thus add the additional constant yields from interest rates to the total investment. We will see that the combination of treasuries and options provides the investor with a bigger "cushion" against losses in the speculative part of his investment without lessening his opportunities. In addition, if stocks are replaced by options, the same expected return can be realized, thanks to the leverage effect of the calls, with a smaller risk. It is also possible to use options to increase the expected return while holding the risk the same. Aside from the protective effects provided by the "cushion" of treasuries, there is another factor to be considered: the options prices of calls move relatively stronger in an "upward" direction than do stock prices, because of the leverage effect which is somewhat asymmetrical. Although the investor can earn his invested capital several times over if the price goes up, he can never lose more than his initial investment, even if the entire market should decline sharply.

Beyond these general reflections, we must consider the practical implications of using options and decide on the relative percentage of options and treasuries in order to keep the risk of the entire portfolio (treasuries and options) in relationship to the risk of a comparable portfolio of stocks and treasuries. To determine this relationship, we will have to rely on a formula presented by Sharpe. Since this formula illustrates the general relationships that have been discussed so far, but does not offer any new results the more practically oriented reader may pass this by. (See the section on risk analysis.)

A beta factor for the options portfolio, which is analogous to the beta factor Sharpe developed for the stock portfolio, can be established. These two beta factors have a linear correlation as has been proved by Ito's theorem. We will then use E_{cv} to measure the elasticity of options prices with regard to stock prices (C = options price, V = stock price):

$$\beta_{ct(options)} = E_{cv} \cdot \beta_{r(shares)}$$

E_{cv} correlates the (relative) changes in options prices with the (relative) changes in stock prices. (In this relationship the stock prices are considered "independent" and the options prices "dependent.") It indicates the percent change in the options price if the corresponding stock price changes by 1%.

E_{cv} is also referred to as "elasticity," well-known in economics, which associates the relative change of one item with the relative change in a second item, where one is dependent on the other (e.g., price elasticity of supply and demand.)

If one wants to apply these theoretical considerations in a practical way, one would first have to figure out the *coefficient of elasticity*.

Example: The coefficient of elasticity E_{cv} is calculated as described in the following hypothetical model:

◇ The average price of the stocks of a maximum diversified portfolio is assumed to be $50 (beta factor $\beta = 1$).

◇ Options relating to the stocks in the portfolio are assumed to have an exercise price $45.

◇ The price of all options is $5; therefore the options are traded without "net" premium.

◇ None of the stocks bear dividends.

◇ The time unit of the calls is assumed to be 2 × 6 months = 1 year.

If the entire market increases by 10%, the average price of the stocks in our portfolio increases from $50 to $55. This increase of the stock price from $50 to $55 has the effect of increasing the options price from $5 to $10 at the same time.

The elasticity would therefore be calculated:

$$E_{CV} = \frac{\Delta C/C}{\Delta V/V} = \frac{5/5}{5/50} = \frac{1}{1/10} = 10$$

where
C = options price
V = stock price
ΔC = change in options price
ΔV = change in stock price

In this example the relative change of the options price from $5 to $10 is ten times bigger than the relative change of the stock price from $50 to $55, although the change in stock prices was the cause of the option price change. The question is now whether the capital asset pricing theory, which recommends that the conservative investor select a combination of stocks and treasuries, rather than the pure stock investment, can be applied to the portfolio if stocks are replaced with options. Furthermore, we must verify that the linear relationship of risk and return for stocks and treasuries is valid for the combination of options and treasuries. In order to be able to make that comparison, and subsequently determine whether it is better to have stocks or options in a portfolio, the returns must be calculated under the premise that both portfolios carry the same risk.

Example: With one-fourth treasuries and three-fourths stocks, the capital asset pricing theory has a beta factor of 0.75, that is, a risk that comes to 75% of the inherent market risk. The inherent market risk is that part of the risk which cannot be minimized any further by diversification. By using the optimum diversified market portfolio, which contains 25% treasuries, and including the elasticity factor 10 of the options as computed in the previous example, the risk of having options in the portfolio becomes:

$$\beta_{ct} = E_{cv} \cdot \beta_r$$
$$\beta_{ct} = 10 \times 0.75 = 7.5$$

where
  E_{cv} = elasticity
  β_r = beta factor of stock portfolio
  β_{ct} = beta factor of option portfolio

From this formula we can conclude that if the stocks in a portfolio are completely replaced by options, the risk (and the rewards) are multiplied by the elasticity factor of the options. Thus, in our example, the risk would be ten times greater. If one wants to reduce the risk of an options portfolio to the level of the stock portfolio, the investor must then invest more capital in treasuries. Assuming a stock portfolio contains three-fourths stocks and one-fourth treasuries, an elasticity factor of 10 for the options allows the options portfolio with the same risk to contain 92.5% treasuries and 7.5% options. When the risk is the same for both portfolios, the deciding factor will be the expected return. Using the following case study, we will investigate this question.

The starting point for the case study is based on the capital asset pricing theory which states that:

$$E(R_P) = R_F + [E(R_M) - R_F] \cdot \gamma$$

where:
  $E(R_P)$ = expected return of the portfolio
  R_F = interest rate on treasuries
  $E(R_M)$ = market return
  γ = percentage of stocks in the entire portfolio (gamma)

First Case

Assuming that the stock price remains stable during the course of the year, we get the following returns for the stock portfolio and for the alternative options portfolio:

1. Portfolio with 75% stocks and 25% treasuries

$$0.07 \times 0.25 = 0.9175 \text{ or } 1.75\% \text{ profit}$$

Since the stock prices had not changed on the average, no return was achieved from the stocks (under the given premises, returns from dividends are not taken into account). We then only have the yield of the treasuries, comprising 25% of the portfolio, at an interest rate of 7%, or 1.75% profit.

2. Portfolio with 7.5% options and 92.5% treasuries

$$0.07 \times 0.925 = 6.475\% \text{ profit on treasuries}$$
$$7.5\% \text{ loss in options (total investment)}$$
$$1.025\% \text{ total loss}$$

With the options portfolio, the total options price was lost because the overall market had not moved. Since options came to only 7.5% of the entire capital, the 7% interest rate for the 92.5% treasuries was not influenced. All together, there is a loss of approximately 1%.

Second Case

The average stock price declines by 10% during the course of the year. This results in the following returns for the stock portfolio and for the alternative options portfolio:

1. Portfolio with 75% stocks and 25% treasuries

$$
\begin{aligned}
E(R_P) &= R_F + (E(R_M) - R_F) \cdot \gamma \\
&= 0.07 + (-0.1 - 0.07) \times 0.75 \\
&= 0.07 - (0.17 \times 0.75) \\
&= \underline{0.07 \quad\ 0.1275} \\
&\quad\ \ 0.0575 \text{ or } 5.75\% \text{ loss}
\end{aligned}
$$

The price decline of the entire market affected the 75% stocks in the portfolio. The loss of 7.5% could only partially be compensated by returns from treasuries, and the result was a net loss of 5.75% for the investor.

2. Portfolio with 7.5% options and 92.5% treasuries

$0.07 \times 0.925 = 6.475\%$ profit from treasuries
7.5% loss from options (total investment)
1.025% total loss

Since the investor can never lose more than the options price, even if the stock prices continue to decline, the total loss is the same as in the first example, approximately 2%.

Third Case

The stock price increases by 10% during the course of the year. This results in the following return for the stock portfolio and for the alternative options portfolio:

1. Portfolio with 75% stocks and 25% treasuries

$$E(R_P) = R_F + (E(R_M) - R_F) \cdot \gamma$$
$$= 0.07 + (0.1 - 0.07) \times 0.75$$
$$= 0.07 + 0.03 \times 0.75$$
$$= 0.925 \text{ or } 9.25\% \text{ profit}$$

The price increase of the entire market affected only the 75% stocks. Together with the return from the treasuries, a total profit of 9.25% is achieved.

2. Portfolio with 7.5% options and 92.5% treasuries

$0.07 \times 0.925 = 6.475\%$ profit from treasuries
$1.00 \times 0.75 = 7.500\%$ profit from options
13.975% total profit

When the market increases, the investor profits by 6.475% from the interest rate on treasuries and also from the effect of great leverage achieved by the use of the options in the portfolio. The total return is 13.975%.

Conclusion

If one looks at the three examples, it can be seen that under the given premises the combination of options and treasuries (92.5% treasuries, 7.5% options) is superior to the use of stocks (75% stocks, 25% treasuries) in the cases in which the stock price declines or moves up. The use of options results in smaller losses and larger gains for the investor. It is only when the stock price stagnates that the stock portfolio has a slight advantage over the options portfolio. It should be noted that these examples used the underlying premise that options have an elasticity of 10. The actual coefficient of elasticity must be determined empirically for the selected portfolios; however, the factor 10 should be relatively close to the actual elasticity when the exercise price is below the stock price.

The above results can be of significant relevance for practical purposes. The capital asset pricing theory already considers it important that the market risk can be reduced by the combination of stocks and treasuries. If the correct balance is calculated with the elasticity factor considered, then the combination of treasuries and options offer still further improvement. When larger market fluctuations occur, the investor will improve his investment performance during both bull and bear trends. That this technique is still widely unknown stems in part from the previously negative attitude of conservative investors toward the options trade. It is also due to the inability of options investors to be satisfied with the investment of only a small portion of their capital in options, with the remainder in treasuries. The emphasis placed on stocks by the capital asset pricing theory becomes even less justifiable if one considers that the assumed interest rate on treasuries of 7% used in the options portfolio can be considerably improved by choosing bonds with a higher rate of interest (10% or more).

The investment strategy discussed here eliminates the necessity for an entry timing system. The investor can come very close to the "buy-and-hold" strategy, if one leaves out the fact that options are tied to expiration dates and that their renewal requires continuous decision making and additional expense.

Simulation of Returns and Risks of Stock and Options Portfolios from 1963 to 1975

In 1976, Merton, Scholes, and Gladstein undertook a study that compared the risks and returns of various options portfolios with those of stock portfolios [Robert C. Merton, Myron S. Scholes, and Mathew L. Gladstein, A Simulation of the Returns and Risk of Alternative Option Portfolio Investment Strategies, unpublished working paper, 1976]. This test series covered the period of 1963–1975. The investigations refer to the return and risk of four stock portfolios. The computed semi-annual average rate of return includes reinvestment of dividends, and it is assumed that there were no commissions or taxes payable and that a semi-annual dividend of 1.5% was paid.

Portfolio No. 1

This portfolio contains 136 stocks, on which options were traded in 1976. The result of the simulation was that a capital of $1000 would

Summary of Semi-Annual Rate of Return Statistics				
	1 136 Stock Portfolio	2 DJ Stock Portfolio	3 S&P 500	4 Commercial Paper
Semi-Annual				
Average Rate of Return	7.9%	4.1%	3.6%	3.3%
Standard Deviation	16.6%	13.7%	13.4%	1.1%
Average Dividend Yield	1.5%	2.5%	1.8%	—
Highest Return	54.6%	49.1%	41.8%	6.2%
Lowest Return	− 21.0%	−16.4%	−19.5%	2.0%
Average Compound Return	6.7%	3.3%	2.8%	3.3%
Growth of $1000	$5043	$2226	$1988	$2239
Coefficient of Skewness	0.73	1.25	0.73	—
Beta	1.17	0.98	1.0	—
Alpha	4.2%	0.5%	.0	—

have increased to $5043 during the period 1963 to 1975. The average beta factor of 1.17 indicates that this portfolio has increased more than the overall market.

Portfolio No. 2

This portfolio contains the 30 Dow Jones stocks. The $1000 invested in this portfolio during the trial run had increased to $2226 by 1975. The beta factor was 0.98 and indicates that the Dow Jones developed nearly parallel to the overall market.

Portfolio No. 3

The portfolio contains the 500 stocks from the S&P 500 index. The $1000 invested in this portfolio during the test run had increased to $1988. The beta factor is 1.0 and indicates that the portfolio developed parallel to the overall market.

Portfolio No. 4

There are no stocks in this portfolio: it consists completely of treasuries. An investment of $1000 in treasuries had grown to $2239 with a semi-annual interest rate of 3.3% after the test period was over.

With the results of the stock portfolios, another test was conducted to check by means of simulation how alternative options portfolios would have developed during that same period. The resulting portfolio containing 90% treasuries and 10% options is now described.

The results of this simulation are extremely interesting in connection with the insights derived from the previous case studies. The case study proved that a portfolio combined with stocks and options (beta factor 1.0)

◇ Brings better results with a rising market.

◇ Does not do as well with a stagnating market.

◇ Again brings better results with a declining market.

The simulation of an options portfolio containing 90% treasuries and 10% options is based on the following premises:

◇ Test period 1963–1975.

◇ Investment of $1000.

◇ Semi-annual rate of interest on treasuries of 3.3%.

◇ Lifetime of options of 6 months.

◇ Premium according to the intrinsic value as computed with the Black and Scholes model.

◇ All options having exercise prices that are 10% below, at par with the stock price, or 10 or 20% above the stock price.

◇ Commission and taxes not included.

Portfolio No. 5

Options were purchased for those 136 stocks on which options were traded in 1976. An investment of $1000 in options with differ-

Summary Statistics for Rate of Return Simulations Options-Paper Buying Strategies				
5 136 Stock Sample				
	Exercise Price = 0.9 Stock Price	Exercise Price = 1.0 Stock Price	Exercise Price = 1.1 Stock Price	Exercise Price = 1.2 Stock Price
Semi-Annual				
Average Rate of Return	6.3%	8.2%	11.1%	16.2%
Standard Deviation	7.8%	10.6%	15.7%	27.2%
Highest Return	25.7%	34.7%	59.9%	121.0%
Lowest Return	− 4.7%	− 5.2%	− 5.7%	− 6.1%
Average Compound Return	6.1%	7.7%	10.1%	13.8%
Growth of $1000	$4370	$6372	$11178	$25670
Coefficient of Skewness	0.83	0.87	1.26	2.26
6 DJ Stock Sample				
Average Rate of Return	4.2%	5.1%	7.2%	10.6%
Standard Deviation	7.3%	10.1%	14.6%	25.7%
Highest Return	27.1%	34.4%	42.6%	88.1%
Lowest Return	− 4.6%	− 5.7%	− 7.5%	− 7.9%
Average Compound Return	3.9%	4.7%	6.3%	8.3%
Growth of $1000	$2627	$3138	$4597	$7287
Coefficient of Skewness	1.26	1.09	1.01	1.64

ent exercise prices showed considerable deviations in the growth of the return. With the exercise price 10% below the stock price, the portfolio increased from $1000 to $4370, but with the exercise price of 20% above the stock price, there was an increase from $1000 to $25,670.

Portfolio No. 6

Options were acquired for 30 Dow Jones stocks. Corresponding to the small increase of the Dow Jones during the test period, the growth of the options portfolio was also smaller. But still, the portfolio increased from $1000 to $2627 with an exercise price 10%

below the stock price and from $1000 to $7287 with an exercise price 20% above the stock price.

Conclusion

The simulation of a portfolio that contains 90% treasuries and 10% options emphasizes the insights gained from the case studies. The high percentage of treasuries provides the portfolio with a large safety margin, if the market declines. The investor will lose much less than he would if he were to take a position with stocks. If prices go up, however, even a small percentage of the entire capital invested in options will result in a much stronger increase in returns than would be the case with stocks because of the leverage effect. It is only when the stock prices stagnate that the stock portfolio has the advantage over the combination treasuries/options. The higher the investor chooses the exercise price of the option, the greater the growth of the options portfolio.

The results of these tests certainly are impressive and informative, but one should be careful not to deduce from them a general validity for the future. During the 12 years of the test, the overall market had increased considerably. Such an increase, however, is never guaranteed. The investor is expected to remain absolutely passive in the market. After the options have been purchased, the development of the market is ignored for the next half year. This could mean that, although the options have realized a considerable profit several times during their lifetime, this profit will have disappeared on the expiration day because prices have declined. It is doubtful whether the investor will have the self-discipline to forego these profits. Another factor is the premise of the model that each option has exercise prices above and below the stock price. Experience has shown that this is not always the case. It is also doubtful that the options can always be purchased at their fair value (computed with the Black and Scholes model), that is, that they are neither over- nor undervalued. The final picture of the options portfolio changes unfavorably, if commissions for the individual transactions are not considered. Despite all these uncertainties, one thing is still true: *the proper use of options can beat any stock investment with regard to return and safety.*

Compared to stocks, options possess quite a number of substantial advantages. It is absolutely wrong to maintain that options do not represent a viable alternative to stocks, because they carry too much risk. The problem with options, rather, stems from the weakness of the investor who does not know his own risk preference. Another aspect is the wide spectrum of investment possibilities. The opportunities with options compared to stocks are much greater, both for the speculator and the conservative investor. It is completely up to the investor to see if he can exploit these advantages. If one looks at the 20% loss in the Dow and at individual stock losses of more than 50% in 1977—Eastman Kodak, and Burroughs, for example—the realistic incorporation of options into each conservatively administered portfolio gains more and more importance. The fact that a properly diversified options-treasury portfolio is superior to any stock portfolio still has not been sufficiently discussed and acknowledged.

CONCLUSION

Considering the results of the case study, and the following simulation by Merton, Gladstein, and Scholes, the question arises as to why big investors or funds do not employ more frequently this strategy of combining approximately 90% treasuries and 10% options. Two of the reasons for this reticence seem fairly obvious:

◇ Lack of knowledge concerning strategies and problems of the option trade

◇ Lack of discipline on the part of the investor who is not able to be consistent once he has chosen a strategy that has to be applied for several months or years

The investor who decides to follow a conservative strategy severely limits his field of action. In the analyses mentioned above, we proceeded from the assumption that 5% of the capital would be invested twice a year in options with a lifetime of 6 months. The investor should plan on wide diversification, so that the options portfolio will move parallel to changes in the general market. In other words, this strategy forces the investor to remain "passive." But as soon as he changes his strategy so that the portion of options in his portfolio rises to 20, 30, or 40% of the total volume, or if he concentrates on only a few stocks thus neglecting a wide market range, he no longer will realize the object he had in mind with this strategy: the results will be either better or worse, but in any case different.

A strategy of enforced inactivity goes against the grain of market professionals. A funds manager is paid for "performance"—and the performance has to be as high as possible. His achievements are the tools that serve to confirm and increase the confidence a customer places in him. The fact that it is usually much more difficult *not* to act whenever the media revel in news in order to obtain favorable results is difficult to accept and usually not appreciated by the investor. In the action of the manager the investor sees a confirmation that he has chosen the proper fund for his investments. If he buys or sells stocks or options at the wrong time, he behaves just like the majority of investors and confirms the theories about investors' behavior. The manager, however, who judged it better to remain inactive will hardly ever be entrusted with new investments if by doing so he missed a strong market movement.

The fund manager is under constant pressure to succeed since he has to compete with his colleagues working for other funds. Furthermore, he has to believe in his own abilities to beat his competitors, and this kind of confidence can only be maintained if his decisions remain profitable.

The discipline necessary to follow through with a system or strategy is at least as important as the system or strategy itself. It becomes a vicious cycle if the investor deviates from his strategy "just once" in order to catch a "safe" opportunity. A decline in stock prices does not preclude the chance that they will recover eventually, but with options the investor cannot indulge in any form of irregularity without penalty. Inexorably, the expiration date moves closer every day, and on the expiration day, the loss is irrevocable.

For generations, the combination of treasuries and stocks has been part of big portfolios. The strategy of combining treasuries and options is only a continuation and further development of this idea. It will be accepted by those investors who see options as a conservative capital investment and who are willing to learn about risks and rewards of this investment mode and to apply it practically.

RISKS AND OPPORTUNITIES OF COMPREHENSIVE OPTIONS STRATEGIES

The combination of options with each other in the form of spreads and straddles has gained considerable importance and status on the exchange; On the one hand, they offer the possibility to profit from changes in prices with limited risk. On the other hand, these combinations carry extremely high commissions, and if handled unprofessionally, they fit more into the category of those investment advisors who are eager beavers where their own profit is concerned but become inexplicably fatigued when it comes to defending the interests of their customers. Many investors simply are sick and tired of the word options and turn off the minute anybody mentions them. This becomes more understandable when one considers the following example which had been published as a serious recommendation by a German market letter. The advice was:

Purchase 1000 shares Amerada Hess (AHC) $34
Purchase 10 AHC 35 puts at $2.50
Write 10 AHC 35 calls at $2.25

The nonprofessional investor can hardly check the disadvantages or advantages of such recommendations. The values of those recommendations is, to say the least, dubious. Without going into detail, the investor, had he followed the advice, would have earned 75¢ or $750 gross at the most on the expiration day, whether the stock price had gone up or down. For taking such a position, however, he would have had to pay $650 alone in commissions, and when the position is closed, he will in all probability have to pay another sizeable lump sum. In other words: the investor will end up with a dead-certain loss unless he receives an 80% discount on commissions from his broker. Naturally, no broker is going to offer that kind of discount. The final outcome of such recommendations therefore will only be this: the investor begins to doubt his own faculties because he cannot estimate and balance the risks and opportunities on his own and will finally stay away from options in general.

From the multitude of possible combinations of options we have selected a number of the most interesting and most frequently traded on the exchange and discuss them in the following.

THE CALL SPREAD

If the investor is convinced that the price of a security is going to rise or decline, he should either buy a call or a put. Opportunities and risks for those two forms of investment are well known. The call promises unlimited profit if the stock price increases. The put, on the other hand, only brings a profit if prices decline. But in both cases the possible loss is limited to the amount of the options price.

Spreads are a combination of calls or puts with the same or different exercise price and expiration date. The investor takes such a position because he would like to limit the risk inherent in a purchase of a call or put. If the risk is limited, however, it follows that the opportunities for making a profit are also limited. Another disadvantage with the spread is that the investor has to pay double in commissions, as opposed to a call or put. The investor also has to watch the clearing modalities and margin requirements imposed by the various brokerage houses on those spread combinations. The multitude of possible combinations between expiration months and exercise prices demand a high degree of know-how. Each combination has a different relation of risk and opportunity. The inexperienced investor should avoid any kind of involvement with spreads.

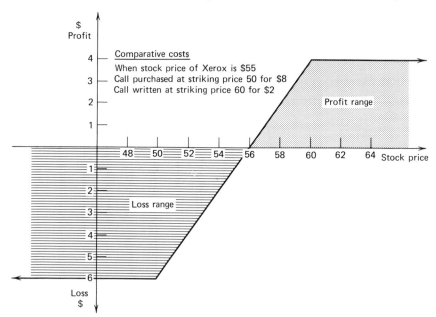

Figure 63   Bullish call money spread.

Strategy VIII: The Bullish Call Money Spread

The bullish money spread consists of a combination of a call purchased at low exercise price and a similar call written at a higher exercise price, both in the same expiration month (see Figure 63).

Goal: The investor enters this combination because he wants to make a profit from a price increase at a lower risk than that with the purchase of a call alone.

Advantage: The danger with the call losing the entire options price if a stock price goes down is reduced by the amount of the options price from the call written at the high exercise price.

Disadvantage: By writing one call with a high exercise price, the potential profit of the call in the low exercise price is limited. It can at the maximum be the difference of the two striking price minus the total option prices paid. Also, the investor has to pay two commissions for this transaction.

The following is an example with Xerox (XRX) from October.

Example:

Stock price Xerox $55
Purchase January XRX 50 calls at $8
Sell January XRX 60 calls at $2

The possible results on the expiration date in figures:

	Call purchased			Call written		
Stock price	Profit + loss with stock exercise price 50	Cost of call	Profit + loss with stock exercise price 60	Income from call	Total profit + loss
64	+1.400	−800	−400	+200	+400
62	+1.200	−800	−200	+200	+400
60	+1.000	−800	0	+200	+400
58	+ 800	−800	0	+200	+200
56	+ 600	−800	0	+200	0
54	+ 400	−800	0	+200	−200
52	+ 200	−800	0	+200	−400
50	+ 0	−800	0	+200	−600
48	− 0	−800	0	+200	−600

The investor who uses this spread counts on a positive price trend. The option written at exercise price 60 for $2 reduces the out-of-pocket cost of the 50 call from $8 to $6. With the call written, he has automatically reduced his chances for expected profit to $4. (difference between exercise prices $10 − $6 = $4.) No matter how much the price rises above $60, the investor can never make more than those $4 with the spread. With a high stock price, on the other hand, he has to reckon with the possibility that the written call 60 may be exercised. Even though there is the possibility of making sure of the $4 profit by exercising the option with the purchased call 50, this profit is considerably reduced by the high commissions payable for these transactions. This combination therefore seems to make little sense. The limited possibilities for making a profit and the danger that the option will be exercised are not counterbalanced by the reduction in price of the option bought by the net premium received at the high exercise price. Added to this, there are the commissions for the spread, which compared with the purchase of a single call are high. This combination only makes sense if the price of the option purchased at low exercise price is at least halved by the return from writing an option in the high exercise price. This, however, presupposes an extremely high net premium at the high exercise price, which happens very rarely. It would seem to be better strategy to simply buy a call. This would apply even more, if the investor does not want to invest fully at this time, but rather buy more later on if the price declines and thus average down his options price.

The rationale for these spreads was propagated by the brokerage houses who use the Black and Scholes model to try to compute whether an option is over- or undervalued (see "The Mathematical Evaluation of Net Premiums"). If the undervalued option is bought at low exercise price and the overvalued option is written at high exercise price at the same time, this deviation from the fair value of options inevitably will have to balance out during the course of time and result in a profit. The question is whether these deviations, based on the strict premises of computer models, actually correspond to reality. Even if these deviations are recognized correctly, the spreads can only help realize the "certain" profit by adjusting the premiums to the over- or undervaluation. A good timing strategy, however, cannot be replaced. This becomes clear if one considers the above example.

The call may be undervalued with the price of $8. If the stock price falls from $55 to $50, the investor will suffer a loss in any case. Exact timing is therefore much more important for an investment decision than the knowledge whether a stock option is over- or undervalued.

The following model will show whether the bullish money spread—since it is used—has any advantages:

	Call	Options Price	Stock Price
Purchase	Xerox Jan. 50	$8	55
Written	Xerox Jan. 60	$2	55
A	Price of option purchased		$8
B	Price of option written		$2
C	Maximum risk $A - B = 8 - 2 =$		$6
D	Difference exercise prices $60 - 50 =$		10
E	Maximum profit $D - C = 10 - 6 =$		$4
F	Risk/profit ratio $\dfrac{C}{E} = \dfrac{6}{4} =$		1.50
G	Profit threshold: C plus exercise price of option purchased $6 + 50$		54
H	Percentage by which stock price has to rise in order to reach profit threshold =		
	$G -$ stock price $= 56 - 55 = \dfrac{1}{55} =$		2%

With this model, every investor can calculate the advantages and disadvantages of that type of spread for himself by inserting the respective figures. The most important figures are:

◇ The return/risk ratio F, which at 1.50 is very bad in this example. With a good bullish money spread, this figure should be 0.70 or less. Such a ratio would be possible if the option in the above example could have been written not for $2 but for $4. But since such a high premium can only rarely be achieved, the prudent purchase of a call would seem in most cases the better strategy, considering all advantages and disadvantages.

◇ The price trend of stocks, which can be checked with a long-term chart. Since the investor only can make a profit with rising prices, he should put on the bullish money spread only—if at all—when a clear upward trend for the stocks is indicated.

A bullish money spread with one call bought at low exercise price but two calls written at the higher exercise price (ratio spread) is much more attractive. For example:

> Dow Chemical February 1978 $25
> Purchase 1 July Dow 25 call at $1.50
> Sell 2 July Dow 30 calls at $1.50

What are the advantages offered by this spread?

The investor proceeds from the assumption that Dow Chemical will increase until July. The entire spread only costs 50¢ (without commission), since the investor buys the call for $1.50 and simultaneously writes 2 calls at 50¢ at exercise price 30. If the stock is quoted at exactly $30 at the time of the expiration in July, the investor makes $3.50 ($5 − $1.50 = $3.50) and receives, in addition, $1 from the written calls with exercise price 30. The maximum profit is therefore $4.50 by an investment of 50¢. If the stock price falls below $25, the maximum loss will be 50¢.

The disadvantage of this spread are the high commissions, which are considerably more than the investor would have to pay for buying a call alone. As long as the stock is below $30, there is no danger of the options at 30 being exercised. However, if the stock price rises above $30, the investor may have to make delivery on the basis of the calls written at 30. After the stock price reaches $34.50, the investor starts to lose money.

Strategy IX: The Bearish Call Money Spread

The bearish money spread is a combination of calls written at low exercise price and calls bought at high exercise price, both in the same expiration month (see Figure 64).

Goal: The investor enters this combination because he wants to profit from writing the call at low exercise price with limited risk when stock prices are declining.

Advantage: The specific danger of the uncovered call—that there is practically an unlimited risk to incur losses when the stock price goes up—is eliminated by purchasing the call at high exercise price. Bearish speculation is also possible with stocks without puts.

Disadvantage: The purchase price of the call at high exercise price diminishes the opportunities to make a profit from the call written. Safety is bought at the price of smaller opportunities to make a profit.

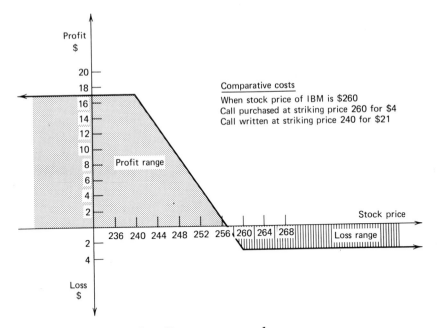

Figure 64   Bearish call money spread.

The double commission and the danger that the option will be exercised for the written call further lessen the attraction of this combination compared to the purchase of a put alone.

An example for this type of spread follows.

Example:

Stock price IBM September $260
Sell Oct. IBM 240 calls at $21   with 1 call   +$2,100
Purchase Oct. IBM 260 calls at $4   with 1 call   −$ 400
                                        profit not realized +$1,700

Stock price	Profit + loss call exercise price 260	Cost of calls	Profit + loss call exercise price 240	Income from calls	Profit + loss total
264	+400	−400	−2.400	+2.100	− 300
260	0	−400	−2.000	+2.100	− 300
256	0	−400	−1.600	+2.100	+ 100
252	0	−400	−1.200	+2.100	+ 500
248	0	−400	− 800	+2.100	+ 900
244	0	−400	− 400	+2.100	+1.300
240	0	−400	− 0	+2.100	+1.700
236	0	−400	− 0	+2.100	+1.700

The investor sells 1 call IBM October 240 at $21, which means he receives $2100. At the same time, he has to pay $400 for purchasing 1 call IBM October 260. The investor's account is credited with the difference $2100 − $400 = $1700. However, the investor cannot draw this money from his account; it has to remain in the account until the spread is terminated, that is, until both options are offset by transaction. The investor must deposit margin in the amount of the maximum possible loss. Since the difference between the exercise 260 and 240 is $20, he has to deposit the difference between the $1700 (which is credited to his account) and $2000 (= difference of exercise prices), i.e. $300 (2000 − 1700) in the margin account of the brokerage house. $300 is the maximum amount the investor can lose with this spread, regardless of how high the stock price goes. With this spread, the investor has to accept the additional risk that he might have to deliver the underlying securities if the written 240 call is exercised. Although he can at any time exercise the option with the IBM October 260 he has purchased, and deliver these shares at exercise price 240, he would in that case not only lose his margin of $300, but also have to pay the commissions due on buying and delivering the securities. How big the danger is that the option will be exercised, and how this danger can be recognized in time, is extensively discussed earlier in this chapter.

The biggest safety factor for the investor with these spreads is that if the stock price goes up indefinitely (contrary to his expectations) he can never lose more than the margin, in our example $300 (without commission). If IBM drops below $260, the profit range is quickly reached. The call 260 cannot decline by more than $4, because this is pure premium. The call 240, however, can decline by $21, because this option consists of the intrinsic value (which moves parallel to the stock price) of $20 and only $1 premium. With a declining price, the investor has an enormous leverage effect for making a profit. He has a maximum risk of $300 with a price increase, but he has a potential to make a profit of maximum $1700 with falling prices.

Bearish money spreads are especially attractive when they require hardly any margin at all. It happens quite frequently that a few weeks before the near expiration date the difference between the written option at high exercise price and the option bought at high exercise price equals the difference between exercise prices when the stock is trading at the high striking price. This would be the case in our example if, with a price of $260, the option exercise price 240 could be written for $22, whereas the option exercise price 260 only trades with $2 ($22 − $2 = $20, which corresponds exactly to the difference between the exercise price 240 and 260). Active traders love to play with these spreads which, although exciting, are also extremely dangerous, as is shown in the following.

Example:

IBM stock price September 1977 $262
Purchase April IBM 260 calls at $15
Sell April IBM 240 calls at $30

Since IBM may fluctuate daily by several dollars, the stock could be at $256 only a few days after the spread has been established, with an options price for the 240 call of $25. The investor now terminates only one part of the spread and repurchases the 240 call for $25. He realizes a return of $5 with this transaction. A short while later, IBM may be quoted at $260. Again, the investor will enter the spread and write another 240 call for $28. The investor will now play with the spread like a yo-yo: through constant buying and writing at low exercise price in the spread, he attempts to take a great number of small profits as quickly as possible. The ''success'' of such activity? Mostly disaster!

Maybe the string of the yo-yo breaks; the stock price does not take an upward move, but drops sharply. Now the 240 call suddenly only yields $14, and the investor has to pay $6 into the margin account, if he wants to try the spread again. Since this often becomes too expensive, the investor will wait and nourish the hope that the price of IBM will eventually take a new upswing. If he waits too long, the premium for the higher exercise price will depreciate. Below the line, the investor will have realized a few good, small profits, but this cannot compensate the big loss he has suffered from the depreciation of the premium for the option purchased at $260. In addition, there are the high commissions he has to put on the table for these quick in-and-out transactions. In the end, the investor will blame options as such, without considering that, given a little bit of patience, the first spread would have been a total success. Bearish money spreads limit the loss to the margin paid into the account. The success of such a combination, however, is greatly dependent on whether the investor can properly judge the price trend; that is, he can only make a profit if the stock price is going down.

The following model will show whether a bearish money spread (since it can be used) will bring a good return:

		Call	Options Price	Stock Price
1	Sell	IBM Jan. 240 call at	$23	262
2	Purchase	IBM Jan. 260 call at	$ 4	262
A		Price of option written		$23
B		Price of option purchased		$ 4
C		Maximum profit 23 − 4 =		$19
D		Difference of exercise price 260 − 240 =		20
E		Maximum risk D − C = 20 − 19 =		$ 1
F		Return/risk ratio $\dfrac{E}{C} = \dfrac{1}{19} =$		0.05
G		Profit threshold C = 19 plus exercise price option written 240 240 + 19 =		$259
H		Percentage by which stock price must fall to reach profit threshold = stock price − profit threshold = $\dfrac{262}{259} =$		1.01%

With this model, every investor can calculate the advantages and disadvantages of an actual spread for himself by inserting the respective figures. The most important criteria are:

◇ The return/risk ratio F, which in the above example is very favorable with 0.05. A bearish money spread is still considered favorable if this figure is not greater than 0.25. The figure could be achieved if, for example, the difference in the exercise prices is only $5 (e.g. 40 to 45). The call 45 is bought at $1, and the call 40 is sold for $4.

◇ The price trend of the stock, which can be determined with a long-term chart. Since the investor can only make a profit with falling prices, a bearish money spread should only be attempted when the price is "high," because at that point the probability for a downward movement is highest.

The bearish money spread is a valuable strategy, if no alternative is given in the form of puts. With this combination, the investor has to keep in mind that commissions are twice the amount of those for puts and that the option written may be exercised at any time.

THE CALL "TIME SPREAD"

With the time spread, the investor has the possibility to purchase an option and to write the same type of option in various expiration months

◇ At the same exercise price.
◇ At different exercise prices.

The investor speculates on the fact that options premiums in the different expiration months will follow different courses. The different development of the premium can be caused by

◇ The effects of the remaining lifetime of the option, which are stronger in the near expiration month than in the distant expiration month.

◇ The varying expectations the investor places on the price development of stocks in the various expiration months and the resulting changes in options.

◇ The different volume, which is usually very much higher in the near expiration month.

The investor who chooses a time spread not only has the choice among the exercise prices, he can also combine them with the various expiration months and thus make decisions, which can both increase the opportunities for profit and the danger of risk. *The investor in a time spread speculates not only on the stock price at a certain expiration date; rather, he is after a quick relative change in the options premium.* When choosing the time spread, the investor can take into consideration both a favorable and unfavorable price trend. If the price trend is favorable, he will choose the bullish time spread; if he thinks the trend is unfavorable, he will select the bearish time spread.

Strategy X: The Bullish Time Spread

The bullish time spread consists of a combination of a call purchased at low exercise price in the near expiration month and the writing of a call at the same or higher exercise price in the distant expiration month.

Goal: The investor wants to profit at low risk from rising prices with the purchase of the call at low exercise price.

Advantage: The danger of losing the entire options price when the stock price declines is minimized by the calls written at the high exercise price. The effect of a short-term price increase is, as a rule, that the call with the low exercise price will increase more quickly than the call with high exercise price.

Disadvantages: The writing of the call in the distant expiration month requires that the full margin, as with an uncovered call (at least 30% of the market value), be deposited.

In October, Xerox was quoted at $54⅞. At that time, the following prices could be achieved:

Example:

Purchase January XRX 50 call at $7	=	$700
Sell April XRX 60 call at $5⅝	=	$562
Cost of the spread		$138

The investor expects the price of Xerox to go up. Since the expiration date of January is still nearly three months ahead, the negative effect of the remaining lifetime of the January option is not yet very strong. The investor buys the call January 50 for $7, because the call will increase in dollars nearly as quickly as the stock, if it goes up, since the net premium is very small with $2⅛ (options price $7 minus intrinsic value $4⅞ = $2⅛). As a protection against a possible price decline, the April call with a premium of $5⅝ is written. Ten days later, Xerox traded at $61¾, and at that point the investor was able to terminate his spread with the following prices:

Sell January XRX 50 calls at $14⅛	=	$1,412
Repurchase April XRX 60 calls at $7⅝	=	762
		650
		138
		$ 512

Profit from spread: $512

With an investment of $138, the investor had realized a profit of $512 within ten days (excluding commissions).

The investor in a bullish time spread buys the call at low exercise price in the near expiration month and writes the call at high exercise price in the distant expiration month, because he wants to profit from a favorable price trend. The written call at high exercise price provides the necessary safety margin, in case he was mistaken in his interpretation of the price development. The investor is after a quick profit, which is supposed to result from the different movements of the premiums in the individual exercise prices. The smaller the cost of the spread, that is, the closer the difference of the options prices in the exercise price 50 and 60 are to each other, the bigger are the opportunities for a profit and the lower the risk. The disadvantage of this combination is that by writing the option in the distant expiration month, the investor has written an uncovered option for at least the period January to April. Therefore, he will have to deposit the full margin for an uncovered option (it varies from broker to broker, but it will be at least 30% of the share value). For that reason, this combination will probably look much less attractive to the investor.

The possibility of establishing the time spread with the same exercise prices and different expiration months, is not discussed. The difference of the net premium change with the same exercise prices is usually so minimal that such a transaction is hardly ever worth the effort, considering the commissions the investor has to pay.

Strategy XI: The Bearish Time Spread

The bearish time spread consists of a combination of a call written in the near expiration month at low exercise price and a purchase of a call at high exercise price in the distant expiration month.

Goal: The investor wants to profit at low risk from falling prices with the call written at low exercise price in the near expiration month

Advantage: The danger of the uncovered call bringing unlimited loss, if the stock price increases, is eliminated by writing the call at high exercise price

Disadvantage: The purchase price of the call at high exercise price diminishes the opportunities for profit from the written call. Safety goes at the expense of opportunity to make a large profit. Double commission and the danger that the option will be exercised for the call written make this combination less attractive

Example: In October, Xerox was quoted at $61¾. The investor is convinced at that time that the price has reached its high for the time being. Since he judges the market trend to be unfavorable, he takes the following spread positions:

Stock price Xerox $61¾		
Sell 1 January XRX 50 call at $14⅛	=	+$1,412
Purchase 1 April XRX 60 call at $7⅝	=	−$ 762
Profit not realized from spread		−$ 650

The investor believes that the price is falling and that the written January 50 call will lose value more quickly than the long April 60 call. With a price decline, the option January 50 call will lose value in dollars nearly as quickly as the stock because it has a net premium of only $2⅜ (options price 14⅛ minus the difference between the stock price $61²/₄ and the exercise price 50, which is 14⅛ − 11¾ = 2⅜), while the 60 call consists nearly entirely of premium and will therefore not deteriorate as rapidly.

On November 7, Xerox was at $54½. The spread could be closed out as follows:

Repurchase 1 January XRX 50 call at $7½	=	−$705
Sell 1 April XRX 60 call at $4¾	=	+$475
Cost of the spread		−$275
Profit not realized		+$650
Profit realized		
(excluding commission)		+$375

The investor has been able to realize a profit of $375, because he had judged the market correctly and exploited the various changes in the premiums. If the investor were to wait for the expiration date January, the following picture would present itself:

If by January the stock price declines to $50 or less, the net premium of $14⅛ for the written January 50 call deteriorates. The buyer of this call will certainly not exercise his option, and the $14⅛ is the profit realized. With the purchased April 60 call, the investor can at the most lose his investment of $7⅝ per share. Since the call purchased still has a lifetime of three months from January to April, there is still a residual value to the option, depending on the current stock price. Assuming that Xerox has a price of $48, the April 60 has a value of about $1 on the expiration date January. The realized profit from the written January 50 of $14⅛ is reduced by the price loss of the April 60, which in this case amounts to $7⅝ − $1 = $6⅝. The realized profit would therefore come to $14⅛ − $6⅝ = $7½.

If until January the stock price continues to rise, the written January 50 call will be exercised at the latest on the expiration day. The investor now can exercise his option with the exercise price at 60 and make delivery of these securities when exercised at the 50. The maximum loss can be computed for this case in advance as follows:

◇ Sold 50 call at $14⅛
  Purchase 60 call at $7⅝
  Profit not realized $6.50

◇ Difference between exercise prices
  $60 − $50 = $10

◇ $10 − $6.50 = $3.50 (maximum loss)

No matter how much the price of Xerox continues to rise, the loss can never be more than $3.50.

It is important for the investor to realize that the profit can never exceed the difference between the options prices of the written and purchased calls when the spread is closed out. In our example, the difference and therefore the maximum profit of the spread, was $14⅛ − $7⅝ = $6½ or $650. At what point the loss range begins depends to a great extent on the trend of options prices and stock prices.

Since in this example the investor has written the call in the *near* expiration month, he does not have to deposit a margin for an uncovered call. Usually the brokerage houses only demand the difference between the individual exercise price minus the credit received from the spread as margin, because that is the only point where the risk might materialize.

If one compares the bearish time spread with the bearish money spread, one will find that the only difference between the two lies in the choice of the expiration month of the option purchased. The advantage of the time spread becomes obvious; when the stock price does not decline too sharply. In that case, the remaining lifetime of the distant expiration month will not influence the net premium of the purchased call as strongly as would be the case with the money spread. If, however, the stock price declines sharply, the net premium in the distant expiration month will also be strongly impaired. In that case, the money spread would be preferable. Which of the two spreads the investor should choose depends entirely on the stock price prognosis. It is not enough to recognize whether the stock price is going to decline; the investor should try to estimate by how much it is going to fall. The possibility of a bearish time spread with the same exercise prices and various expiration dates is not discussed, because attractive combinations with that strategy are very rarely found.

Strategy XII: The Butterfly Spread

Goal: Both with rising and falling stock price, the loss is limited by purchasing calls at highest and lowest exercise price. The investor will make a profit as long as the stock price moves within a range which is determined by the exercise prices.

Advantage: The loss can be kept very small both with rising and falling prices.

Disadvantage: The investor has to pay four times the amount of commission he would have to for the purchase of a single call or put, and this considerably diminishes the attraction of this combination. The profit is limited and can only be realized within a range which is determined by the exercise prices.

Example: On November 12, Halliburton traded at $139½. The following butterfly spread (see Figure 65) could be put on (excluding commission):

1. **Bearish Money Spread**

Purchase 1 HAL April 180 call at $1½	=	−$ 150
Sell 1 HAL April 160 call at $4⅞	=	+$ 488
profit not realized from spread		+$ 338

2. **Bullish Money Spread**

Sell 1 HAL April 160 call at $4⅞	=	+$ 488
Purchase 1 HAL April 140 call at $11½	=	−$1.150
Cost of the spread		−$ 662
Cost of the butterfly spread 662 − 338	=	−$ 324

	Purchase 1 Call Exercise Price 180			Written 2 Calls Exercise Price 160			Purchase 1 Call Exercise Price 140
Stock price	Profit + loss stock		Cost of call	Profit + loss stock		Income from calls	Total profit + loss
184	+4	−1½	−48	+9¾	−11½	+44	− 3¾
180	0	−1½	−40	+9¾	−11½	+40	− 3¾
176	0	−1½	−32	+9¾	−11½	+36	¾
172	0	−1½	−24	+9¾	−11½	+32	+ 4¾
168	0	−1½	−16	+9¾	−11½	+28	+ 8¾
164	0	−1½	− 8	+9¾	−11½	+24	+12¾
160	0	−1½	0	+9¾	−11½	+20	+16¾
156	0	−1½	0	+9¾	−11½	+16	+12¾
152	0	−1½	0	+9¾	−11½	+12	+ 8¾
148	0	−1½	0	+9¾	−11½	+ 8	+ 4¾
144	0	−1½	0	+9¾	−11½	+ 4	¾
140	0	−1½	0	+9¾	−11½	+ 0	− 3¾
144	0	−1½					

With the bullish money spread, the biggest profit is achieved if the market trend is favorable. With the bearish money spread, on the other hand, the investor will be successful if the market trend is unfavorable. The results with a butterfly spread are as follows.

In our example, the profit range is between the highest and the lowest exercise price (180 − 140). As long as the stock price moves between $14 and $176, the investor will always realize a profit. If on the expiration date the stock price is exactly at the level of the medium exercise price 160, in which the two calls had been written, the investor will achieve the highest possible profit of $16¾ at

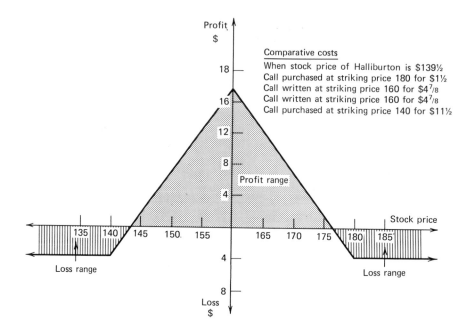

Figure 65   Butterfly spread.

this point. At prices above $176 or below $14, he will inevitably incur a loss. The loss, however, cannot surpass $3¾ no matter how high or low the stock price is. It is always possible to terminate the butterfly spread before the expiration date, if a change in the net premiums indicates that this can be done profitably.

These combinations are suitable only for the investor who can really follow all the ramifications of the spread on his own and, above all, is able to compute exactly the risks and opportunities involved, since he has to pay commissions on four options.

THE PUT SPREAD

As with a call spread, the put spread is a combination of the purchase and writing of options of the same type at the same or different exercise prices and in the same or different expiration months. Put spreads are, like call spreads, used to reduce the risk either by means of puts purchased or written. They can be established either with a credit or debit, just like call spreads. Profit or loss depends on price fluctuations of the underlying securities.

Strategy XIII: The Bullish Put Money Spread

The bullish put money spread is a combination of a put purchased at low exercise price and a put written at high exercise price in the same expiration month.

Goal: The investor takes this position because he wants to profit from writing the put at high exercise price with limited risk when stock prices are rising.

Advantage: The specific danger of the uncovered put, namely, that there is a practically unlimited risk when the stock price falls, is eliminated by purchasing the put at low exercise price.

Disadvantage: The purchase price of the put at low exercise price diminishes the chances with the written call. The investor pays for security with a smaller opportunity to make a profit. Double commissions and the danger that the option will be exercised with the put written lessen the desirability of this combination, as compared to the purchase of a call.

All the details from the bearish money spread in calls can be transferred to this put strategy, with the exception of the evaluation of the market trend, which is exactly the opposite, and we therefore forego a detailed description. The table on page 278 will offer some indications as to when it would be profitable to put on a bullish put money spread.

With this model, every investor can calculate the advantages and disadvantages of an actual spread for himself if he inserts the respective figures. The most important figure here, too, is the optimum risk/return ratio, 0.08 in this example. This can only be achieved because the margin (and at the same time the maximum loss) of $1.50 is really very small compared to the potential profit of $18.50.

Combinations with a risk/return ratio of 0.25 can still be considered extremely good. The important points the investor absolutely must not forget with these spreads are the calculation of commissions, on the one hand, and the danger that the option on the written put can be exercised at any time.

Bullish Put Money Spread

	Put	Options Price	Stock Price
Sell	IBM January 280 at	$31	$250
Purchase	IBM January 260 at	$12½	$250
A	Price of option written		31
B	Price of option purchased		12½
C	Maximum profit 31 − 12½		18½
D	Difference of exercise prices 280 − 260 =		20
E	Maximum risk $D - C = 20 - 18\frac{1}{2} =$		1½
F	Return/risk ratio $\dfrac{E}{C} = 1\frac{1}{2} =$		0.08
G	Profit threshold = risk (E)		
	1½ plus exercise price of option purchased		
	260 260 + 1½ =		261½
H	Percentage of stock price increase necessary to reach profit threshold =		
	261½ − stock price 250 − 11½ = $\dfrac{11\frac{1}{2}}{250}$		5½

Strategy XIV: The Bearish Put Money Spread

The bearish put money spread combines a put purchased at high exercise price with the writing of a similar put at low exercise price during the same expiration month.

Goal: The investor establishes this combination because he wants to profit from falling prices, but at less risk than with the purchase of a put as above.

Advantage: The danger with the put of losing the entire options price in case the stock price goes up is reduced by the amount of the options price from the put at the low exercise price.

Disadvantage: By writing a put at low exercise price, the potential return from the put purchased at high exercise price is limited. Thus the investor pays for the advantage of losing less with the written put with a diminished opportunity to make a profit. In addition, he has to consider the double commission he has to pay for this transaction.

Example: IBM was quoted at $250, and the following spread could be put on with the same expiration month:

Purchase IBM 260 put at $11
Sell IBM 240 put at $3

With this spread, the risk of the 260 put purchased is reduced by writing the 240 put from $11 to $3 = $8. No matter how much the stock price goes below 240 until the expiration date, the investor has achieved the highest possible profit with $20 − $9 = $11. If the investor was mistaken in his price forecast and the stock rises above 260, both options will expire. The loss, however, can never surpass $8. The following table will give some indications as to when and under what circumstances it would be profitable to enter a position with the bearish put money spread:

Bearish Put Money Spread

	Put	Options Price	Stock Price
Purchase	IBM January 260	$11	$250
Written	IBM January 240	$ 3	$250
A	Price of option purchased		$11
B	Price of option written		$ 3
C	Maximum risk $A − B = 11 − 3 =$		$ 8
D	Difference exercise prices $260 − 240 =$		$20
E	Maximum return $D − C = 20 − 9 =$		$11
F	Return/risk ratio $\dfrac{C}{E}\ \dfrac{9}{11}$		0.82
G	Profit threshold = exercise price of written option 260 plus c (a) $= 240 + 9 =$		249

With this model, every investor can calculate the advantages and disadvantages of an actual spread for himself if he inserts the respective figures. The most important figure here is the return/risk ratio (F), which in this example is acceptable at 0.82. It would be better still if the figure were smaller. This spread only becomes a viable alternative to simply purchasing a put if the purchase price of the entire spread is very low, which would happen if the option written at the low exercise price carried a sufficiently high net premium.

CONCLUSION

It would not be surprising if the investor were both astonished and confused by the number of possible options strategies. How efficient these strategies are is another question, one that would have to be answered negatively in most cases. Aside from the high commissions and the sort of transaction that is very hard to unravel, *not one of these strategies offers real and concrete advantages compared with the well-considered purchase of puts and calls alone.* This collection of strategies could easily be enlarged upon. Each strategy has its advantages and disadvantages, and the investor should only consider following such a strategy when he is totally and conclusively familiar with its ins and outs.

5 *THE EUROPEAN OPTIONS EXCHANGE IN AMSTERDAM*

As soon as it became fairly obvious that the Chicago Board Options Exchange (CBOE) would be a success, the Americans tried to sell their freshly acquired know-how to the Europeans. Delegates first turned to the biggest European exchange, the London Exchange. When negotiations there dragged along, the Dutch Amsterdam Exchange took the initiative and tried to analyze what the chances would be for a European Options Exchange. The idea was no longer to establish an options exchange as part of the stock exchange, as was initially the case in London, but rather to establish an independent European options exchange in Amsterdam. The Dutch exchange invested several million dollars in the advance financing of this project, and this alone proved that they were determined to open the exchange in any case. This happened on April 4, 1978.

THE STRUCTURE OF THE EUROPEAN OPTIONS EXCHANGE

The European Options Exchange (EOE) was set up as a holding company in the form of an association with a body corporate accountable to Dutch laws. Members of European or other stock exchanges, members of the CBOE and companies which comply with the conditions set up by the exchange, are allowed to acquire interests. Each seat on the exchange represents one vote. The price for one seat is approximately 25,000 Gulden for members (banks, American brokers, or companies that had been involved from the beginning). European Option Clearing Corporation is a 100% owned subsidiary of the EOE with a fully paid in stock capital of at least 1,000,000 hfl. It is the issuer of the options and the central clearing house. It guarantees the financial safety of all transactions. In addition, it has the responsibility to see that the options buyer can at all times exercise the option and that the options writer will at all times accept the obligation to make delivery if the options buyer chooses to exercise his option.

On the following securities out of the different European countries calls and puts are to be traded:

The Netherlands

ABN Bank   call
Akzo   call
Amro Bank   call
Hoogovens   call
KLM   call & put
Philips Gloeilampen   call & put
Royal Dutch   call & put
Unilever   call & put
Nationale Netherlands
    call & put
Heineken   call & put

France

Thomson CSF   call
Saint-Gobain   call
PSA, Peugeot/Citroën   call

Great Britain

British Petroleum   call
General Electric   call
Imperial Chemical Industries
    call

United States

Boeing   call
Eastman Kodak   call

Belgium

Compagnie Financière   call
Gevaert Photo   call
Petrofina   call & put
Source Perrier   call
Union Minière   call

Germany

Mannesmann   call
Siemens   call
Volkswagen   call
Thyssen   call
BASF   call

Citicorp   call
General Motors   call
IBM   call
Occidental Petroleum   call
Polaroid   call
Sears, Roebuck   call
Schlumberger   call
American Telephone & Telegraph
  call
Exxon   call
Xerox   call

The American securities were included in the trade in order to create additional liquidity. Furthermore, this left the door open for arbitrage transactions at a later time between the CBOE and the EOE. With the establishment of the European Options Exchange, it was intended to create an options exchange for European stocks that had the necessary depth, continuity, and liquidity. As in Chicago, this intention is to be realized by the combination of two levels of transactions; that is, first opening an options contract between buyer and writer and then, on the second level, the secondary market where investors who hold options contracts can terminate their positions on the exchange by the corresponding countertransaction. The efficiency of the options exchange is to be increased by standardizing the conditions of the options contract. Here, the EOE strictly follows the rules developed by the CBOE (see Chapter 4).

Expiration Months

As with the CBOE, the Amsterdam exchange at first introduced the expiration months January, April, July and October, and only three expiration months are open for trading at any one time.

Exercise Prices

Once a new expiration month is released for trading, the Clearing Corporation determines the exercise price close to the current stock price. If the stock price fluctuates, the corporation introduces new exercise prices which are adapted to the fluctuations.

Size of Contract

Unlike the CBOE, which prescribes that each options contract contains 100 shares, the EOE standardizes options contracts only to a certain extent and the investor can set up the contract in various ways, depending on the stocks. This seems sensible, since stocks such as Hoffmann La Roche, Nestle (Switzerland), Bayer (Germany) or Royal Dutch (The Netherlands) show wide differences as far as stock prices and trading volume are concerned.

Commissions

The Exchange intended to take the minimum commission as set up and prescribed by the CBOE until April 1975 as a model.

It is still too early to say whether the Options Exchange in Amsterdam will prove to have the necessary depth, liquidity, and continuity in the long run. In the final analysis, it will be a question of the readiness and willingness of all participants to coordinate the different laws, exchange rules, and—last but not least—their political preferences that will determine the success or failure of options in Amsterdam.

Elimination of the Currency Risk

The present currency risk could best be eliminated if a European economic unification (Common Market) were realized with one reserve currency only. That is still not the case. In Amsterdam, therefore, the procedure is to try to balance the discrepancies by clearing each option in the currency in which the respective shares are traded. German stock options have to be paid in deutschmark, Swiss securities in Swiss franks, and the Dutch values in gulden.

Trouble-Shooting Is Necessary

Each country has its own clearing house for conducting international exchange transactions. In Germany it is the *Arbeitsgemeinschaft Deutscher Kassenverein* and the *Auslandskassenverein*, in France the *Sivovam*, Switzerland the *S.E.G.A.*, Belgium the *C.I.K.*, and in Amsterdam the *Necigef*. All delivery notifiers for options that are exercised are supposed to go through these clearing houses. The problems and troubles that are caused by the different rules for portfolio administration and for the exchange in the various countries, and the different margin requirements with the writing of uncovered options (semicoverage in Germany), still await resolution in all of the European countries.

The rules the EOE is considering for governing restrictions go far beyond those of the CBOE. The intention is to prevent market manipulation by imposing restrictions on both opening and closing transactions at certain times. However, any kind of restriction can cut down on liquidity. A restriction on closing transactions can throw the entire market out of kilter, since not only liquidity but also continuity and market depth are gone if the market participant no longer has the choice to even up his position according to his own preferences.

How important these kinds of deliberations and thought processes may eventually become is evident from the ongoing discussion in the United States about the extent to which options influence the prices of stocks. Even though a general and continuous effect of options on the stock price has not been proven so far, they do have a partial influence which cannot be denied. This becomes particularly obvious on the expiration day of options when short-term influences which are due to arbitrage transactions of brokerage houses can be noticed.

New Investors' Groups

The run of investors to the CBOE showed that there was a real demand for this form of investment. It was not only the speculator who wanted to achieve the biggest potential return with the leverage effect while investing only small amounts, who showed the greatest interest. The conservative investors and funds who used the writing of options as a defensive strategy still carry home the profit from options. The European Options Exchange could have a positive influence on the securities traded here. Compared with the United States, the European investors still show relatively small interest in options. However, through options, new investors could be won for the stock market, and people could be induced to learn about this form of investment. The possibility to establish covered writers positions can help concentrate the interest in certain stocks and thus provoke a much higher volume. This could have a favorable effect on the companies insofar as there would be better possibilities for new issues because of the broader market for the stocks.

A further considerable advantage from a tax point of view could result from buying stocks and writing options against them at the

Since the European Option Clearing Corporation has to take liability for the financial security and the practical processing of the options trade, it should have the right to exercise control over its members. But the big banks have until today refused specifically to grant this right to the CBOE and EOE. The policy of the big banks with respect to options, and their readiness to recommend options investment to their customers, varies drastically. Although some of the banks have since decided that it would be better to inform their customers about all the aspects and details of options and print brochures and detailed information pamphlets, others still try to disqualify options as being too risky and refuse to recommend that form of investment. Since poor recommendations and orders of nonqualified investment advisors can lead a bank into such an internal muddle which it can hardly unravel, this reticent attitude becomes more understandable. Additionally, there is the danger that the customer will seek restitution from the bank. The amount of time and effort one has to put into options can be incredibly great. There is not only the "German options trade" with the possibilities of put and call options, and the "Swiss Future Trade" with its special rules. The technical, organizational, and training problems will be the first on the list of difficulties encountered with the options trade and will have to be solved if the European Options Exchange is to function properly. Success in the options business depends more on the qualifications, dedication, responsibility and adaptability of the co-workers than on anything else.

Restrictions on Trading Options Contracts

The EOE is permitted to place restrictions on trading as necessary so as to protect the investor, maintain a functioning market, and be in the public interest. Certain transactions, such as taking a position by buying or writing uncovered options, could be suspended from trading at certain times, and existing contracts may not be terminated under certain circumstances and for defined periods. The EOE has found one of its rules very useful, namely, that opening transactions cannot be conducted if the difference between stock price and exercise price ("out of the money") is more than $5 and if the option trades below 50¢. These restrictions can be considered very useful, since they encourage concentration and increase the liquidity in the exercise prices near the current stock price. Closing transactions are always possible on the EOE.

same time. Although premiums from covered writers transactions are definitely subject to income tax in Germany, since they cannot be liquidated, the same combination opens completely new perspectives for all investors if the transaction were to be conducted through the options exchange.

One of the decisive factors that will make it possible for the options exchange in Amsterdam to function profitably will be the readiness of all banks to participate in this new form of investment. As long as the interest is there, all technical problems can be solved. The CBOE was founded not because the brokers were looking for new sources of income. The experiment was successful, and both investors and brokers are profiting from it. This compulsion to make a profit from the securities business is not as pronounced in Europe. But the competition among the banks, which becomes ever more aggressive in order to gain new customers, could be an inducement to get more deeply involved in Amsterdam.

6 *CONCLUSION*

At the beginning of the book we had asked ourselves whether the investor can in the long run achieve a better return on his investment in stocks and options than commonly thought possible. With some reservations, this question can be answered with yes. The possibility of realizing an above-average return may not be open to the majority of the investors who have neither the know-how nor the analytical tools for a dependable price prognosis. However, it is exactly this lack of knowledge on the part of the majority that presents the few qualified investors with the possibility to work for, and finally achieve, a return which is considerably above average, and that for a sustained period of time.

The long-term oriented investor especially has to have knowledge both of overall economic developments and of developments in the various industries in order to make a qualified price forecast. He will only be able to predict the development of stock prices with a certain degree of accuracy if he has that background and can interpret and understand the economic ramifications. Whether the investor should rely on charts or on fundamental analysis should not lead to a battle between the followers of two diverging opinions and beliefs. Both methods have their specific advantages and weaknesses, and they can be used together and thus complement each other. The strategy of the market technicians is a synthesis of the two methods that requires a lot of time when applied practically. An absolutely infallible price prognosis, however, is not **288** guaranteed with this method either.

Since there are no analytical tools for prognosis that are absolutely perfect, every system contains a degree of uncertainty and unknown factors. This uncertainty factor cannot be reduced arbitrarily, but it can be included methodically in the calculation. The prerequisite for that would be a risk factor that really works. The investor could, for example, use the variability range of the expected price fluctuations which can be estimated by means of frequency distribution of past price quotations, that is, the highest and the lowest of the past years. Securities with a great range of difference between the highest and the lowest in the past are quite attractive for those investors who have a high risk preference because they pin all their hopes on a strong price increase and tend to forget about the risk of a price deterioration. On the other hand, the investor with a strong inclination toward safety will favor those stocks which had a narrow trading range in the past. Any investment counseling that does not take into account this difference between investment risk per se and investor's risk preference, but simply recommends certain forms as the absolute "optimum," can only be called dangerous and irresponsible. It is too easily done, under the pretense of rational thinking and know-how, to recommend investment forms that are absolutely contrary to the actual risk preference of the individual investor.

Markowitz' and Sharpe's models indicate how investment risk in a portfolio can be controlled. With them, an optimum mixture for any given risk preference can be computed mathematically. However, these models are in part based on data that are dependable only to a certain extent and that do not contain all information necessary.

The investor can also switch back and forth between stocks and other forms of capital investment or cash holdings, depending on the trend of the stock market. For that reason, stock price forecasts gain additional importance. Not only does the investor have to predict long-term trends as accurately as possible, but it becomes necessary to figure out the point at which the fluctuation lines within that trend reach their highs and lows. If the investor choses an investment strategy with timing, the investment risk becomes dependent on the timing. The investor invites a much higher risk if he buys stocks at a high price, since these are much more likely to decline than stocks with a low price, where the probability of an upswing is much greater. Thomas referred to these interrelations in his *Risk and Opportunity* method (Dow Jones Irwin, Inc., Homewood, Ill., 60430, 1974), and the investor can only afford to disregard them if he leaves the securities in the portfolio for a longer period of time.

Although the stock market alone offers a wide spectrum of investment strategies, the stormy development of the options market in the United States showed that a great number of investors still were not satisfied with the strategic possibilities offered. Many investors obviously welcomed the many forms of trading with options and considered them a worthwhile and valuable expansion of their operating field. This expansion, however, contains dangers as well. It is much more complicated to make decisions about buying and writing of options than about stock transactions. The investor not only has to select the security and the time of the transaction, but also has to make a decision about the exercise price and expiration month. If the investor wants to be successful in options investing, he has to have more information, be more careful and thorough in his analysis, and spend more time on it than a stock investment requires. He always must remember that he can suffer a total loss even if he made a basically correct stock prognosis, if he is tied to an unfavorable expiration month.

The buyer of calls and puts has a wide strategic field in which he can pick and choose the strategy best suited to his taste and preferences. The investor who considers the stock market a game of chance and only sees two possibilities—that is, either to multiply his capital within the shortest time possible or to lose all according to the maxim "all or nothing"—can have the time of his life in options, particularly if he "puts all his eggs into one basket" and neglects timing that would safeguard and justify a risky speculation, since it would give the appropriate buying or selling signals. Nobody can force his luck with options. It will hurt the investor if he loses on his stocks because of a forecast that went wrong, but he will always have the hope that the stocks will go up again. Not so the options buyer—his expectations and hopes come to an end with the expiration date of the option.

In practice, one can often observe a sort of inverted investor's behavior; the more the investor speculates on exercise prices and expiration months, the fewer auxiliary aids he uses for price prognosis, and he invests more in options compared to the total capital on hand. The daily press comments regularly on those occurrences when somebody gains several 100% in options within a few days, but somehow they never report on the following transactions of those lucky ones. Since these speculators jump from one option to the other, on top of everything else, and depend on their emotions or tips they stumble on, these portfolios usually do not last out the first year. It is not just a question of the losses. The investor must also pay heavily in commissions with this kind of fast in-and-out trading. Even though options commissions are not as high as those the investor has to pay on stocks, they mount up extremely fast to the highest level if the investor wants to force his luck by steady gambling.

The investor only rarely follows an investment plan systematically, even if he does have such a plan, but very often he destroys the basically sound strategy by constantly changing the premises. It is extraordinarily difficult to put aside all subjective feelings and thoughts and to follow an objective strategy without reservation, and most investors are simply incapable of it. *Know-how* and *discipline*, those are the two criteria that determine success or failure, especially with in options. Discipline, of course, cannot be measured and has different meaning for each type of investor, but the know-how can be acquired.

One requirement, of course, is our initial capital (which does not even have to be tremendously big!)—but there are three points the investor should always keep in mind if he wants to be successful with his strategy.

Michael Ott has summarized these three requirements as follows (Aktientrend Nr. 51–52, 1977):

1. Set up a definite goal!

You have to know beforehand what you want to achieve. You think that is self-explanatory? Certainly not—just ask anybody about concrete ideas and you will never get any other answer but that he wants to make a profit. How much? As much as possible. And in what time? Well, at once, if you please. But: If you are after a short-term success in the market, your strategy has to be different from the one you would apply if you were more interested in a long-term success. If you want a high continuing return, again you will have to follow other strategies than the ones you would use if you only wanted price returns without dividends for tax reasons.

If you are unable to supervise your portfolio daily, you should not try short-term speculations. If, however, you are bored to tears because your present strategy only requires attention and action every few months or years, you should get into short-term speculation right from the beginning.

But: you will certainly fall flat on your nose if you proceed without a definite plan and simply react to news and give in to sudden impulses. Therefore: *Make up your mind what goal you want to reach.* Narrow it down as far as possible, don't just flounder around. Put it down in writing. And be realistic—don't run after a dream!

2. Determine your strategy!

The choice of your strategy depends on the goal you have set up for yourself. You have to take various factors into account, but above all, be realistic about your own personal circumstances and possibilities.

If you only have the weekend to work on your portfolio, that is no reason for despair or to give up hope to get rich eventually. In that case you simply have to stay away from strategies which require daily decisions.

If you are dependant on a regular income derived from your portfolio, you have to plan differently than would be the case if you only wanted to play around with a portion of your capital. And if you have a regular income which you have to invest in the market, you will not follow the same strategy as you would apply for a one-time investment decision.

You first have to decide which form of capital investment would be right for you. If you think options, commodity investments, etc. are uncanny and strange things—hands off! And if you just want to combine stocks and bonds or cash, adjust your strategies to that concept right from the start and don't waver!

You can also combine several strategies and divide your portfolio accordingly. Following a long-term strategy, you could invest 75% of the capital in such a way that it only requires very little attention and work, but promises good returns. Use the other 25% in a short-term, more speculative strategy that will provide the necessary (?) excitement.

Remember: there are many beautiful strategies which are extremely intricate and complicated and promise good returns—but they eat up all of your time! There are other strategies which require much less time and bring results which are nearly as good. *The main thing is not to find an optimum strategy, but to discover one that is absolutely tailored to your needs and resources.* Stay away from a strategy that smothers you with work and gives you such a disgust of the market that you only want to forget about it. Better use a less time-consuming strategy which you can follow without reaching your wit's end! The strategy you have selected should also be put down in writing—it will help avoid temptations. . . .

3. Be consistent in the use of your strategy!

This is one of the most important requirements. It sounds so trite that you may think it absurd that this point is emphasized so strongly, but this is exactly where most investors come to grief.

Why? Why should anyone who has found a good strategy that brings success stay away from it and engage in silly experimentation? Why should that require a special effort? Well—it does, you can depend on it.

There are many reasons for that. For one thing, every strategy is a chain of single decisions, some of which turn out to be correct. Others, however, fail. Only the sum of the individual decisions makes up the favorable result. Every single decision can be wrong. It may sound all right in theory, and the investor accepts the possibility. However when it is applied practically, he will nonetheless try to evade failure and will think up clever little bypasses. Suddenly he will discover "special circumstances" which justify the deviation from the strategy—"just this once" for this "special" case. But there are hardly ever any "special cases" that happen only once—and the damage is done and the investor has to live with that "extra" loss, which he certainly had not reckoned with.

Miracles may happen in the market once in a great while, but it would be an even greater miracle if fortune would smile on you of all people! So don't give in to daydreams; stay with realities. Another tip: it might prove helpful if you were to formulate your expectations in figures: don't say you want to achieve as much as possible but: I expect 10 or 15 or 20% return on the average per year, with that I'll be satisfied. Such a fixed point could save you from a fruitless chase after the last dollar in profit—which in any case would only end in disaster. And it might prove just as useful if you were to divide your portfolio as suggested above. If you—like the majority of investors—tend to give in to your speculative tendencies more often than not, you could satisfy your adventurous longings and play with the speculative part of your portfolio. In this way the loss—which is inevitable anyway—will at least be limited.

If this happens several times, the investor has to stand up against another temptation: he might try to replenish his portfolio with all his might and force his luck by engaging in the most risky speculations. That is the beginning of the end. Or: one has followed the strategy systematically and religiously, but for weeks it looks as if the last decision had been wrong. Sure, afterwards it turns out that there was no reason to worry, but "wait a few weeks" is more easily said than done, and the situation looks quite different if you have to undergo that experience in reality. The investor has too much time to indulge in doubts and consequently make the wrong decisions—he gives in to temptation, and again the damage is done.

Another situation: somewhere one stumbles across a "sure thing"; the manufacturers of such stories develop such an enormous amount of convincing and fascinating power, and, more often than not, the investor loses his head and thinks: the system maybe okay, but it has its deficiencies. And here is that incredible chance—and confidential on top of it—to make real money. Well, the consequences are known. . . .

This is the really important point: you have to remember, once and for all, that nobody can *always* make a profit with *any* strategy. Whoever tells you differently is a liar. You must accept the fact that you will always buy above the lowest and sell below the highest price. Don't even try to overcome that handicap. There is absolutely no strategy that will enable you to do that. Again, whoever tells you differently does not tell the truth. Always keep in mind: it is a real success, if you make 10% on the average on the market over the long run. That is more than the normal interest rate, and it is more than the rate of growth of the entire economy. If you have made more than 20% on the average per year, you have been extremely successful. Beware of whoever promises you to make 100% per year—with your money, of course—, because he is the biggest liar of them all.

(A simple calculation for those who doubt it: Slogan: 100% every year. Initial capital: 10 million dollars (many funds have more!), and off they go: after one year, it is 20 million; after two years, 40; after three, 80; four, 160; five, 320; after six, 640 million. And here you begin to make a profit: after seven years 1.28 billion; after eight, 2.56 billion; after nine, 5.12; and after only ten measly years, the investor is sitting pretty with more than 10 billion dollars. We would need only one of those market geniuses and our public debts would be taken care off!)

Whoever wants to trade in options has to know the rules of the stock market backward and forward. Exercise months and exercise prices of the individual options are merely auxiliary means for sharpening the strategy. Whoever thinks he can pass over the stocks and still make his fortune with options without previous knowledge will pay heavily for his "boast". And he will have to pay just as heavily if he entrusts his capital to one of those investment funds which boast in advertisements that once again the big profit of 50% has been achieved. These companies should be approached with the necessary caution, because there is simply no investment form where you can make a big profit that does not carry a high risk. But if these investment companies interpret their own advertisement in such a way that they themselves are the ones who make the fast and big profit of 50% from the entire customers investment in their account (because they gain more commissions from their customers jumping in and out of transactions,) one could very well believe them. Every investor should get detailed information as to what the risk would be for his investment and which auxiliary means are employed to protect the capital from risk before he appoints a third person to administer his capital. Nobody needs an unknown third person to gamble away his capital.

The simple options transactions such as calls and puts are still relatively complicated compared to stock transactions. With combined options transactions, such as spreads or straddles, the investor has to deal with further difficulties. The beginner will at first find these combinations of strategies irritating and confusing. As a consolation: neither spreads nor straddles offer opportunities that are beyond what calls or puts would not bring either. Under certain circumstances, they might prove helpful as auxiliary strategies. Their practical usefulness, however, is limited, since they involve high commissions, and the investor in the short option is constantly under pressure, since the option might be exercised.

Like stocks, options can be combined with other forms of investment. The combination of options with treasuries is especially attractive, because treasuries contain a very low risk and can safeguard options to a certain degree without destroying the opportunities. There are some very convincing arguments for the contention that combinations of treasuries and options are superior to those of stocks and treasuries. If one were to calculate the optimum combination of stocks and treasuries on the basis of a given risk preference and with certain data, and repeat the same calculation with options and treasuries, one will find that with the options portfolio the risk is smaller and the opportunities greater than with the stock portfolio.

The attraction of such a strategy is evident, and of course that leads to the question of why so few investors favor this form of investment. The answer is relatively simple: the strategy is too conservative for the investor who likes high risk, and, in addition, demands a degree of reticence and discipline, which apparently is too much for most investors who would basically be interested in options. Besides, it is quite possible that those arguments with which the advantages of a combination of options and treasuries, described and emphasized in this book, are still widely unknown.

Compared with the Options Exchange in Chicago, the European Options Exchange in Amsterdam offers the European investor two real advantages: the investor can make his transactions with options on stocks from companies that are well known to him, and he can avoid the currency risk to a great extent. A successful participation in European options, of course, presupposes a fundamental knowledge of options—and that in fact means work! The investor who has read this book down to the last paragraph should be very close to fulfill this requirement and will find himself at an advantage over other investors—and that should be worth the time and effort to him.

APPENDIX
TAX CONSIDERATIONS

Everyone who participates in the options market must look to the "risk-reward" ratio, that is, how much money is being risked in terms of the potential reward. This is true of the most conservative options participant: the writer of covered calls who is looking for income enhancement. It is equally true of the speculator who writes naked calls, naked puts and is also true—in a special way—of the purchaser of options, because this investor has 100% of the premium cost at risk.

Because taxes *erode* a part of the reward, the options purchaser or writer subject to the income taxes of the United States should review these tax considerations before embarking on a program of options investment.

These considerations reflect the tax changes made by the Revenue Act of 1978.

PRINCIPAL CONSIDERATIONS

◇ In general, profits from the sale of options that expire are short-term capital gains. Such short-term capital gains are fully taxed as though they were current income. Thus they add a tax liability—dollar for dollar—at the client's "marginal tax rate." This may be as high as 70%, because such short-term capital gains are unearned income.

◇ Losses from the purchase of options that expire as worthless (with one exception that is explained later) are short-term capital losses. Short-term capital losses—up to $3000 in any tax year—receive preferential tax treatment in that taxpayers may deduct from income a portion of net securities losses.

◇ The most advantageous options participant is the writer of covered calls: if a call is exercised against the writer, the premium becomes part of the proceeds and takes on the holding period of the underlying stock. Thus the premium may become part of a long-term capital gain if the underlying stock has been held long-term when the stock is delivered against the call.

We shall treat all of the tax considerations individually, but the investor should understand that the tax laws of the United States are complex. There is no substitute for professional tax advice, especially if the investor has other sources of unearned income because under the Revenue Act of 1978 there is a minimum tax requirement if such unearned income exceeds certain statutory amounts.

PROFIT OR LOSS

For those readers who give their tax computation to professional tax consultants, it will be useful to review a basic principal:

$$\frac{\text{Net proceeds of any}}{\text{security transaction}} - \frac{\text{adjusted cost of}}{\text{acquisition}} = \text{profit or loss}$$

This is an important concept, because the Internal Revenue Service has specific rules regarding the premium paid for an option and for the premium received from the sale of an option. These premiums will be added to the net proceeds—or the cost of acquisition or subtracted from the proceeds or cost of acquisition, depending on the circumstances of the options transaction. We treat of these in detail.

OPTION BUYING

Let us start with the investor who buys an option for $300. Here are all of the possible situations.

1. **Investor buys a call;** *the call expires.*

   Example: Investor buys a call on ABC for $300. Option expires as worthless.

$$\begin{array}{ccc} \text{Net proceeds } (NP) - \text{adjusted cost of} \\ \text{acquisition } (ACA) \\ 0 \quad - \quad \$300 \quad = -\$300 \end{array}$$

   The investor has suffered a $300 short-term loss.

2. **Investor buys a call;** *the investor resells the call.*

   Example: Investor buys a call on ABC for $300. The investor resells the call for $500.

$$\begin{array}{ccc} NP & - & ACA \\ \$500 & - & \$300 & = +\$200 \end{array}$$

   The investor has a short-term gain of $200.

3. **The investor buys a call** *and exercises it!*

$$\begin{array}{ccc} NP & - & ACA \\ \text{Transaction} & & \text{Strike price } plus \\ \text{incomplete} & & \text{the premium} \end{array}$$

   There is no tax consequence, because the investor has not yet sold the stock acquired by exercising the call. The investor acquired the stock as of the day he exercised the call. The tax consequences—either a gain or loss—will depend on the sale price of the security when it is sold. Remember: investor's cost is strike price plus premium.

4. **Investor buys a call and** *is short the underlying stock.* The Internal Revenue Service considers these as two independent transactions.

   Example: investor sells 100 ABC short at 55. When stock drops to 45, investor buys a call for $300 at 45. Stock is now at 41 and call expires.

   (a) Short account:

$$\begin{array}{ccc} NP & & ACA \\ \$5500 & - & \text{transaction} & = & \text{no tax con-} \\ & & \text{incomplete} & & \text{sequence until} \\ & & & & \text{short is covered} \end{array}$$

(b) Option account

0	−	$300	=	− $300 short-term loss

5. **Investor buys a put, and has no position in the underlying stock.** *The put expires.*

NP		ACA		
0	−	$300	=	− $300 short-term loss

6. **The investor *buys a put on the same day* that he bought the underlying stock. The Internal Revenue Service considers this a "marriage".** *The put expires.*

(a) Put account

0	−	0	= no tax consequence

(b) Long account

Transaction incomplete	− price of stock *plus* put premium	= no tax consequence until long stock sold

In other words, the investor who "hedges" a long position on the same day with a put (the option to sell) in effect adds the put premium to the purchase price of the underlying stock to get an adjusted cost of acquisition. The investor may not take a short-term capital loss when the put expires. Instead, the investor has an adjusted cost of acquisition. This adjusted cost will determine the investor's gain or loss when the underlying stock is finally sold.

7. **The investor owns the underlying stock and *subsequently* buys a put.** *The put expires.*

(a) Put account

0	−	$300	=	$300 short-term capital loss

(b) Long account

Incomplete	−	original cost	= no gain or loss until sold

This is important: if an owner of the underlying stock (or its equivalent, for example, a convertible security) hedges it while the underlying stock is a short-term holding, the application of a hedge wipes out the holding period of the underlying stock. Let us put this concept into specific terms:

1/2/80 Client buys 100 ABC at 55 . . . stock subsequently rises to 71.

8/7/80 To hedge paper profit (when stock is at 71), client buys a put at 70 for a premium of $300 that will expire in April 1981.

Apr. '81 Put expires as worthless

June '81 Client sells original stock at 95.

Tax consequences:

(a) Put account: short-term loss of put premium of $300

(b) Long account: *short-term gain* of 40 on ABC. Reason: client hedged long account while it was short-term. Original holding period was wiped out, and holding period began again the day after the put expired in April, 1981. It was short term when client sold in June, 1981. This may seem unfair, but the IRS is adamant: you cannot play "both sides of the street" and try for a short-term loss and a long-term gain on what is, in effect, an offsetting transaction.

If the client hedges a long-term paper profit with a put, the IRS allows the long-term holding period to stand, and the premium paid for the put is an independent transaction which may result in a gain or loss depending on the resale value of the put.

8. **The investor owns the underlying stock and buys a put. Subsequently, he puts the stock.**

$$\underbrace{\text{Strike price } minus \text{ the premium}}_{NP} - \underbrace{\text{original purchase price of security}}_{ACA} = \text{gain or loss}$$

The gain or loss will be long or short term depending on the holding period when investor purchased the put. Refer to the discussion in 7. If stock was long term when put was purchased, it remains long term. If stock was short term when investor purchased the put, it remains short term.

OPTION WRITING

Here are all the possible situations in which an investor writes an option.

9. **The investor writes a call, the call expires.**

NP		ACA	
+$300	—	0	= short-term capital gain of $300

10. **The investor owns the underlying stock and writes a call. Later, the call is exercised against the writer.**

NP		ACA	
Strike price plus the premium	—	original purchase or security	= gain or loss

The gain or loss will be long or short term depending on original purchase date of underlying security and the day investor receives exercise notice. (There is still some confusion on this point: settlement date is actually four business days later. Professional advice is recommended if there is a problem of long versus short term or the tax year if a gain is involved.)

11. **The investor writes an uncovered call and the call is exercised against the writer.**

NP		ACA	
Strike price plus the premium	—	cost of acquiring the security	= short-term loss

Use the total cost: the market price of the security plus two brokerage commissions; one to purchase the security; one to deliver it against the call.

12. **An investor writes a call (it makes no difference whether the call is covered or uncovered) and subsequently makes a closing purchase transaction.**

NC		ACA	
Proceeds from writing the call	—	total cost to close out short option	= short-term gain or loss

13. **An investor writes a put, the put expires.**

NP		ACA	
Proceeds from writing the put	—	0	= short-term gain

14. **An investor writes a put that is uncovered; then the underlying stock is put to the investor.**

    NP   *ACA*
    Incomplete transaction − strike price *minus*
                                 the put premium

    In other words, there are no tax consequences until the stock acquired from the put is sold. The investor's acquisition price is the strike price minus the premium.

15. **An investor writes a put against a short position in the underlying security. The stock is put to the investor and the stock is used to close out the underlying short position.**

    NP   *ACA*
    Proceeds of short sale − strike price minus = short-term gain
                             the put premium   or loss

16. **An investor writes a put that is covered by a long put. The stock is put to the investor and he uses the long put to put the stock.**

    NP   *ACA*
    Proceeds from exercising − cost of acquiring   = gain or loss
    the long put *minus*   the stock put to him
    premium paid for the   *minus* the premium
    long put   he received when he
                                  wrote the put

    Technically, this is two independent transactions, but the tax consequences will be short term and will be a gain or loss based on these considerations:

STRADDLES

17. **The Internal Revenue Service considers both long and short straddles as two independent transactions. The tax consequences are computed separately.**

    Example: investor writes a straddle. Premium on put $300; premium on call $400. Stock is put to investor; the call expires.

(a) put account

Incomplete transaction – strike price *minus*
put premium

No tax consequence until the stock is sold

(b) call account

+$400   –   0   = $400 short-term
gain

SPREADS

18. **Because spreads are established at a "net credit" or a "net debit" in effect, they become one transaction. There will be either a net gain or loss (short term) on the entire transaction.**

SUMMARY

Although professional tax advice should be sought for complex problems (and this series of situations may seem complex!), there is a simple approach: under a plus sign place all money that comes to you; under a minus sign place all money that you pay out on the transaction. The offsetting of "money in" and "money out" will tell you whether you had a gain or a loss (or an incomplete transaction if money has not yet come to you).

On completed transactions, you can have a long-term capital gain only:

◇ you write a call and the underlying stock is long term when it is called;

◇ you own the underlying stock, buy a put after the underlying stock is long term, and then exercise the put.

HOLDING PERIOD CONSIDERATIONS

The tax law gives preferential tax treatment to long-term capital gains. Under the Revenue Act of 1978, 40% of net long-term gains are added to income and taxed at the taxpayer's "marginal tax bracket". This may be as high as 70% in some circumstances because it is considered "unearned income."

The 60% of the net long-term gain that is excluded becomes preference income and—under certain circumstances—is subject to a minimum tax, but it does not reduce the amount of "personal service income" (earned income) subject to the maximum tax of 50%.

The Revenue Act of 1978 made a trade off: it dropped the 25% effective maximum tax on the first $50,000 of net long-term capital gains; lowered to 40% (from 50%) the amount subject to the taxpayer's marginal tax bracket; kept the excluded portion as *preference income* (subject to a minimum tax in certain circumstances) but does not let this source of preference income reduce the amount of the taxpayer's earned income subject to the 50% maximum tax on that category of income.

The net result is that the Revenue Act of 1978 *enhanced* the preferential tax treatment of net long-term capital gains. We shall treat of such long-term gains briefly.

A long-term capital gain results from the acquisition of an asset (whether by purchase or gift) and its *subsequent* sale at a profit after the asset is held "more than one year".

The holding period is computed as follows:

◇ take the day after the purchase (or the day after the donor's purchase date in case of a gift). That same calendar date one year later begins the long-term holding period.

◇ if a security is acquired by a stock split, stock dividend, or by conversion, use the same method: the acquired security is considered as acquired when the original security was acquired;

◇ if a security is acquired by an option (right, warrant, call, or a short put) the date of exercise begins a new holding period! Reason: you paid out new money—so, new holding period.

Except for a gift, the IRS follows a simple concept: if the money out is less than the money in, and the money was out longer than one year, you have a long-term capital gain. (In the case of a gift, someone else's money was out; it became your money; so, they use the original purchase date.)

One final point: a long-term gain can only arise from a purchase (or gift) followed by a sale! It can never arise from a sale followed by a purchase.

Now, let's look at the possibility of long-term gains from option transactions. You write (sell) an option, and it expires or you re-purchase the option. Since this is a sale followed by a purchase, there is no circumstance in which this could become a long-term gain!

REFERENCES

Bail, Ray, and Philip Brown, "An Empirical Evaluation of Accounting Income Numbers," *Journal of Accounting Research*, Vol. 6 (Autumn 1968), pp. 159–178.

Black, F., and M. Scholes, "The Valuation of Option Contracts and a Test of Market Efficiency," *Journal of Finance*, Vol. 27, pp. 399–417.

Consensus of Insiders, "Stock Splits . . . Boon or Bane?" P.O. Box 10247, Ft. Lauderdale, Fla. 33305, October 7, 1977.

Cragg, John G., and Burton G. Malkiel, "The Consensus of and Accuracy of Some Predictions of the Growth of Corporate Earnings," *Journal of Finance* (March 1968), pp. 41–46.

Durand, David, "Growth Stocks and the Petersburg Paradoxon," *Journal of Finance*, Vol. 12, No. 3 (September 1957), pp. 348–363.

Fama, Eugene, Fisher, Jensen, and Roll, "The Adjustment of Stock Prices to New Information," *International Economic Review*, Vol. 10, No. 1 (February 1969), pp. 1–21.

Friend, Irwin, "A Study of Mutual Funds," Securities Research Unit, Wharton School of Finance and Commerce, University of Pennsylvania (1962).

Galai, D., "Pricing of Options and the Efficiency of the Chicago Board Options Exchange," unpublished Ph.D. dissertation, University of Chicago (1975).

Granville, Joseph E., *A Strategy of Daily Stock Market Timing for Maximum Profit*, Englewood Cliffs, N.J.: Prentice-Hall, 1960.

Jensen, Michael C., "The Performance of Mutual Funds in the Period 1945–1974," *Journal of Finance*, Vol. 23, No. 2 (May 1974), pp. 389–415.

Kaufman, P., *Technical Analysis in Commodities*. New York: John Wiley & Sons, 1979.

King, Benjamin, "Market and Industry Factors on Stock Prices Behavior," *Journal of Business* (January 1966).

Levy, Robert A., "Relative Strength as a Criterion for Investment Selection," *Journal of Finance*, Vol. 22 (1967), pp. 595–610.

Little, Ian, M.D., and A. C. Rayner, "Higgledy, Piggledy Growth," Institute of Statistics, Oxford, Vol. 24, No. 4 (November 1962).

Lorie, James H., and Lawrence Fisher, "Some Studies of Variability of Returns on Investment in Common Stocks," *Journal of Business* (April 1970).

Lorie, James H., and Victor Niederhoffer, "Predictive and Statistical Properties of Insider Trading," *Journal of Law and Economics*, Vol. 11, pp. 35–53.

Malkiel, Burton G., *A Random Walk Down Wall Street*. New York: W. W. Norton, 1975, p. 140.

Merton, Robert C., Myron S. Scholes, and Mathew L. Gladstein, "A Simulation of the Returns and Risk of Alternative Options Portfolio Investment Strategies," unpublished working paper.

Niederhoffer, Victor Osborne M. F. M., "Market Making and Reversal on the Stock Exchange," *Journal of the American Statistical Association*, Vol. 61 (December 1966), pp. 897–916.

Ott, Michael, *Aktientrend*, No. 51-52 (1977).

Russo, Robin J., "Compare—A Technical Timing System," Dean Witter Reynolds, New York, 1976.

Schweitzer Wirtschaftsrevue Bilanz, "Welcher Indikator ist der beste?," November 11, 1977.

Schweitzer Wirtschaftsrevue Bilanz, "Hauptsache die Zinsen fallen," March 3, 1978.

Sharpe, William F., "Capital Asset Price, A Theory of Market Equilibrium under Conditions of Risk," *Journal of Finance*, Vol. XIX (September 1964), pp. 425–442.

Sharpe, William F., "Mutual Funds Performance," *Journal of Business, Security Prices*, A Supplement, Vol. 39, No. 1, Part 2 (January 1966), pp. 119–138.

Smith, Adam, *The Money Game*. New York: Random House, 1967, p. 240.

Thomas, Conrad, *Risk and Opportunity*. Homewood, Ill.: Dow Jones Irwin Inc., 1974.

Treynor, Jack L., "The Trouble with Earnings," *Financial Analyst's Journal*, Vol. 28, No. 5 (September–October 1972), pp. 41–46.

Valentine, Jerome I., "Investment Analysis and Capital Market Theory," *The Financial Analyst*, Research Foundation (1975), p. 33.

Yasicek, Oldrich, and John A. McQuown, "The Efficient Market Model," *Financial Analyst's Journal*, Vol. 28 (September–October 1972), p. 358.

INDEX

Numerals in italic indicate illustrations.

309